SURGERY AND SELFHOOD IN EARLY MODERN ENGLAND

Offering an innovative perspective on debates concerning embodiment in the early modern period, Alanna Skuse examines diverse kinds of surgical alteration, from mastectomy to castration, and amputation to facial reconstruction. Body-altering surgeries had profound socio-economic and philosophical consequences. They reached beyond the physical self, and prompted early modern authors to develop searching questions about the nature of body integrity and its relationship to the soul: was the body a part of one's identity, or a mere 'prison' for the mind? How was the body connected to personal morality? What happened to the altered body after death? Drawing on a wide variety of texts including medical treatises, plays, poems, newspaper reports, and travel writings, this volume will argue that the answers to these questions were flexible, divergent, and often surprising, and helped to shape early modern thoughts on philosophy, literature, and the natural sciences. This title is also available as Open Access on Cambridge Core.

ALANNA SKUSE is the Wellcome Trust Research Fellow for the Department of English at the University of Reading. She was previously the Wellcome Trust Postdoctoral Research Fellow at the University of Reading and long-term research fellow of the Folger Shakespeare Institute, Washington, DC, and is also the author of *Constructions of Cancer in Early Modern England: Ravenous Natures* (2015).

T0371468

SURGERY AND SELFHOOD IN EARLY MODERN ENGLAND

Altered Bodies and Contexts of Identity

ALANNA SKUSE

University of Reading

CAMBRIDGE
UNIVERSITY PRESS

Shaftesbury Road, Cambridge CB2 8EA, United Kingdom

One Liberty Plaza, 20th Floor, New York, NY 10006, USA

477 Williamstown Road, Port Melbourne, VIC 3207, Australia

314–321, 3rd Floor, Plot 3, Splendor Forum, Jasola District Centre, New Delhi – 110025, India

103 Penang Road, #05–06/07, Visioncrest Commercial, Singapore 238467

Cambridge University Press is part of Cambridge University Press & Assessment,
a department of the University of Cambridge.

We share the University's mission to contribute to society through the pursuit of
education, learning and research at the highest international levels of excellence.

www.cambridge.org
Information on this title: www.cambridge.org/9781108826181

DOI: 10.1017/9781108919395

© Alanna Skuse 2021

This work is in copyright. It is subject to statutory exceptions and to the provisions of
relevant licensing agreements; with the exception of the Creative Commons version
the link for which is provided below, no reproduction of any part of this work may
take place without the written permission of Cambridge University Press.

An online version of this work is published at http://dx.doi.org/10.1017/9781108919395
under a Creative Commons Open Access license CC-BY-NC-ND 4.0 which permits re-use,
distribution and reproduction in any medium for non-commercial purposes providing
appropriate credit to the original work is given. You may not distribute derivative works
without permission. To view this license, visit https://creativecommons.org/licenses/by-nc-nd/4.0

All versions of this work may contain content reproduced under license from third
parties. Permission to reproduce this third-party content must be obtained from
these third-parties directly. When citing this work, please include a reference to the
DOI: 10.1017/9781108919395

First published 2021
First paperback edition 2023

A catalogue record for this publication is available from the British Library

Library of Congress Cataloging-in-Publication data
NAMES: Skuse, Alanna, 1986– author.
TITLE: Surgery and selfhood in early modern England : altered bodies and contexts of identity /
Alanna Skuse, University of Reading.
DESCRIPTION: Cambridge, United Kingdom ; New York : Cambridge University Press, 2021. |
Includes bibliographical references and index.
IDENTIFIERS: LCCN 2020040209 (print) | LCCN 2020040210 (ebook) | ISBN 9781108843614
(hardback) | ISBN 9781108826181 (paperback) | ISBN 9781108919395 (epub)
SUBJECTS: LCSH: Surgery–Europe–History. | Body image. | Mind and body.
CLASSIFICATION: LCC RD27 .S48 2021 (print) | LCC RD27 (ebook) | DDC 617.094–dc23
LC record available at https://lccn.loc.gov/2020040209
LC ebook record available at https://lccn.loc.gov/2020040210

ISBN   978-1-108-84361-4   Hardback
ISBN   978-1-108-82618-1   Paperback

Cambridge University Press & Assessment has no responsibility for the persistence
or accuracy of URLs for external or third-party internet websites referred to in this
publication and does not guarantee that any content on such websites is, or will
remain, accurate or appropriate.

Contents

Figures

Acknowledgements

This book is the result of a Medical Humanities Research Fellowship from the Wellcome Trust (H5213000). My sincere thanks go to them for their support throughout my career. Preliminary research was carried out during a long-term fellowship at the Folger Shakespeare Library, the most welcoming place in which I have had the pleasure to study. During this project, I have been fortunate in meeting a great many people who gave freely of their time and wisdom. My mentor at the University of Reading, Michelle O'Callaghan, helped to make this book better and bolder in myriad ways, not least through her encyclopaedic knowledge of early modern texts. My colleagues Andrew Mangham and Rohan Deb Roy read and gave advice on endless iterations of funding applications. Hannah Newton provided knowledge, friendship, and tea. In the public engagement activities which accompanied the research for this book, I met academics, artists, and practitioners who shaped my thinking in ways I could not have foreseen. These include Verity Burke, CN Lester, Maggi Stratford, Tracey Harwood, Camille Baker, and Jane Boston. I am also grateful to my editor at Cambridge University Press, Emily Hockley, and to the anonymous readers who provided insightful and constructive feedback. A section of Chapter 3 originally appeared as '"Keep Your Face out of My Way or I'll Bite off Your Nose": Homoplastics, Sympathy, and the Noble Body in the *Tatler*, 1710' in *Journal for Early Modern Cultural Studies* 17, no. 4 (2017), 113–32. I would like to thank the University of Pennsylvania Press for permission to reprint that material here

Last, but by no means least, are my friends, family, and husband, who take a faintly bemused but ever tolerant approach to my macabre research interests.

Introduction

In 1686, John Moyle published *An Abstract of Sea Chirurgery*, a book for aspiring ships'-surgeons who had yet to actually work at sea. Moyle gave instructions for many kinds of minor surgeries and physic. Particularly striking, however, was his advice for a surgeon preparing for engagement day:

> Imagine that you are at Sea now in a Man of War, and in sight of the Enemy; and all men are clearing their respective quarters, and fitting themselves for fight; at what time you, as you are Chyrurgeon of the Ship, must prepare as followeth.

> First you must see that your platform be laid as even as may be, with a Sail spread upon it, which you must speak to the Commander to order . . .

> On this platform you must place two Chests, to set your wounded men on to dress them, one for your self to perform the greater operation on, and the other for your mate to dress slighter wounds on. You are likewise to have by you two Tubs with water; the one to throw amputated Limbs into until there is conveniency to heave them over-board; and the other to dip your dismembring Bladders in.[1]

The scene brings home the dangers which attended military service in this period. Moyle fully expected that at each engagement with the enemy, he would be required to amputate so many arms and legs that he would need a designated barrel in which to stow the disembodied parts. Nor was Moyle some reckless sawbones; it was hard, he admitted, to ignore the 'sad schreeking' of the men under the knife, but it had to be done.[2] The text gives detailed instructions for conducting amputations, and for tending to the patient immediately afterward. However, it leaves many questions unanswered. What happened to Moyle's patients when they got back to shore and re-joined civilian society? How did they view their radically

---

[1] John Moyle, *Abstractum Chirurgiae Marinae, or, An Abstract of Sea Chirurgery* (London: Printed by J. Richardson for Tho. Passinger, 1686), pp. 21–2.
[2] Ibid., p. 25.

changed bodies? What did they make of the fact that a part of themselves had been tossed overboard by Moyle and his mate?

This book is about questions such as these, and about people whose bodies were permanently changed by medical intervention. Patients of all kinds frequently disappear from recorded history after undergoing surgery. Seventeenth- and eighteenth-century medical texts like Moyle's generally focussed intently on the act of operation and its immediate aftermath, but infrequently followed up their cases. Yet surgery created an extraordinary range of bodily anomaly. Castration, amputation, mastectomy, facial surgery: all had life-changing psychic and social effects about which we know remarkably little. In recent years, the history of people with disabilities in the early modern period has begun to be studied. These works have told us something of the experiences of people with congenital and acquired disabilities and diseases, particularly from an economic point of view.[3] This book takes a different approach, focussing on how anomalous bodies shaped and were shaped by more metaphysical concerns: beliefs about the nature of embodiment, about soul and body, and about personal identity.

In his *Sea Chirurgery*, Moyle's concern was with the short-term survival of his patients. His disposal of the amputated limbs, however, recalls a situation envisioned by John Donne half a century earlier, as he worried about how the risen body would be (re)constituted:

> What cohaereance, what sympathy, what dependence maintaines any relation, any correspondence, between that arm that was lost in Europe, and that legge that was lost in Afrique or Asia, scores of yeers between?[4]

Donne's vision was one in which the body was endlessly susceptible to partition. While this malleability was frightening – one might literally fall apart over the course of a lifetime – it was also thrilling, hinting at new corporeal possibilities in which the body could be remade. Thus, narratives about bodily dismemberment emphasised construction as well as

---

[3] See, for instance, David J. Appleby, 'Unnecessary Persons? Maimed Soldiers and War Widows in Essex, 1642–1662', *Essex Archaeology and History* 32 (2001): 209–21; Rebecca A. Kahl, 'Dog-Faced Deflores: Disability in Early Modern Literature' (MA thesis) (Northern Michigan University, 2013); Eric Gruber von Arni, *Justice to the Maimed Soldier: Nursing, Medical Care and Welfare for Sick and Wounded Soldiers and Their Families during the English Civil Wars and Interregnum* (Aldershot: Ashgate, 2001); Mark Stoyle, '"Memories of the Maimed": The Testimony of Charles I's Former Soldiers, 1660–1730', *History* 88:290 (2003): 204–26.

[4] John Donne, 'A Sermon Preached at the Earl of Bridge-Waters House in London at the Marriage of His Daughter, the Lady Mary, to the Eldest Son of the Lord Herbert of Castle-Iland, November 19 1627', in *The Sermons of John Donne*, ed. Evelyn Simpson and George Potter, vol. VIII (of 10), no. 7 (Berkeley: University of California Press, 1956), pp. 4–5.

destruction. Only a few years after Moyle wrote of discarding amputated limbs, Rabelais' *The Life of Gargantua and Pantagruel* was published in English, and described the reattaching of a severed head:

> Vein to vein, sinew to sinew, vertebra to vertebra … And suddenly Episthemon began to breathe, then to open his eyes, then to yawn, and then to sneeze; and then he let off a loud, homely fart, at which Panurge said, 'Now he is certainly healed.'[5]

Satirist, ship's-surgeon, preacher-poet – the issues of 'coheareance' raised in discussion of altered bodies affected all those concerned with personal identity, and this book will work across genres to reconstruct attitudes to bodily alteration. Texts which are not traditionally 'literary' have a central place here, as I argue that documents from newspapers to receipt books contributed to a cultural milieu in which bodily difference was both a tool for thought and a social issue. However, paying close attention to the role of the altered body in early modern society also reveals just how many such bodies populate the canonical literature of the sixteenth, seventeenth, and eighteenth centuries. I will show that understanding the material circumstances of bodily difference in this period can shed new light on familiar texts by Hester Pulter, Joseph Addison, William Shakespeare, John Donne, and René Descartes, among others. This in itself is not entirely new; the 'bodily turn' among early modern literary scholars has been underway for some time.[6] However, this book will take a particularly integrative approach, drawing from medical history, disability studies, and phenomenology in order to focus intently on issues of embodiment. Thus, for example, in my reading of *Titus Andronicus* I focus on the fine detail of Lavinia's disability (her use of the writing staff) in conjunction with phenomenological theories of prosthesis which interrogate the identity-forming powers of such 'auxiliary organs'. Similarly, Donne's interest in contemporary science is well known. By paying particular attention to his writings on the matter of bodily identity after death, however, one can detect a conflict between Donne's academic orthodoxy on the matter of bodily resurrection and his personal horror of bodily partition and decay.

---

[5] François Rabelais, *Gargantua and Pantagruel*, trans. M. A. Screech, new edition (London: Penguin, 2006), p. 146.
[6] On Shakespeare's *Titus Andronicus*, for example, see Nicola M. Imbracsio, 'Stage Hands: Shakespeare's *Titus Andronicus* and the Agency of the Disabled Body in Text and Performance', *Journal of Literary and Cultural Disability Studies* 6:3 (2012): 291–306; Farah Karim-Cooper, *The Hand on the Shakespearean Stage: Gesture, Touch and the Spectacle of Dismemberment* (London: Bloomsbury, 2016).

To consider metaphysical and pragmatic concerns as thus closely inter-
twined is particularly apt to a period in which the arts and sciences had not
yet been separated. Curious minds such as Donne's read omnivorously in
medicine, philosophy, religion, and politics, adopting good ideas and
idioms wherever they found them. Moreover, if early modern thinkers
were wide-ranging in their intellectual vocabulary, I argue that they were
similarly fluid in their thinking about embodiment. As I discuss below, it
has often been suggested that over the course of the seventeenth and
eighteenth centuries, a monist view of embodiment, in which flesh and
mind were virtually indistinguishable, gave way to a dualist model influenced by Descartes. While that trajectory holds true in places, this book
will show that if one listens to the stories told by early modern people, it is
equally evident that there was no clean division between old and new
modes of thought. Castrato bodies were treated as commodities, but
castrati were also viewed as characterologically different on account of
their physical difference. Flesh could be grafted from one individual to
another, but apparently retained a sympathy for its original owner even
over vast distances. The faithful declared their belief that God would make
their bodies anew, yet feared being buried without all their body parts. By
examining the altered body in a variety of contexts, I will contend that
attitudes to bodily anomaly pushed the boundaries of thinking about
embodiment and identity. Through their varied responses to bodily difference, we see that early modern people were epistemologically multilin-
gual, strategically employing a view of embodiment which was more
monist, more dualist, or somewhere in between, depending on the circumstances in which they found themselves. Moreover, their stories often
show how messily these different models fit together. The body may seem
at once to be mechanistic object, and acting, feeling subject – the mind's
prison and its mode of expression. Scholastic, economic, and social back-
ground all made a difference, but the end result was improvisational,
flexible, and heteroglossic.

   To consider these questions as provoked in particular by the *altered*
body is to engage with the question of bodily normalcy and disability in
general. My focus in this book on bodies which were altered by surgery is
motivated by several factors. This category is, pragmatically speaking, a
more manageable subset than that of 'people with disabilities', which
might include the temporarily impaired, the chronically unwell, and the
elderly among others. People with acquired impairments were less subject
to providentialist narratives in which disability was understood as a divine
portent or punishment, and discourses around such people were therefore

more open to other kinds of metaphysical questions. Perhaps most importantly, looking at people with surgically altered bodies opens a space for considering early modern categories of bodily difference and disability. In this book are amputees and other people we would readily identify as 'disabled', and who were recognised in the early modern period as unfit for work and eligible for welfare assistance. However, the category of 'altered bodies' also includes people whose bodies could not straightforwardly be categorised as impaired. Castrati, for example, were certainly physically anomalous, but their bodies were created as a means to an end, and in some cases served to bring them fame and fortune. The matter is complicated further when one considers that the very term 'disabled' is culturally inflected. Disability scholarship of the past decade has increasingly questioned the terms in which we can address past experiences of bodily difference. Lennard J. Davis, for instance, has long contended that we should 'assume that disability was not an operative category before the eighteenth century'.[7] 'Disability', he argues, emerged as a concept in relation to industrialisation, and before that point, 'deformity' was a more commonly used term. Moreover, he contends, congenital 'deformities' were differentiated from bodily differences acquired later in life.[8] Irina Metzler likewise grapples with the difficulties of using modern terminology to describe medieval conceptions of difference, arguing that '"Disability" is a term that only makes cultural sense in the present.'[9] Her analysis, like those of Elizabeth Bearden and Chris Mounsey, searches for a phrase which will encapsulate the high degree of individual variation between people who were all, in the modern sense, 'disabled'.[10] For Metzler the idea which best fits is that of 'liminality', a sense of being not only on the edge of a category but in between the categories of sick and well, static and

---

[7] Lennard J. Davis, 'Dr Johnson, Amelia, and the Discourse of Disability in the Eighteenth Century', in *Defects: Engendering the Modern Body*, ed. Helen Deutsch and Felicity Nussbaum (Ann Arbor: University of Michigan Press, 2000), p. 57.

[8] Ibid., pp. 58–9.

[9] Irina Metzler, *A Social History of Disability in the Middle Ages: Cultural Considerations of Physical Impairment* (London: Routledge, 2013), p. 4.

[10] See Elizabeth B. Bearden, 'Before Normal, There Was Natural: John Bulwer, Disability, and Natural Signing in Early Modern England and Beyond', *PMLA* 132:1 (2017): 33–50, https://doi.org/10.1632/pmla.2017.132.1.33; Elizabeth Bearden, *Monstrous Kinds: Body, Space, and Narrative in Renaissance Representations of Disability* (Ann Arbor: University of Michigan Press, 2019); Chris Mounsey, 'Variability: Beyond Sameness and Difference', in *The Idea of Disability in the Eighteenth Century*, ed. Chris Mounsey (Cranbury: Bucknell University Press, 2014), pp. 1–28. See also David M. Turner, *Disability in Eighteenth-Century England: Imagining Physical Impairment* (Abingdon: Routledge, 2012), especially pp. 16–34.

dynamic.[11] For Mounsey and Bearden, the concept of 'variability' most appropriately describes the wide experiential differences which exist between sensory impairments, intellectual disability, physical disability, and so on.[12] Variability, argues Mounsey, is 'a concept that enshrines uniqueness, has the patience to discover the peculiarities of each individual and by doing so captures particular people rather than an "institutionalized representation of disabled people"'.[13]

While such formulations encourage nuance, they are not always up to the task of describing what was common, as well as different, between people with various kinds of bodily difference. Disability studies has traditionally been an activist discipline, which has advocated for people with disabilities based on treating them as a group with similar social and economic concerns. Thus, at the same time as emphasising variability, Mounsey contends that 'each person's disability (under whichever banner it may subtend) is unlike any other person's, while the experience of being disabled is the same for each disabled person'.[14] The term 'disability' may be a blunt instrument but it is often a politically expedient one. With this in mind, both Bearden and Metzler thus adopt a disability studies model in which 'impairment' describes the biological fact of physical difference, while 'disability' denotes the restrictions that impairment involves, which are determined by environmental and socio-cultural factors (the provision or otherwise of assistive items, or equality legislation, for example). This approach too has its problems, and in their *Cultural Locations of Disability*, Sharon Snyder and David Mitchell collapse the impairment/disability distinction in order to 'recognize disability as a site of phenomenological value that is not purely synonymous with the processes of social disablement'.[15] As they argue, 'Environment and bodily variation . . . inevitably impinge upon each other.'[16] In the scenarios described in this book, social and environmental factors are so deeply imbricated in constructions of embodiment as to make sharp distinctions unhelpful. I therefore use 'impairment' and 'disability' here more or less interchangeably, alongside the more precise term 'bodily alteration'.

---

[11] Metzler, *A Social History of Disability in the Middle Ages*, p. 5.
[12] See also Allison Hobgood and David Houston Wood, 'Early Modern Literature and Disability Studies', in *The Cambridge Companion to Literature and Disability*, ed. Clare Barker and Stuart Murray (Cambridge: Cambridge University Press, 2017), pp. 32–46.
[13] Mounsey, 'Variability: Beyond Sameness and Difference', p. 17.   [14] Ibid., pp. 1–2.
[15] Sharon L. Snyder and David T. Mitchell, *Cultural Locations of Disability* (Chicago: University of Chicago Press, 2010), pp. 6–7.
[16] Ibid.

Though they remain unresolved, these debates demonstrate that there are multiple ways in which the distinction between normatively bodied and other-bodied might be configured, and multiple axes along which normalcy and non-normalcy might be plotted. One aspect of disability history which remains underdeveloped is the intersection of disability, deformity, or other degrees of 'impairment' with race and gender.[17] The difficulty for early modern scholars attempting to develop this intersectionality is immediately apparent in the fact that most chapters of this book feature far more writing by and about men than by and about women – and no writing by people of colour. This is instructive in itself; in my sources, the white male body is, as ever, the paradigm for considering subjectivity. Nonetheless, considerations of gender and race also inform the stories in this book in subtler ways. Chapter 2, for instance, considers how the 'exotic' one-breasted body of the Amazon woman teetered between abjection and erotic spectacle. In Chapter 5, the appearance of the raced body in discourses about bodily resurrection is connected to uncertainty about the spiritual status of non-whites and non-Christians.[18] Altered bodies could be radically different in their affects depending on what kind of body was being altered, as well as on what kind of alteration took place.

As this lability indicates, the body in early modern culture is a particularly slippery subject (or object). The definitional status of the body is bound up with material practices that reshape the flesh and cultural mores which determine its uses, such that the body may be seen both as individuated and as interacting with a socio-cultural ecology. The topic is further complicated by the dominance in much early modern thought of the humoral model, which has loomed large in literary criticism of the past two decades. According to the neo-Galenic model of bodily function, ebbs and flows in the body's fluids, or humours, might affect not only one's physical state but one's mental processes, a symbiotic relationship so close

---

[17] Notable exceptions to this rule include Felicity Nussbaum, *The Limits of the Human: Fictions of Anomaly, Race and Gender in the Long Eighteenth Century* (Cambridge: Cambridge University Press, 2003); Helen Deutsch and Felicity Nussbaum, 'Introduction', in *Defects: Engendering the Modern Body*, ed. Deutsch and Nussbaum, pp. 1–30; Roxann Wheeler, *The Complexion of Race: Categories of Difference in Eighteenth-Century British Culture* (Philadelphia: University of Pennsylvania Press, 2000).

[18] As Stephen Burwood points out, the ability to 'forget about' one's body is often not afforded to those deemed 'Other', particularly when that Otherness is deemed to include a greater susceptibility to bodily appetites (Stephen Burwood, 'The Apparent Truth of Dualism and the Uncanny Body', *Phenomenology and the Cognitive Sciences* 7:2 (2008): 263–78, https://doi.org/10.1007/s11097-007-9073-z).

as to be impossible to pull apart into 'body' and 'mind'. Thus Gail Kern Paster, a leading proponent of the 'bodily turn' in Renaissance literary studies, describes how

> physiological knowledge intersects with early modern behavioral thought to produce somatically based theories of desire and affect. The penetration of flesh by spirit that was accomplished by the vessels had the effect of distributing needs and affects outward to every part, of radically decentralizing what might be called the body's intentionality or even the physiology of its ensoulment.[19]

Paster sees somatic and emotional experience in this period as indivisible; early modern people, she argues, would have found it odd to differentiate between mental and physical health. Because emotions were not experienced in isolation, health itself was also profoundly relational. As such, she contends, in studying early modern literature and history we should be thinking less of the embodied soul and more of the ensouled body. The maelstrom of somatic, relational, emotional, and cognitive experience was apprehended as an 'ecology of the passions', in which each aspect depended on relationships within and without the bodily envelope.[20]

Paster's work has been seminal in understanding aspects of early modern culture and literature; this emphasis on bodily materiality has produced a whole genre of Shakespearean criticism, often intersecting with the study of gender and race.[21] At the same time, however, other scholars have warned against overlooking the importance of the immaterial soul in early modern culture. Jonathan Sawday and Angus Gowland are foremost among those who analyse descriptions of the emotions, and even of the body itself, in terms of intellectual and spiritual curiosity.[22] Gowland, for

---

[19] Gail Kern Paster, 'Nervous Tension: Networks of Blood and Spirit in the Early Modern Body', in *The Body in Parts: Fantasies of Corporeality in Early Modern Europe*, ed. David A. Hillman and Carla Mazzio (New York: Routledge, 1997), p. 118.

[20] Mary Floyd-Wilson et al., 'Shakespeare and Embodiment: An E-Conversation', *Literature Compass* 2:1 (2005), https://doi.org/10.1111/j.1741-4113.2005.00180.x.

[21] See, for example, Dympna Callaghan, *Shakespeare without Women: Representing Gender and Race on the Renaissance Stage*, Accents on Shakespeare (London: Routledge, 2000), on the production of gender difference in early modern theatre; Karim-Cooper, *The Hand on the Shakespearean Stage*; Carol Thomas Neely, *Distracted Subjects: Madness and Gender in Shakespeare and Early Modern Culture* (New York: Cornell University Press, 2004); Katharine A. Craik and Tanya Pollard, eds., *Shakespearean Sensations: Experiencing Literature in Early Modern England* (Cambridge: Cambridge University Press, 2013), on the affective and humoral impacts of reading and viewing plays; Michael C. Schoenfeldt, *Bodies and Selves in Early Modern England: Physiology and Inwardness in Spenser, Shakespeare, Herbert, and Milton* (Cambridge: Cambridge University Press, 1999).

[22] Jonathan Sawday, *The Body Emblazoned: Dissection and the Human Body in Renaissance Culture* (Abingdon: Routledge, 2013); Angus Gowland, 'Melancholy, Passions and Identity in the

example, insists that 'What was fundamental in conceptions of passions and the human subject was not materialistically conceived "embodied emotion", but the relationship between the functions of the body and those of the soul.'[23] For these critics, the embodied soul retains supremacy over the ensouled body.[24] The 'subject', they argue, is the thinking soul; the body is objectified by comparison. Comparing early modern 'passions' with modern 'affect', Benedict Robinson offers a third option, in which the passions are 'kind[s] of cognition', 'qualities of a substance' rather than substances in and of themselves.[25] Moreover, all these scholars position the difference between ensouled bodies and embodied souls as, to some extent, one of chronology. What is being described here is a shift, over time, from a monist to a dualist conception of the body. The reasons for this shift have been explored in great detail in works including Roy Porter's influential *Flesh in the Age of Reason*, which identifies a number of contributing factors to the conceptual division of soul from body.[26] Descartes' *Meditations* is, of course, prominent among these factors. However, the popularity of Cartesian dualism depended on a raft of social, cultural, and economic changes, many of which are touched upon in this book. The following chapters will show how the new science of the seventeenth century arguably encouraged natural philosophers to think of the body as a composition of parts which might be removed and replaced, and how a mechanistic view of the flesh was likewise fostered by the rise of automata. The execution of Charles I, and later, the Glorious Revolution, brought into question the idea of the noble body, while the later seventeenth century witnessed a 'crisis in paternity' which lent new urgency to issues of inheritance.[27] Economic factors loom particularly large here; I will argue that with the rise of consumer culture, the body might be viewed as a commodity to be bought and sold, manipulated, and enhanced. Such changes were communicated and facilitated by the rise of print culture, particularly advertisements and newspapers. Most crucially, all these

Renaissance', in *Passions and Subjectivity in Early Modern Culture*, ed. Freya Sierhuis and Brian Cummings (Farnham: Ashgate, 2013), pp. 75–94.
[23] Gowland, 'Melancholy, Passions and Identity in the Renaissance', p. 87.
[24] See also Scott Manning Stevens, 'Sacred Heart and Secular Brain', in *The Body in Parts: Fantasies of Corporeality in Early Modern Europe*, ed. David A. Hillman and Carla Mazzio (New York: Routledge, 1997), pp. 263–84.
[25] Benedict S. Robinson, 'Thinking Feeling', in *Affect Theory and Early Modern Texts: Politics, Ecologies, and Form*, ed. Amanda Bailey and Mario DiGangi (New York: Palgrave Macmillan, 2017), pp. 111, 113.
[26] Roy Porter, *Flesh in the Age of Reason* (London: Allen Lane, 2003).
[27] Mary Elizabeth Fissell, *Vernacular Bodies: The Politics of Reproduction in Early Modern England* (Oxford: Oxford University Press, 2004), pp. 197–242.

changes took place against a backdrop of innumerable armed conflicts which created a steady supply of amputee or otherwise anomalous bodies.

This is not to imply that conceptions of embodiment followed a neat track from Renaissance to Enlightenment. It is very often the case that procedures or phenomena which are commonly taken to have contributed to the segregation of body from mind may, under the right circumstances, be read in the opposite direction. When the body was carved up, augmented, or examined, discussions emerged which might as easily insist on the 'person-ness' of the body as on its 'thing-ness'. The contested boundaries between things and people have been recognised in recent scholarship in a number of works on subject–object relationships in the early modern period. In particular, scholars have noted the ability of objects to shape subjectivity, acting as interfaces between the flesh and the wider world which transform the potentialities and boundaries of the body. In Margreta de Grazia, Maureen Quilligan, and Peter Stallybrass's *Subject and Object in Renaissance Culture*, they explain:

> The very ambiguity of the word 'ob-ject,' that which is thrown before, suggests a more dynamic status for the object. Reading 'ob' as 'before' allows us to assign the object a prior status, suggesting its temporal, spatial and even causal coming before. The word could thus be made to designate the potential priority of the object. So defined, the term renders more apparent the way material things – land, clothes, tools – might constitute subjects who in turn own, use, and transform them. The form/matter relation of Aristotelian metaphysics is thereby provisionally reversed: it is the material object that impresses its texture and contour upon the noumenal subject. And the reversal is curiously upheld by the ambiguity of the word 'sub-ject,' that which is thrown under, in this case – in order to receive an imprint.[28]

As this book will explore, when the categories of object and subject are interrogated, the body itself may appear as either or both object and/or subject, a shaping influence on the mind or a constitutive part of it.

This flexibility can be difficult to envision from within the confines of a post-modern society which has embraced a mechanistic view of both flesh and, increasingly, experience. One of the ways in which this book seeks to access the different dimensions of early modern selfhood is through the application of phenomenological theory. Branches of phenomenology are almost as numerous as phenomenological critics, but here I borrow from

---

[28] Margreta de Grazia, Maureen Quilligan, and Peter Stallybrass, 'Introduction', in *Subject and Object in Renaissance Culture*, ed. de Grazia, Quilligan, and Stallybrass (Cambridge: Cambridge University Press, 1996), p. 5.

Maurice Merleau-Ponty, Paul Ricoeur, Drew Leder, and Valerie Sobchack in viewing embodiment, and ontology, as a combination of biological facticity and experiential, relational biography. These scholars have in common that they view the self as a 'double-sided' entity. As physical beings with senses, they argue, we possess both thing-ness and the capacity to apprehend other things in the world; that is, 'intentionality'. Various phenomenologists describe this double-sidedness in different ways. In Merleau-Ponty's formulation, he writes of the subject body (*corps sujet*), lived body (*corps vécu*), or one's own body (*corps propre*).[29] The body is, he finds, both 'me' and 'mine', that which is experienced and that from which all experience takes place.[30] In Ricoeur's formulation, selfhood is divided into *idem* and *ipse*: the first, the quality of material sameness, and the second, encompassing tastes, values, and the continuation of character over time.[31] Whatever the terminology – and I have largely avoided specialist terms in this book – the ramifications of this double-sidedness for the study of depictions of embodiment are primarily ones of elucidating what is already felt to be true. The body, according to phenomenology, has the curious property of being both 'here' and 'there' – both that which experiences things and that which is experienced *as* a thing by others. Neither of these facets is divisible from the other, and therefore, as Stephen Priest observes, 'body-subject and world are dialectically related: they are mutually constituting'.[32] Moreover, phenomenology is itself mutually constituting with much work in the history of emotions and sensory history which I have described above. Bruce Smith, who coined the term 'historical phenomenology' to describe his work on histories of sex and sound, argues that this method 'directs attention to the sentient body ... positioned among the cultural variables set in place by new historicism and cultural materialism'.[33] The same might equally be said of many works by historians of disability, literature, sensation, or emotion seeking to reconstruct how it felt to have a particular kind of body in the past.

---

[29] Jenny Slatman, 'Is It Possible to "Incorporate" a Scar? Revisiting a Basic Concept in Phenomenology', *Human Studies* 39:3 (2016): 351, https://doi.org/10.1007/s10746-015-9372-2.

[30] Pascal Dupond, *Le vocabulaire de Merleau-Ponty* (Paris: Ellipses Marketing, 2001), p. 9.

[31] David M. Kaplan, *Ricoeur's Critical Theory* (New York: State University of New York Press, 2003).

[32] Stephen Priest, *Merleau-Ponty* (Abingdon: Routledge, 1998), p. 74.

[33] Bruce R. Smith, 'Premodern Sexualities', *PMLA* 115:3 (2000): 326, https://doi.org/10.2307/463453. For another example of the use of phenomenology to explore Renaissance ideas of the body, see Bearden, *Monstrous Kinds*, especially pp. 19–21.

In light of the flexibility which I argue characterised early modern approaches to embodiment, it seemed inappropriate to order this book in terms of chronological or even generic categories. Rather, it is – to borrow Mark Breitenberg's phrase – a 'collection of interventions', themed around varieties of bodily alteration.[34] Each chapter thus ranges widely over different kinds of texts from different points in the late sixteenth, seventeenth, and eighteenth century. Though I have tried to provide a sense of change over time where this is evident, I repeatedly found that textual influences behaved less neatly, light-footedly skipping generations and genres.

Bodily alterations in this period often took place through necessity – the need to save the patient by removing an arm or leg, for example. However, this was not always the case. Chapter 1 considers the use of castration as a means of turning the body into a money-making instrument. Elective castration for the purposes of creating castrato singers was a relatively rare but culturally prominent means of changing the body. As I argue, the procedure created a body with unique erotic and commercial capital, which was bound up with the rise of commercialised forms of literature. In this respect, therefore, the (literally) instrumental nature of this altered body promoted a vision of embodiment in which the body appeared as an object that could be exploited, whether for monetary gain or sexual pleasure. Hostility towards castrati arose because such men were felt to violate not only the categories of male/non-male, but those of master/ servant; castrati worked for a living, but were perceived to have power over those whom they entertained. Even accounts of the sexual potency of castrati were, I argue, opportunities to objectify these anomalous bodies. The subjective experience of the castrato emerges only rarely: first, in narratives of castrato marriages, and second, in operatic roles which embrace the castrato's sexual liminality.

Chapter 2 examines another sexually altered body, that of the female mastectomy survivor. Such women may, I argue, be viewed as correlates to castrati in that they too were often exoticised: the figure of the one-breasted Amazon was an erotic and ethnographic spectacle. In this guise the mastectomied woman was also, like the castrato, sexually dangerous and functionally unique, with her bodily alteration believed to confer martial advantages. Unlike castrati, however, the altered status of the Amazon body was consistently obfuscated, and was never linked to

---

[34] Mark Breitenberg, *Anxious Masculinity in Early Modern England* (Cambridge: Cambridge University Press, 1996), p. 28.

instances of medical mastectomy. This occurred in spite of the fact that mastectomy was well known as a cure for breast cancer in the early modern period; indeed, the cancerous body and the Amazonian body had troubling parallels, both being perceived as rejecting or perverting maternal function. The absolute exclusion of one-breasted bodies from the stage and from domestic narratives reveals how far the status of the altered body was determined by patriarchal social structures.

The theme of morally interpreting the altered body continues in Chapter 3, where I look to varieties of facial surgery and prosthesis. Facial surgery in this period was frequently a grim necessity, and was often framed as such. Nonetheless, the early modern period saw the development of medical procedures aimed as much at the augmentation and transformation of the face as at its restoration to 'normality'. As I show, these advanced procedures – which included tooth transplants – brought into question the morality of changing one's appearance. These issues were heightened in discussions of a rare but fascinating operation, the Tagliacotian rhinoplasty. Promising to graft a new nose on to the faces of men afflicted by syphilis, this operation potentially, and controversially, disguised the results of sexual licentiousness. In the hands of satirical authors, however, the Tagliacotian rhinoplasty became something even more rich and strange. It was suggested not only that the graft might be taken from another person's flesh, but that the grafted part might retain a sympathetic connection to its original 'owner'. Once again, the nature of the connection (or lack thereof) between a person's flesh and their 'true' identity was foremost in such discussions. Hester Pulter's poem on the subject is a witty, sharply satirical admonition against sexual incontinence. Anticipating later works by Butler and Addison, it demonstrates how rhinoplasty became a vehicle for voicing larger concerns about embodiment, sociability, and morality.

Chapter 4 turns to a more common form of bodily alteration: amputation. This procedure is well documented in early modern medical literature, but attitudes towards amputees remain obscure. Looking to descriptions of prostheses in this period, I argue that prosthetic arms and legs were ideally imagined as articulate and mobile. They were strongly linked to a narrative of rehabilitation in which the amputee regained the ability to walk, ride, and in general to 'perform' able-bodiedness. This trend at once indexed a person's character to their bodily abilities and suggested similarities between the prostheticised human body and a machine or automaton. In the latter section of the chapter, this reading of prosthetics informs a detailed analysis of Shakespeare's *Titus Andronicus*.

Focussing on Lavinia's plight after her hands and tongue are amputated, I argue that her use of a staff to write the names of her attackers is, pragmatically speaking, unnecessary. What is necessary, however, is that Lavinia utilises objects in order to resist her own object-ification. That is, by making signs, she resists others' reading of her mutilated body as a passive sign, and regains a degree of agency. As ever, however, objects have meaning as well as people. Lavinia's staff may allow her to reclaim her subjectivity, but it can as easily recast her as the perpetual rape victim or freakish supercrip.

All kinds of bodily alteration in this period were inflected by the spiritual question of what happened to the body after death. In Chapter 5, I look to the problematics of the altered body in relation to the doctrine of bodily resurrection. Beginning with a scholarly and literary perspective, I show how theorists attempted to square the fact of bodily change with belief in the resurrection of the same body. In John Donne's poetry and sermons, this conflict is both anguished and productive, yielding rich depictions of the body's scattered parts and their heavenly reunion. Issues of embodiment surfaced in a refracted form in miracle accounts which featured the supernatural restoration or replacement of amputated limbs. The 'Miracle of the Black Leg' was one such account; this unique tale featured a saintly surgery in which a diseased white limb was replaced with a leg from a black corpse, prompting questions about whether that flesh could really 'belong' to its new body. Finally, I look to burial practices. Theoretical expositions of the body's fate after death often contrasted with the way in which 'real' people chose to bury their bodies and body parts; the latter often demonstrates the flexibility with which they considered embodiment.

Chapter 6 examines a different kind of bodily anomaly which informed some of the early modern period's most influential thinking on cognition and nociception – phantom limb syndrome. This curious phenomenon is clearly described in texts by Ambroise Paré. It comes to the fore, however, in the work of René Descartes, who found in this bodily anomaly a fascinating test case for his theory of 'non-resemblance' in the senses. As I explore, the nature of phantom limbs seemed to Descartes to confirm his idea that pain sensations occurred in the mind rather than in the body, thus reaffirming his notion of the body as object. In this capacity, phantom limbs occur in other contemporary texts, including in the first known autobiographical description of phantom limb syndrome. Looking closely at Descartes' published works and correspondence, however, we can see how the strangeness of phantom limbs challenged this philosopher to re-examine his own thinking about perception and the 'hard problem' of consciousness. Finally, in the book's Conclusion I consider what early modern narratives of bodily alteration might tell us about the twenty-first-century desire to augment and transform the natural body.

CHAPTER I

The Instrumental Body: Castrati

For most of the people in this book, bodily alteration was not a choice. Those who underwent amputations, mastectomies, and facial surgeries generally did so as a last resort. By contrast, this chapter deals with a group of people for whom surgery was a calculated decision, made by somebody close to them. The castrato – a man gelded in childhood to preserve his youthful singing voice – provides a rare example of a body which was 'created' by surgery to fulfil a purpose.

In examining writings about castrati, I will show how close attention to the altered body sometimes precluded engagement with the person who *lived* that body as something more than a singer and sex object. Stories about the lives and loves of castrati were almost exclusively told from an outsider's perspective. They are thus an apt reminder, at the beginning of this book, of the difficulties we face as readers when trying to imagine what it was like to live with, in, and through an anomalous body. Those who wrote about castrati described them in terms which emphasised their physical difference and their value as 'instruments', but obscured or denied their subjectivity as human beings. Even when castrati made themselves rich, famous, and adored, they were denigrated by those who resented such assertions of agency and sought to represent them purely as objects, moveable goods to be pored over and acted upon rather than engaged with. Literary-historical study can make visible this whitewashing, but can only partly reveal an alternative story. The embodied experience of castrati is fragmentarily glimpsed through their art, and through the rare incursions of castrati into that most heteronormative of institutions, marriage.

Manufactured Men

At the most basic level, the manufacture of castrati – that is, the removal of testes and scrotum from pre-pubescent boys – was a money-making exercise. In this respect, it was unusual; as this book will show, most kinds of bodily alteration had economic consequences, but the path from bodily difference to social and economic difference was seldom so clearly mapped. The majority of castrati came from Italy, often from humble families, and the gelding of young boys flourished during times of economic hardship.[1] Gelded boys could be sent to live with a singing master, freeing their family of a financial burden, and it was hoped that in later life they might repay both master and parents by becoming famous and commanding vast fees for their singing. Whether the child had any say in the matter was in most cases unclear – it is difficult to imagine how a small child could possibly give consent to such a procedure, but castrati generally remained tight-lipped about their experiences. This was in large part because all castrati were illegal creations; gelding for other than medical reasons had been banned on pain of excommunication by Pope Sixtus V in 1587.[2] Many castrati questioned about their state would claim to have lost their testicles in an accident or to have had them removed in a hernia operation.[3]

The gelding operation held dangers, as did any invasive surgery in this period. In the absence of effective anaesthesia, it must also have been excruciatingly painful. By the standards of the time, however, this was a fairly minor procedure. Numerous medical texts of the period give instructions for the removal of testicles from adult males on medical grounds (usually hernias or tumours), and they typically report a speedy recovery.[4] However, gelding was only the beginning of the castrato's bodily alteration. As they matured, castrati developed distinctive physical features marking them out from other men and rendering them easy targets for all kinds of satire. The archetypal castrato had no beard and little body hair, but might possess a particularly full head of hair. His skin was softer than that of other men, and he tended towards plumpness, particularly around the hips. As gelding interrupted the hormones responsible for the closure of the growth plates, castrati tended to be unusually tall, with long limbs. Moreover, the intensive training to which the castrato was

---

[1] John Rosselli, 'The Castrati as a Professional Group and a Social Phenomenon, 1550–1850', *Acta Musicologica* 60:2 (n.d.): 143–79.
[2] Helen Berry, *The Castrato and His Wife* (Oxford: Oxford University Press, 2012), p. 13.
[3] Rosselli, 'The Castrati as a Professional Group and a Social Phenomenon, 1550–1850'.
[4] Daniel Turner, *The Art of Surgery: In Which Is Laid down Such a General Idea of the Same, as Is . . . Confirmed by Practice*, 6th edition, vol. II (of 2) (London: printed for C. Rivington and J. Clarke, 1741), pp. 274–5; Hugh Ryder, *New Practical Observations in Surgery* (London: printed for James Partridge, 1685), p. 55–8; Ambroise Paré, *The Workes of That Famous Chirurgion Ambrose Parey . . .* ed. Th. Johnson (London: printed by Th. Cotes and R. Young, 1634), p. 877.

subject – often up to ten hours a day – changed his body further.[5] Through a combination of vocal exercises and hormonal factors, castrati possessed a large chest cavity that provided their voices with more power than those of female sopranos.[6]

The craze for castrati in England started relatively late. From the sixteenth century, castrati had entertained the Italian and, to a lesser extent, the German court, first in church singing and later in opera.[7] It was not until the mid-seventeenth century, however, that castrati began to visit and work in Britain, and they remained a rarity, accessible only to the privileged.[8] Thomas King reports how:

> In 1667 and 1668 ... Samuel Pepys recorded hearing castrati at the Catholic Queen's Chapel at St James's Palace and in a rare, much anticipated appearance at the King's Playhouse. Twenty years later, on 19 April 1687, Pepys could invite his friend, the virtuoso John Evelyn, to a private performance, in Pepys's own lodgings, by Giovanni Francesco Grossi.[9]

Castrati typically occupied the mezzo-soprano range, but the quality of their voice was famously unlike any other. John Bulwer praised the 'smalness and sweetnesse' of their tone, while the Frenchman Charles Ancillon enthused that 'It is impossible to give any tolerable idea of ... the Beauty of their several voices: in short, they are above description, an[d] no one can possibly entertain any notion of them but those who have had the pleasure to hear them.'[10]

Being both rare and talented, castrati inevitably became valuable. Exactly *how* the castrato was to be valued, however, was a complicated matter. As Pepys' efforts to secure a private castrato performance

---

[5] I am indebted here to CN Lester for their explanation of classical vocal training and insight into the range of music performed by castrati. Of particular note, CN pointed out that their own ribcage had expanded by several inches after beginning operatic vocal training as an adult.

[6] For a detailed medical explanation of the castrato's vocal ability and physical distinctiveness, see Enid Rhodes Peschel and Richard E. Peschel, 'Medical Insights into the Castrati in Opera', *American Scientist* 75:6 (1987): 578–83.

[7] Rosselli, 'The Castrati as a Professional Group and a Social Phenomenon, 1550–1850', 146–7.

[8] Rosselli estimates that there were around 120 castrati living in Rome in 1650 (ibid., 157).

[9] Thomas A. King, 'The Castrato's Castration', *SEL Studies in English Literature, 1500–1900* 46:3 (2006): 563.

[10] John Bulwer, *Anthropometamorphosis: = Man Transform'd: Or, the Artificiall Changling* (London: printed by William Hunt, 1653), p. 355; Charles Ancillon, *Italian Love: Or, Eunuchism Displayed. Describing All the Different Kinds of Eunuchs; Shewing the Esteem They Have Met with in the World, and How They Came to Be Made so, Wherein Principally Is Examined, Whether They Are Capable of Marriage, and if They Ought to Be Suffered to Enter into That Holy State ... Occasioned by a Young Lady's Falling in Love with One, Who Sung in the Opera at the Hay-Market, and to Whom She Had like to Have Been Married. Written by a Person of Honour*, 2nd edition (London: printed for E. Curll, 1740), p. 30.

demonstrate, to hear these singers was a matter of social prestige as well as personal aesthetics. Being seen at castrato performances – better still, hosting castrato performances – was a marker of one's wealth and good taste, tied up with the vogue for all things continental. In the early days of castrati, argues Helen Berry,

> To be able to hear a castrati sing was an elite privilege, a private pleasure reserved for powerful men whose bodily senses were attended to with all forms of luxury. What pepper and spices did for the tongue, and furs did for the touch, the castrato did for the ear, and sometimes the eye as well.[11]

As an extension of this logic, particularly fine castrato singers were often patronised by wealthy members of the nobility. Occasionally, they were sent from one court to another in a sort of gift exchange, and in this respect they acquired a status analogous to that of unmarried women – that is, a tool for making bonds between powerful men.[12] Unlike most such women, however, castrati were capable of building fortunes to rival many of those whom they entertained, and in so doing, they demonstrated a degree of intersubjective agency which made it more difficult to treat them as objects or even as servants. Contemporary accounts make clear that while the majority of castrati never achieved fame, a very select few became superstars. In England, arguably the most feted were Carlo Maria Michelangelo Nicola Broschi (1705–82), or 'Farinelli', Franceso Benardi (1686–1758), or 'Senesino', and Nicola Francesco Leonardo Grimaldi (1673–1732), also known as 'Nicolini'. All these men were capable of commanding astronomical sums for their appearances, and all more or less managed their own careers. In 1734, for instance, it was reported that 'The famous Singer, Farinelli, who is just arriv'd here from Italy, has contracted with the Nobleman Subscribers, to sing at the Opera House in the Hay-Market 50 Nights, for 1,500 Guineas and a Benefit.'[13] This sum represented around £170,000 in modern terms, or the equivalent of 15,000 days of skilled labour for an early modern tradesman.[14] Later that year, the *London Evening Post* described how the royal family had come to see the superstar sing, and the following year, the *General Evening Post* reported his performance at one of innumerable society parties.[15]

---

[11] Berry, *The Castrato and His Wife*, p. 16. [12] Ibid.
[13] 'Farinelli Sings at the Haymarket', *London Evening Post*, 12 October 1734.
[14] Conversion calculated using www.nationalarchives.gov.uk/currency-converter.
[15] *London Evening Post*, 29 October 1734; *General Evening Post*, 16 January 1735. On castrati's salaries, see Cheryll Duncan, 'Castrati and Impresarios in London: Two Mid-Eighteenth-Century Lawsuits', *Cambridge Opera Journal* 24:1 (2012): 43–65.

The wealth accrued by famous castrati troubled many of those who wrote about these men in periodicals, satires, and newspapers. As Martha Feldman has shown, making money allowed castrati to participate in society, and potentially to leave a legacy in spite of their infertility:

> Politically castrati compensated for being infertile through a number of strategies ... adoption, often of nephews; extended international friendship networks with patrons, royals, writers, singers, artists, and others ... careful acquisition of goods and money; and careful management of their estates, heirs, and bequests ... They were apt to align themselves with male power, including rulership, if they could sing at court or in important churches or opera houses. In all this we can see them engaging in concrete forms of male social reproduction.[16]

Not all of the options Feldman describes would have been available to castrati in England, but nonetheless many commentators were deeply troubled by the extent to which English society appeared to have embraced castrati. In 1734, for instance, a letter-writer to *The Prompter* was led to opine that: 'I have heard sensible People express – their Astonishment at the Countenance – and Reception Eunuchs meet with in *England*. I am told Lords and Dukes are to be seen at their Levees.' This reception, he argued, was out of keeping with the treatment of such men elsewhere – notably, even in hedonistic Italy:

> Bless the *Prince of Modena*, who shewed us the other Day how *our Nobility* ought to use them. I heard, in a Company of Persons, illustrious for Sense and good Breeding, that *S—en—s—no* [Senesino], having got permission to wait on that Prince, (when he entered the Room) fell *prostrate* and *licked the Dust*; and tho' he did so three times, the *noble-minded* Prince used him as *Nobles* do in other Countries; he did not descend so *low* as to *speak to him*, did not *look at him*, did not *seem to know* that the *propudious Creature* was in the Room. Surely 'tis enough that they are paid so *abundantly*; why make *Companions* and *Equals* of them? No *Man* converses with an *Eunuch* any where but in *England*, unless he has a Mind to *Marry it*, as Nero did Sporus.[17]

The hyperbole of this letter was typical; the popularity of castrati was blamed for all manner of moral and economic ills. One common tactic among critics of castrati was to claim that their rise was directly indexed to the decline of the 'honest poor', complaining, for instance, that 'A Lady can't find Half a

---

[16] Martha Feldman, *The Castrato: Reflections on Natures and Kinds* (Oakland: University of California Press, 2015), p. xvii.
[17] 'Letter to the Editor', *Prompter*, 19 December 1735.

Guinea on a *Saturday* morning, for a poor Shoemaker ... that at Night will untye her purse-strings, and with *Greediness* bestow it at the Opera.'[18] Outraged pamphlet- and letter-writers complained that castrati's devotees reneged on debts, sold property, and even stole in order to afford tickets to their performances.[19] One eighteenth-century pamphlet attested that:

> A Woman of the first Quality *in England*, fearing lest *the Senor* should be affronted at receiving a Bank Note of 50l *for one* Ticket, if presented without Disguise, thought of a lucky Expedient, to prevent his Anger; which was, to purchase a Gold Snuff-box of Thirty Guineas Value, in which having inclosed the Note, she ventured, with Fear and Trembling, to make her Offering at the EUNUCH'S Shrine.

> ... *a Widow Lady of a very moderate Fortune, with two or three Children to take care of*, said, *with great Concern*, SHE HAD STOLE A TICKET FOR FIVE GUINEAS. If she had said, *She had Robbed her Children of Five Guineas*, she had spoke the Truth.[20]

The notion that money given to castrati was siphoned directly from more deserving causes was widespread.[21] Moreover, the fact that the gift-givers in all these encounters were women was no coincidence. Women's supposed fascination with castrati was linked to a perceived lack of manly authority and noble feeling among aristocratic young men, particularly in the late seventeenth and early eighteenth century (see Chapter 3). Thus in 1735, the author of the pamphlet *A Trip through the Town* decried the inability of young men to keep women properly in check and away from castrati: 'Is there no Spirit left in the young Fellows of the Age? No Remains of Manhood? Will they suffer *the Eyes, Ears, Hearts, and Souls* of their Mistresses, to follow *an Eccho of Virility?*'[22] The culpability of the fop or rake in the rise of castrati is implied once again in the second plate of Hogarth's 1735 *A Rake's Progress* (see Figure 1.1). In a chaotic room full of lavishly dressed men, a long piece of paper hangs over the back of a chair; it is titled 'A list of the rich Presents Signor Farinelli the Italian Singer condescended to Accept of the English Nobility & Gentry'.

Suspicion and resentment of the popularity and wealth of castrati were clearly widespread. Week after week, angry letters and columns appeared in publications such as the *London Evening Post*, *The Prompter*, *The Daily Post*, and others, all complaining of the money and attention 'squander'd'

---

[18] *A Trip through the Town. Containing Observations on the Customs and Manners of the Age*, 4th edition (London: printed for J. Roberts, 1735), p. 63.
[19] Ibid., pp. 61–62.   [20] Ibid.   [21] *Daily Post*, 16 February, 9 May 1738.
[22] *A Trip through the Town*, pp. 61–2.

Figure 1.1   William Hogarth, *A Rake's Progress*, Plate 2: *Surrounded by Artists and Professors*, Engraving, 1735.

on Farinelli and his ilk.[23] Moreover, such complaints were not based on the unnaturalness or barbarism of castrating young boys. Indeed, very few critics of castrati objected to their creation per se. Rather, what vexed these writers so much was the socio-economic liminality of the castrato. The castrato was a commodity; his body was created specifically for the entertainment of the rich. Unlike other commodities, however (and unlike the ultimate human commodity, the slave), castrati resisted their objectification by acting in ways which made apparent their status as agential subjects – specifically, making money and gaining influence. The castrato thus occupied a curious position: he was not chattel, but neither could he be admitted as a subject within a heteronormative, patrilineal society. For commentators to admit the phenomenological experience of the castrato would therefore have required them to admit the discord that existed between fixed, idealised social structures and varied, anomalous lived bodies.

---

[23] 'Letter to the Editor', *Daily Post*, 16 February 1738.

Sex Objects

Given how entwined the castrato's socio-economic status was with his gender identity, it is unsurprising that complaints about castrati's place in society bled into complaints about their sexual activity, and vice versa. What is perhaps surprising is the range of sexual vices attributed to castrati. Abuse directed at castrati figured them as sexually deviant in every direction. They were variously accused of being incapable of sex and sex mad, homosexual and (excessively) heterosexual, passive and predatory. Predictably, many of the insults levelled at castrati were homophobic; Valeria Finucci describes how 'Castrati provoked homophobic reactions and were subject to taunts, verbal abuse, coercion, physical retaliation, and psychological intimidation.'[24] It was certainly the case that some castrati engaged in homosexual relationships with their patrons or other men. In such pairings, the distinctive body of the castrato once again became a commodity, this time as a novel sexual object.[25] Roger Freitas has argued that the castrato's sexual appeal stemmed in part from his mixture of juvenile and adult sexual characteristics: 'Sexually speaking – and this is an essential point – the castrato would have been viewed as equivalent to the boy.'[26] To a greater extent, however, it seems to have been the castrato's combination of stereotypically masculine and feminine physical features which shaped his representation as a sex object. This notion is evident in the letter to *The Prompter*, above, which refers to Nero marrying Sporus: Nero famously castrated Sporus, a slave, in order to have Sporus act as his 'wife', a phrase which here implied both submission within the romantic relationship and being sexually penetrated.[27] Similarly, Casanova – himself an icon of sexual excess – famously mistook for a woman a castrato who then promised that 'he will serve me as a boy or a girl, whichever I choose'.[28]

---

[24] Valeria Finucci, *The Manly Masquerade: Masculinity, Paternity, and Castration in the Italian Renaissance* (Durham: Duke University Press, 2003), p. 239.

[25] Katherine Crawford, 'Desiring Castrates, or How to Create Disabled Social Subjects', *Journal for Early Modern Cultural Studies* 16:2 (2016): 59–90.

[26] Roger Freitas, *Portrait of a Castrato: Politics, Patronage, and Music in the Life of Atto Melani* (Cambridge: Cambridge University Press, 2009), especially pp. 101–48; Theo van der Meer, 'Sodomy and the Pursuit of a Third Sex in the Early Modern Period', in *Third Sex, Third Gender: Beyond Sexual Dimorphism in Culture and History*, ed. Gilbert Herdt (New York: Zone Books, 1994), pp. 137–212.

[27] David Woods, 'Nero and Sporus', *Latomus* 68:1 (2009): 73–82.

[28] Quoted in Freitas, *Portrait of a Castrato*, 29. Associations between castrati and homosexuality were always coloured by the association between castrati and Italy, and between Italians, pederasty, and sodomy. A vituperative 1747 text in favour of gelding Catholic priests argued that this method of

The presumed homosexual activities of castrati were evidently of concern to commentators, but they were seldom openly named in the period's
newspapers and periodicals, which shied away from discussing the possibility of sex between men. The insinuation of such activities, however, was
part of a continuum in which castrati were imagined to pose a wider threat
to sexual morality. Thus, a large volume of literature, ranging from the
satirical to the polemic, was dedicated to detailing the alleged affairs of
castrati with aristocratic women. In some such works, castrati were figured
more as emotional partners than in explicitly sexual terms. For instance, in
a satirical poem about Nicolini, published in 1711, the singer is imagined
as a replacement for a lapdog:

> Ye blooming *Nymphs* who warily begin
> To *dread the Censure*, but to *love the Sin*,
> Who with *false Fears* from your *Pursuers* run,
> And *filthy Nudities* in *Picture* shun,
> From *Scandal* free, this *pretty PLAY-THING* meet,
> . . .
>
> Who gently leaning on the *Fair Ones* Breast,
> May sooth *her Griefs*, and lull her into Rest.
> And should *He*, should *He* like *her* Squirrel creep
> To *her* soft Bosome when *she's* fall'n asleep;
> Ev'n then she's safe. Nor need *she* fear *Him* more
> Than those *kind Aids* which eas'd *her* Heart before.[29]

There is a hint here that in replacing 'kind Aids', Nicolini may be
providing sexual gratification. In the main, however, the castrato is represented here as, in Helen Berry's terms, '[a] life-size doll, safe for women to
dress up, buy presents for, and play with'.[30] To correspond with, express
devotion to, or meet with a castrato was, as Berry points out, far less
scandalous than to similarly engage with an 'intact' man.

In many other cases, however, relationships between castrati and
women were represented as far less innocent. It was obvious that the
greatest part of the castrato's appeal was that he could not impregnate

tackling the Popish threat would be particularly appropriate, since 'it is a common practice in *Italy*
and other popish countries with the meaner sort of people, to *geld* their own sons to make the better
market of them for singing-boys, and musicians, or to be catamites to cardinals, and other
dignitaries of the *Romish* church' (*The priest gelded: or popery at the last gasp. Shewing ... the
absolute necessity of passing a law for the castration of Popish ecclesiastics* (London: A. M'Culloh, 1747),
pp. 12–13).

[29] *The Signior in Fashion: Or the Fair Maid's Conveniency. A Poem on Nicolini's Musick-Meeting*
(Dublin, 1711).

[30] Berry, *The Castrato and His Wife*, p. 81.

his partners. Women might, it was feared, engage in sexual activity with a castrato without producing any evidence of their wrongdoing. Under this guise, 'Constanzia' [Constance] Mullman, a woman whom Berry describes as 'a notorious prostitute', was rumoured to have engaged in an affair with the talented and immensely famous Farinelli, a topic which provided ample fodder for satirists.[31] In mock epistles between the lovers, 'Constanzia' explains that the eunuch appeals to women because he offers extra-marital sex without consequences:

> Eunuchs can give uninterrupted Joys,
> Without the shameful curse of Girls and Boys:
> The violated Prude her Shape retains,
> A Vestal in the publick Eye remains;
> Shudders at the remotest shew of Vice,
> And Bashfulness out-blushes, she's so nice:
> With eager Fondness yet can yield her Charms,
> When raptur'd in her darling Eunuch's Arms.
>
> These love the Deed, but seem to hate the Name,
> Indulge Love's Pleasure, but avoid the shame:
> Well knowing Eunuchs can their Wants supply,
> And more than Bragging Boasters satisfy;
> Whose Pow'r to please the Fair expires too fast,
> *While F—lli* stands it to the last.[32]

The castrated man was here viewed as facilitating female sexual agency, in the form both of extra-marital sex and of unsanctioned kinds of sexual activity.[33] There were persistent rumours that some castrati were unaltered men in disguise, exploiting their talents to gain access to adoring women. Elsewhere, it was said that castrati were in fact women, seeking to cover up their licentious behaviour towards both sexes.[34] Crawford notes that it was even suggested at one point that Farinelli was pregnant, a narrative made possible in part by the effeminising effect of the above poem: where Constantia Philips (allegedly) affected masculine agency, Farinelli assumed

---

[31] For her part, Mrs Mullman claimed that rumours of the affair, and the 'correspondence' between the pair, had been cooked up by her estranged husband, and that she had never so much as seen Farinelli, having been ill with a 'pleuritic fever' the entire time he was in England (Teresia Constantia Mullman, *An Apology for the Conduct of Mrs Teresia Constantia Phillips*, vol. II (of 2) (London: printed for the booksellers of London and Westminster, 1748), pp. 91–2.)

[32] Teresia Constantia Mullman, *The Happy Courtezan: Or, the Prude Demolish'd. An Epistle from the Celebrated Mrs C- P-, to the Angelick Signior Far–n–Li* (London: printed for J. Roberts, 1735).

[33] George Sebastian Rousseau and Roy Porter, *Sexual Underworlds of the Enlightenment* (Manchester: Manchester University Press, 1987), pp. 57–8.

[34] Berry, *The Castrato and His Wife*, p. 84.

the feminine role.[35] Even if one accepted that castrati were who they claimed to be, it was often said that castrati could maintain erections despite their infertility. Marten's 1737 *Gonosologium Novum*, for instance, argued that

> experience has shewn that such men as have been deprived of their testicles, have, notwithstanding, been able to shew their prowess by diverting themselves with women, and defiling the nuptial beds of others ... It cannot be express'd to what point [eunuchs] will push their irregular desires, when their fancy is once inflam'd, and a kind of aqueous seed in the prostate or seminal bladders irritates their privities.

'Constanzia's' epistle buys into this idea, and implies that her castrato lover not only can engage in penetrative sex, but is more virile than other lovers, 'stand[ing] it to the last'. Though it was not explicitly stated, the much-vaunted fondness of women for castrati also hints at non-penetrative practices such as masturbation and oral sex; Freitas cites Casanova as having mentioned that castrati employed the 'secret des Lesbiennes'.[36]

Allegations of castrati's heterosexual affairs may at first seem to contradict suspicions about their homosexual activities. However, both these narratives relied on one thing – the objectification of the castrato's body. Just as was the case in his professional life, the perceived value of the castrato in his personal relationships was based on his bodily alterity. Whether because of his novel aesthetic attributes or his infertility, the castrato as lover had an instrumental value which informed both sympathetic and hostile accounts of his activities. By contrast, the emotional and physical experience of the castrato was entirely absent from written accounts of either homosexual or heterosexual encounters. His subjectivity was once again erased, while his value as a commodity was continually reinscribed. As we shall see elsewhere in this book, the visual spectacle of the anomalous body was a source of fascination. Bodily alteration was horrifying, but it was also exciting and potentially erotic. The castrato was unique, however, in the extent to which his spectacular body was interpolated as a money-making device.

In part, this interpolation was facilitated by contemporary market forces, and specifically by changes to the economics of printing in the

---

[35] Crawford, 'Desiring Castrates, or How to Create Disabled Social Subjects', 74.
[36] Freitas, *Portrait of a Castrato*, p. 141. This 'secret' was apparently observed by Casanova during an orgy in Rome at which abbés (Roman Catholic clergymen) were also present, reflecting both the anti-Catholic nature of these rumours and the erotic potential of racial, religious, and bodily otherness.

years in which castrati were most popular. The rise of castrati took place broadly concurrently with the expansion of the market in newspapers and periodicals.[37] Moreover, the height of castrato fever was attained after the lapse of the Licensing Act in 1695, and therefore in tandem with the sharp rise in the numbers of newspapers and periodicals printed from that date.[38] This rise arguably fostered intense scrutiny of all kinds of bodies. As Mark Dawson points out, the need to concisely and vividly describe physical features in newspaper reports led to the employment of a physiognomic and humoral shorthand in which attributes such as complexion or height were made to stand in for moral and social status.[39] Increased print advertising also encouraged focus on the body by homing in on physical shortcomings in order to sell medicines, cosmetics, and assistive technologies such as canes. Castrati were part of this marketisation; breathless accounts of their lavish lifestyles and scandalous affairs helped to shift newspapers. However, the positioning of castrati as items for ocular as well as auditory consumption reached its apex in a far odder form – namely, a series of advertisements for the 'Anodyne Necklace Shop' which appeared in 1745.

The anodyne necklace was, as Chapter 3 discusses, a piece of 'sympathetic' medicine, aiming to cure everything from teething pains to fevers using the atoms which allegedly flowed from the amulet.[40] The aim of this piece appears to be to get customers through the door of the premises on Drury Lane, London. Rather than promising the most effective or cheapest goods, however, the proprietor of the Anodyne Necklace Shop offers a different incentive: the chance to look at and in some measure interact with the castrato Farinelli:

---

[37] On advertising and the newspaper trade, see Michael Harris, 'Timely Notices: The Uses of Advertising and Its Relationship to News during the Late Seventeenth Century', in *News, Newspapers and Society in Early Modern Britain*, ed. Joad Raymond (Abingdon: Routledge, 2013), pp. 141–56. On the role of newspapers and the circulation of the *London Gazette*, which peaked in the late 1690s, see Natasha Glaisyer, 'The Most Universal Intelligencers', *Media History* 23:2 (2017): 256–80, https://doi.org/10.1080/13688804.2017.1309971. For a general overview of newspaper and periodical culture in this period, see Gerhild Scholz Williams and William Layher, *Consuming News: Newspapers and Print Culture in Early Modern Europe (1500–1800)* (Amsterdam: Editions Rodopi, 2008); James Raven, *Publishing Business in Eighteenth-Century England* (Woodbridge: Boydell and Brewer, 2014), pp. 118–32; James Sutherland, *The Restoration Newspaper and Its Development* (Cambridge: Cambridge University Press, 2004).

[38] Raymond Astbury, 'The Renewal of the Licensing Act in 1693 and its Lapse in 1695', *The Library* 5th series, 33:4 (1978): 296–322, https://doi.org/10.1093/library/s5-XXXIII.4.296.

[39] Mark S. Dawson, 'First Impressions: Newspaper Advertisements and Early Modern English Body Imaging, 1651–1750', *Journal of British Studies* 50:2 (2011): 277–306.

[40] Francis Cecil Doherty, *A Study in Eighteenth-Century Advertising Methods: The Anodyne Necklace* (Lewiston: Edwin Mellen Press, 1992).

The Interpretation of Women's Dreams

With the Prints of these DREAMS, Finely Engraved, And, the Application of them to Men.

Of Which, If a Maid Dreams the 34th Dream, She may as Well Wed FARINELLI, *At One* ----- With *A Curious Print* of FARINELLI, Finely Engraved, Plainly and Visibly Shewing, (to Plain, Open, and Clear View) the Apparently *Visible* MARKS of His CASTRATION.

With a LOTTERY,

For HUSBANDS for Young MAIDS,

With the Prints of these *Husbands*, finely Engrav'd.

Not One Blank, but ALL Prizes, the *Lowest* of Which, Is a Very HANDSOME and RICH *Young* Gentleman, that Keeps his COACH.

And, If She Draws of the 6th Class of Tickets, She is Then, SURE to be, MY LADY.

Any *Maiden*, that will Put off TWO *Tickets,* shall have ONE, for *Her Self,* To Put Her in Fortuna's Way. To be Drawn, as Soon, as Full.

'Tis GIVEN GRATIS ------- At the ANODYNE NECKLACE Shop, in LONG-ACRE.[41]

The author of this advertisement was clearly targeting young women. Enter the necklace shop, and one could experience both the thrill of viewing Farinelli's nakedness and the dubious benefit of being entered in a sort of fortune-telling raffle. Farinelli's body functions in this text as an object of ocular desire, a man whose physicality provokes equal lust and repugnance in those who examine his image. In this respect he is not dissimilar to the anatomies which Jonathan Sawday identifies as having had erotic potential for seventeenth-century audiences, joining 'morbid fears' with 'barely suppressed desires'.[42]

In such advertisements, the objectification of castrato bodies reached its zenith. Ironically, given the way in which he made his living, the castrato was entirely voiceless in the texts which traded on his image. Elsewhere in this book, we will see how bodily alteration was often shown to provoke a renegotiation of the relation between mind and body, such that the terms in which one 'lived one's body' were brought into question. Popular representations of castrati largely sidestepped such negotiations by simply declining to acknowledge that the castrato *had* a mind, and instead focussing obsessively on the potential of his unusual body. Fleeting affairs

[41] 'The Interpretation of Women's Dreams (Anodyne Necklace)', *Penny London Post or The Morning Advertiser*, 8 April 1745.
[42] Jonathan Sawday, *The Body Emblazoned: Dissection and the Human Body in Renaissance Culture* (Abingdon: Routledge, 2013), p. 49.

with castrati were viewed as physical rather than emotional exchanges, and thus the issues raised by those affairs were ones of the castrato's socio-economic liminality rather than deeper crises of gender; the matter at stake was how to conceive of the castrato's status as a commodity, rather than how to conceive of him as male or female. Ultimately, however, this objectification was not sustainable. Castrati made their voices heard, and in the process provoked discussion of their gender status. They did so by seeking to become 'real men' – that is, by seeking to marry.

Beyond Instrumentality

If castrati's illicit affairs were disconcerting to commentators, their encroachment on licit areas of sexuality – namely, the institution of marriage – was viewed as potentially catastrophic. It is telling that although such unions occurred only a handful of times during the seventeenth and eighteenth centuries, they attracted as much interest as any of the castrato's professional activities. Two cases of castrato marriage stand out as having garnered particular attention. The first occurred in Dresden in 1667, between Bartolomeo Sorlisi (1632–72) and Dorothea Lichter. The second took place between Giusto Ferdinando Tenducci (1736–90) and an Irishwoman, Dorothea Maunsell, in 1766. Both cases have been explored in detailed studies, and I will not rehearse their specifics here.[43] It is worth noting, however, that both instances provoked hostility from religious and secular authorities. In Sorlisi's case, initial misgivings from Dorothea Lichter's family were overcome, but it took years to persuade the Lutheran Church to marry the pair. The case of Tenducci and Maunsell was more complex. Maunsell, aged fifteen, eloped with Tenducci as a means to avoid betrothal to another suitor favoured by her family, though she also claimed to be passionately in love with the singer. Her relatives reacted with fury, accusing Tenducci of abducting their daughter, and they pursued his imprisonment and the dissolution of the marriage until 1767, when they finally capitulated. By 1771, however, Dorothea had borne at least one child which was widely accepted to have been fathered by William Kingsman. She married Kingsman in 1772, and a trial followed in which she successfully contended that her marriage to Tenducci had

---

[43] For a detailed study of Tenducci, see Berry, *The Castrato and His Wife*; on Sorlisi, see Mary E. Frandsen, '"Eunuchi Conjugium": The Marriage of a Castrato in Early Modern Germany', *Early Music History* 24 (2005): 53–124.

never been valid, and that she was not therefore guilty of bigamy.[44] As I explore below, this decision by the courts reflected a longstanding belief in some quarters that castrato marriages were illegitimate because of the liminal status of the castrate body.

Why were castrati forbidden – or at least, very strongly discouraged – from marrying? The answer to this question is less obvious than it appears. Officially, castrati had been forbidden to marry in the same 1587 Papal 'cum Frequenter' which had barred the castrating of boys to become singers. This, however, does not seem to have been the main issue which prevented acceptance of Sorlisi's and Tenducci's marriages. Neither, it appears, was the castrato's inability to beget children. Though critics often argued that castrati were unfit for marriage because they were unable to procreate, Sorlisi and Tenducci both pointed out that this consideration did not prevent marriages between men and women past childbearing age. Likewise, it was not usual (though not unheard of) for marriages to be dissolved when one of the parties proved to be infertile. Rather, the objection to castrato marriages that was stressed in court accounts and popular reportage was once again linked to the liminality of the castrato. Those who argued against such marriages questioned whether castrati could rightly claim to be men.

For English readers, this question was treated in most detail in a text translated from French, Charles Ancillon's *Italian Love: Or, Eunuchism Displayed* (1740; first published 1718). This text was framed as an advisory to a friend's daughter who had become enamoured with a castrato, though there is no evidence that this was more than a conceit. Ancillon's attitude to castrati was much coloured by his reading on eunuchs, who appeared in various ethnographic texts throughout the seventeenth century. Eunuchs were said to be created by the rulers of Middle Eastern or Oriental countries in order to serve as administrators or as guards for harems.[45] Following these texts, Ancillon asserted that eunuchs' bodily difference conferred on them particular, mostly undesirable, character traits:

> An Eunuch . . . is a person which has not the faculty or power of generation,
> either through weakness or coldness of nature, or who is any wise deprived

---

[44] 'Maunsell [Married Name Kingsman], Dorothea (b. 1749x51), Figure of Scandal | Oxford Dictionary of National Biography', accessed 4 December 2019, https://doi.org/10.1093/ref:odnb/104868.

[45] See, for instance, *The New Atlas, or, Travels and Voyages in Europe, Asia, Africa, and America* (London: J. Cleave and A. Roper, 1698), pp. 20–1; Bulwer, *Anthropometamorphosis*, pp. 354–62; Ottaviano Bon, *A Description of the Grand Signour's Seraglio or Turkish Emperours Court*, trans. John Greaves (London: Jo. Ridley, 1653), pp. 95–100.

of the parts proper for generation ... Such who can by no means propagate and generate, who have a squealing languishing voice, a womanish complection, and soft down for a beard, who have no courage or bravery of soul, but ever timerous and fearful: In a few words, whose ways, manners, and customs, are entirely effeminate.[46]

This list emphasised the character of the castrato in a way which was entirely absent from discussions about those singers' social lives and casual affairs. Once again, however, such a formulaic depiction of castrati assigned to them as a group courses of action based entirely on their bodily difference, and thus sought to exclude the possibility of their individual, subjective agency. Ancillon's desire to stereotype and stigmatise castrati was far from unique. In so doing, he echoes the tone of earlier texts which, in their most antagonistic forms, treated castrato singers as not only less than male, but less than human. *A Trip through the Town* described Farinelli as a mixture of exotic beast and apparition, one 'whose CRIES have a sort of MAGICK CHARM in them, that takes Possession, at once, of the MOV'D Listener's Soul ... The *Hyaena*, who is said, by its feigned Cry of Misery, to attract Traveller's Steps towards itself, has not so sure an Effect as that of this AMPHIBIOUS ANIMAL.'[47] Similarly, Nicolini was described in dehumanising terms as a '*Plump, Tender Thing*', member of 'A *tuneful Race*'.[48]

This discourse was soon brought to bear on discussions of the castrato's legal rights, which culminated in public wrangling over the castrato's right to marry. In *Italian Love*, Ancillon argues, predictably, that castrated men should not be allowed to marry because the purpose of marriage is procreation. In his elaboration on this argument, however, the author strays from that utilitarian view and into the question of the castrato's gender identity. Ancillon seems to assume that no woman would knowingly marry a eunuch, even though this is precisely the scenario around which he bases his 'epistles'. Reinforcing once again the potential commodity value of human bodies, he argues that marriage is a contract in which each party 'buys' the other's body. Castrati, he argues, misrepresent their bodies, and thus any marriages they contract ought to be considered fraudulent: 'The marriages then of eunuchs never were truly marriages, because there never was a true conjunction.'[49] His objections to castrati go even deeper, however, when he asserts that 'they put on the appearance of

[46] Ancillon, *Italian Love: Or, Eunuchism Displayed*, p. 8.   [47] *A Trip through the Town.*
[48] *The Signior in Fashion: Or the Fair Maid's Conveniency.*
[49] Ancillon, *Italian Love: Or, Eunuchism Displayed*, p. 158.

men, when they are not so in reality'.[50] From claiming that the castrato
was not a procreative man, Ancillon moved to claiming that they were not
men *at all*.

Discussions of castrato marriage thus show how castrati could be
considered sexually as well as socially liminal. Nonetheless, while these
debates still mostly took place about rather than with castrati, they show a
greater engagement with castrati as agential subjects. Ancillon characterised
castrati in terms of their bodily difference, but he at least acknowledged
that castrati *had* characters, whereas elsewhere they were represented as
practically devoid of an inner life. Paradoxically, sexual liminality provided
the best platform for castrati to forge their own identities. In arguing for
their status as marriageable, Sorlisi and Tenducci spoke up in a way few
castrati managed. Furthermore, the castrato's aesthetic distinctiveness was
founded on gender fluidity. For the most part, as scholars of opera have
shown, the castrato voice was a heroic voice. Composers such as Handel
wrote leading heroic male parts with the high, powerful voice of the
castrato in mind:

> a voice in the soprano range, singing floridly composed lines with lavish
> interpolated embellishments, came to represent the sound of the hero. This,
> perhaps, is one of the key points, that the hero *sounded* a particular way that
> was most associated with castrato and *travesti* voices.[51]

This allocation, however, was complicated. At times, castrati also played
women on stage, a role in which Naomi André argues that 'some could
sustain the illusion of belonging to either gender outside of the opera
house, despite the men's or women's clothing they wore'.[52] Equally, when
a castrato could not be found, soprano female singers might fill the same
roles, acting as *travesti* (female singers who dressed as men). Overall, the
castrato's appearances on stage played to, and played with, his indeterminate status outside the theatre. André relates the castrato's position to that
of the transvestite boy actor, and in particular, to Majorie Garber's
contention that 'transvestism is a space of possibility structuring and
confounding culture'.[53] Rather than perpetuating this sort of representa-
tional crisis, however, André sees the castrato's ability to play male or

[50] Ibid., p. 148.
[51] Freya Jarman, 'Pitch Fever: The Castrato, the Tenor and the Question of Masculinity in Nineteenth-Century Opera', in *Masculinity in Opera*, ed. Philip Purvis (Abingdon: Routledge, 2013), p. 52.
[52] Naomi Adele André, *Voicing Gender: Castrati, Travesti, and the Second Woman in Early-Nineteenth-Century Italian Opera* (Indianapolis: Indiana University Press, 2006), p. 49.
[53] Quoted in ibid., p. 49.

female on or off stage as 'a performance practice that is part of a larger aesthetic'.[54] In that aesthetic, the use of soprano voices for male and female parts fostered a 'one-sex' view of anatomy which was antithetical to strict sexual dimorphism. Both castrati and, later, *travesti* possessed

> a voice that was heard as being gendered masculine *and* feminine without different aural markers. The voices of these women, as well as the earlier operatic castrato, were heard as sometimes male and sometimes female, depending on the surrounding context. In looking back, it is also possible to imagine their voices as neither man nor woman in an exclusive sense, but regard that as a combination of something in between: a 'third' option for gendering the singing voice.[55]

The same artistic distinction which led to the castrato's prestige as a performer, and therefore to his commodification, opened up a space in which he could be imagined as *living* his body. While the castrato's phenomenological experience might still be only dimly imagined, within the aesthetic of gender fluidity, an alternate mode of living was, at least, thinkable.

Conclusion

It is clear that for many onlookers, the castrato body was something very strange. Was it also strange to the castrato? When critics objectified castrati as commodities, and denied their subjectivity, they acted in a way consistent with what Drew Leder terms 'social dys-appearance'. Leder explains:

> As long as the Other treats me as a subject ... mutual incorporation effects no sharp rift. But it is different when the primary stance of the Other is highly distanced, antagonistic, or objectifying. Internalizing this perspective, I can become conscious of my self as an alien thing. A radical split is introduced between the body I live out and my object-body, now defined and delimited by a foreign gaze.[56]

'Highly distanced', 'antagonistic', and 'objectifying': these are all fitting terms to describe the attitudes of most seventeenth- and eighteenth-century writers towards castrati. We cannot know, however, whether such attitudes had the effect of alienating castrati from their own bodies, because those same attitudes excluded castrato voices. As so often in our study of people with bodily difference, the only perspective which remains

---

[54] Ibid.   [55] Ibid., p. 48.
[56] Drew Leder, *The Absent Body* (Chicago: University of Chicago Press, 1990), p. 96.

is that of the bodily and socially normative. Nonetheless, some evidence remains for castrati asserting their right to live fully rounded lives which incorporated their experience as gelded men. This includes the rare phenomenon of castrato marriage, in which the potential for meaningful relationships outside patrilineal structures is glimpsed. It also includes castrati's readiness to play a variety of on-stage roles in which male and female voices were interchangeable, and thus in which sexual dimorphism receded from view.

There is one further oddity about early modern accounts of castrati. Whilst 'facts' about eunuchs were sometimes used as bases to make claims about the bodies and characters of castrati, things which were supposedly known about castrati (for instance, their alleged sexual appetites) were not used to make claims about other gelded men. As I have described elsewhere, the gelding of adult men for medical or other reasons occurred within a cultural framework which included religious and folk references, but castrati were very rarely seen among those references.[57] There were no jokes about 'singing an octave higher' in ballads about castration or medical accounts of orchiectomy. Admittedly, castrati were not uppermost in the mind of most early modern people of the 'middling sort'. Nonetheless, this absence implies that the foreignness of castrati, their manifold physical differences, and their exoticised sexuality made them, for most people, entirely alien. Accounts in which castrati were dehumanised were not exceptions to the rule, but rather reflected a general view in which these singers were profoundly unlike 'normal' men.

[57] Alanna Skuse, '"One Stroak of His Razour": Tales of Self-Gelding in Early Modern England', *Social History of Medicine*, 33, no. 2 (2020), 377–93, https://doi.org/10.1093/shm/hky100.

CHAPTER 2

Invisible Women: Altered Female Bodies

In 1711, William Beckett, a well-respected surgeon, provided the readers of his *New Discoveries Relating to the Cure of Cancers* with instructions for performing a mastectomy operation:

> Let the Patient be placed in a clear Light, and held steady; then take hold of the Breast with one hand, and pull it to you; and, with the other, nimbly make Incision, and cut it off as close to the Ribs as possible, that no Parts of it remain behind. But if any *cancerous Gland* should remain, be sure to have actual Cauteries of different sizes, ready hot by you, to consume it, and to stop the Bleeding; or otherwise apply, for restraining the Hemorrhage, Dorsels dipp'd in scalding hot *Ol. Terebinth* [turpentine oil] . . . then with good Boulstring and Rolling, conveniently place the Patient in Bed, and at night give her an *anodine Draught*, then the second or third Day open it, digest, deterge, incarn and siccatrize.[1]

Though the procedure was a grim one, Beckett knew more about treating cancer than almost any of his contemporaries, and his instructions represented best practice for an aspiring surgeon. In one respect, however, Beckett's account – and his entire text – was lacking. Neither this, nor any other account of mastectomy which I have found, mentions what happened to the patient after they healed.[2] This is in stark contrast to other kinds of body-altering operations which I describe in this book. There was, as Chapter 4 explores, a rich discourse about prostheses for limb amputees and their functionality. As Chapter 3 shows, descriptions of facial surgery and prostheses emphasised the

---

[1] William Beckett, *New Discoveries Relating to the Cure of Cancers, Wherein a Method of Dissolving the Cancerous Substance Is Recommended, with Various Instances of the Author's Success in Such Practice, on Persons Reputed Incurable, in a Letter to a Friend. To Which Is Added, a Solution of Some Curious Problems, Concerning the Same Disease* (London, 1711), pp. 69–70.

[2] See Alanna Skuse, *Constructions of Cancer in Early Modern England: Ravenous Natures* (Basingstoke: Palgrave Macmillan, 2015).

social rehabilitation of patients. When it came to mastectomy survivors, however, there were no such descriptions, no mentions of padding or prostheses to replace the lost breast, and no clues about whether women with one breast went on to have more children, to marry or remarry, or to work. In this chapter, I will argue that women whose bodies were altered by surgery became invisible in early modern texts, and will explore why this might be the case.

In many ways, the sexually altered female bodies which I will describe here are correlates to the castrato body discussed in the previous chapter. Both were exoticised and often dehumanised, and in both cases, contemporary texts demonstrated a fascination with the (dis) abilities which such bodily alterations might confer. However, where the castrato body was hypervisible and overdetermined (notwithstanding the determined lack of attention paid to castrati's own experiences), the altered female body was underdetermined, and viewed only within specific textual contexts. Ethnography provided a space within which the phenomenological implications of altering the female body might be explored. However, such bodies were kept at arm's length. The combination of femininity and disability was a disturbing, ultimately abject prospect.

Altering the Female Body

The main sex-specific way in which the female body was surgically changed in the early modern period was by mastectomy, the removal of the breast, in whole or part, usually as a treatment for cancer.[3] Such surgeries have often been overlooked by medical historians, who have understandably assumed that these operations were too dangerous to have been attempted on any regular basis. Removing a breast to treat a slowly spreading cancer was, after all, a quite different prospect to amputating a limb which was mangled beyond repair and bleeding dangerously; the former required a prior commitment to excruciating pain and danger which is now almost unthinkable. Nonetheless, as this book discusses elsewhere, early modern people were, remarkably, prepared to undergo non-emergency surgeries in order to secure both longevity and quality of life. This was particularly the case for women facing cancer, a disease feared by patients and physicians alike, and

[3] Ibid.

known to cause a slow, agonising death if left untreated. As the French surgeon Pierre Dionis put it:

> If we believe *Hippocrates*, Cancers are not to be touch'd, for in touching them, observes that Author, you aggravate the Evil, and hasten the Death of the Patient.

> But how are you to resist the Persecutions of a poor suffering Patient, which implores your help? Are you to abandon her to the Rigour of her Distemper, which torments her Day and Night? No, a Chirurgeon must not be so cruel: He must search out Means to cure her.[4]

Mastectomy was, therefore, a recognised part of the surgical repertoire: though not common, it was an option available to most experienced surgeons. Methods for the operation are detailed in numerous prominent medical textbooks, including those by Richard Wiseman, James Cooke, and William Salmon.[5] They usually follow a similar method to that described by Beckett above. The breast was cut around the base, most commonly with a knife similar to that used in limb amputations, but sometimes with a sharp wire. With the breast removed, the surgeon would attempt to remove any tumour that remained visible, either by excision or using a hot iron cautery. They then used cautery or styptic powders to stem the flow of blood, before dressing the wound and hoping for the best. As is often the case for this period, what we know of patient experiences of this procedure is pieced together from second-hand accounts. There are no autobiographical accounts from this period from women who underwent mastectomies – the first known example is Frances Burney's evocative description of her mastectomy in 1811.[6] It is abundantly clear, however, that such surgeries were immensely traumatic for everybody involved. Many surgeons admitted that they dreaded these operations, during which the life of the patient and the reputation of the practitioner were in imminent danger, and in which the suffering of the patient could disturb even a hardened operator. One *Medical Dictionary* advised readers that

---

[4] Pierre Dionis, *A Course of Chirurgical Operations, Demonstrated in the Royal Garden at Paris. By Monsieur Dionis, Chief Chirurgeon to the Late Dauphiness, and to the Present Dutchess of Burgundy. Translated from the Paris Edition* (London, 1710), pp. 249–50.

[5] Richard Wiseman, *Several Chirurgical Treatises* (London, 1686), pp. 108–10; James Cooke, *Mellificium Chirurgiæ, or the Marrow of Many Good Authors Enlarged: Wherein Is Briefly, Fully, and Faithfully Handled the Art of Chirurgery in Its Four Parts, with All the Several Diseases unto Them Belonging: Their Definitions, Causes, Signes, Prognosticks, and Cures, Both General and Particular* (London: printed by T.R. for John Sherley, 1662), pp. 308–12; William Salmon, *Ars Chirurgica* (London, 1698), p. 98.

[6] Frances Burney, 'Letter from Frances Burney to Her Sister Esther about Her Mastectomy without Anaesthetic, 1812' (Paris, 1812), Berg Coll. MSS Arblay, British Library.

women undergoing mastectomy might 'shriek and cry in a manner so terrible, as is sufficient to shock and confuse the most intrepid surgeon, and disconcert him in his operation'.[7]

Notwithstanding the evident sympathy many surgeons had for their patients, however, medical accounts of mastectomy also show that these operations were an exercise in which groups of professional men exerted their power to control the female body, even to the extent of granting life or death.[8] As was the case for castrati, this dynamic was manifested in texts' inattention to the phenomenological experience of the person whose ordeal they described, either from a somatic or a psychological perspective. Accounts of cancer surgery in medical textbooks sometimes talk in detail about the symptoms and living situation of the patient prior to surgery; as I discuss below, cancer was linked to a number of causes including mastitis and amenorrhea. In descriptions of the mastectomy itself, however, the subjectivity of the patient is pointedly erased. By their own admission, surgeons operated not on a person, but on a breast, assiduously seeking to 'devide the good from the evill'.[9] As this book will demonstrate at various points, there was a general tendency in early modern accounts of surgery to objectify the person under the knife. In cases of mastectomy, however, this tendency seems to be have been amplified. Dionis, for instance, assured the readers of his *Chirurgical Operations* that '[t]his Operation is easier than is imagined before 'tis performed; for the Breast separates as easily from the Ribs, as when we divide the Shoulder from a Quarter of Lamb'.[10]

This impulse to deny both the psychological and physical experiences of mastectomy patients extended beyond the operation itself. Moreover, this is not only an effect of scarcity of evidence. Mastectomy surgeries were less common than (for example) limb amputations, but there is evidence that they were taking place semi-regularly throughout the seventeenth and eighteenth centuries. From the 1700s, newspapers reported the operations of the great and good: on 8 February 1728, for instance, an announcement in the *London Evening Post* reported that 'the lady of Sir Challenor Ogle'

[7] Robert James, 'Amputation', in *A Medicinal Dictionary*, 3 vols. (London, 1743), vol. I, sig. 5GV.
[8] As I have observed elsewhere, cancer surgeries, being relatively unusual, tended to attract students and other observers. For instance, Richard Wiseman recorded operating on cancers alongside or in front of other professionals including including Walter Needham, 'Mr Nurse', Doctor Bate, Doctor Thomas Cox, Doctor Micklethwaite, Jacques Wiseman (his 'kinsman'), and Mr Hollier, Mr Arris, Edward Molin, Mr Troutbeck, and Mr Shunbub (all chirurgeons). Wiseman, *Several Chirurgical Treatises*, pp. 101–2.
[9] Philip Barrough, *The Method of Physick* (London, 1583), p. 232; see also Johannes Scultetus, *The Chyrurgeons Store-House*, trans. E.B. (London: printed for John Starkey, 1674), p. 171.
[10] Dionis, *Chirurgical Operations*, pp. 254–5.

had undergone an operation to remove a cancer in her breast, 'and there is great Hopes of her Recovery'.[11] The obituary pages also recorded the deaths of numerous women during or shortly after surgery.[12] However, despite the fact that mastectomy survivors existed, they are virtually invisible in the historical record. Medical texts may detail the dressings and medicines used in the days and weeks after surgery, but they end abruptly thereafter. This is a stark contrast to narratives of limb amputation described in Chapter 4, which emphasise return to functionality as part of the recovery narrative. Neither do mastectomy survivors appear in the popular texts which valorised, demonised, mocked, and sympathised with other kinds of 'altered bodies'. In short, they are conspicuous by their absence.

Amazons

In one arena, however, the effects of mastectomy *were* being discussed. As colonial activity burgeoned in the sixteenth and seventeenth centuries, lurid tales reached England of unimammarian women living in remote parts of the world, often in gynocentric societies. Such accounts often blended mythology, history, and ethnography, and could be found in a variety of texts. From the fourteenth century, manuscript copies of Sir John Mandeville's *Voyages and Travailes* circulated in French, and later in English translations and editions, including a printed edition in 1582.[13] John Bulwer's *Anthropometamorphosis* (published in 1650 and in an enlarged edition in 1653) featured a comprehensive catalogue of human variation and bodily modification, which included Amazons.[14] Likewise, Thomas Heywood's 1624 *Gynaikeion* sought to provide a 'history of women' arranged under the names of the nine classical muses. Throughout these varied reports, however, the main features of Amazons and Amazon society remained the same. Most authors agreed that the Amazons were an ancient society, though their exact origins, and their current geographical location, were confused. Prose histories of the

---

[11] *London Evening Post*, 8 February 1728.
[12] *Daily Gazetteer*, 3 November 1736; *Daily Journal*, 28 October 1736; *London Evening Post*, 15 February 1729.
[13] John Mandeville, *The Voyages and Trauailes of Sir John Maundeuile Knight Wherein Is Treated of the Way towards Hierusalem, and of the Meruailes of Inde, with Other Lands and Countries* (London: printed by Thomas Este, 1582), sig. L2r–v.
[14] John Bulwer, *Anthropometamorphosis: = Man Transform'd: Or, the Artificiall Changling* (London: printed by William Hunt, 1653), pp. 321–5.

seventeenth century repeatedly asserted that the Amazons were an offshoot of the Scythian people. Heywood, for instance, attested that the Amazons were originally Scythian women who migrated while their husbands were away at war and formed their own society, while others believed that the Amazons warred with the Scythians or bore children by them.[15] Many texts drew on the works of Plutarch and Virgil, in which numerous stories circulate of couplings between Western heroes and Amazonian princesses. In some versions, Theseus abducts and then marries Antiope, sister of the Amazonian queen Hippolyta; in others, he weds Hippolyta herself.[16] Alexander the Great was also reputed to have been visited by and fathered a child with the Amazon queen Thalestris.[17]

Whatever their origins, authors were clear that Amazons lived either entirely without men, or with men in subservient roles. In 1582, for instance, Mandeville's *Voyages and Travailes* was printed and described (with considerable imaginative licence) how a New World tribe of warrior women would 'suffer no men to live among them, nor to have rule over them', instead periodically inviting men to copulate with them.[18] Fourteen years after Mandeville's account appeared in print, Sir Walter Raleigh published his own, more detailed version of the Amazon story as part of the *Discovery of the Large, Rich, and Beautiful Empire of Guiana*. It stated confidently that Guianese Amazons partnered with local kings for one month each year, during which they would 'feast, daunce, and drinke of their wines in abundance, and the Moone being done, they all depart to their owne Provinces'. Moreover,

> It was farther told me, that if in the wars they tooke any prisoners that they used to accompany with those also at what time soever, but in the end, for certaine they put them to death: for they are said to be very cruell and bloodthirsty, especially to such as offer to invade their territories.[19]

Amazons' famously ferocious and gynocentric societies were closely indexed to their most distinctive bodily feature: the removal of one breast. Though Raleigh noted that 'that they cut of[f] the right dug of the brest

[15] Thomas Heywood, *Gynaikeion: Or, Nine Bookes of Various History. Concerninge Women Inscribed by Ye Names of Ye Nine Muses* (London, 1624), 220; Gaultier de Coste La Calprenède, *Hymen's Præludia, or Loves Master-Peice Being That so Much Admired Romance, Intituled Cleopatra: In Twelve Parts* (London: W.R. and J.R, 1674), p. 159.
[16] Plutarch, *Plutarch's Lives.* (London: Jacob Tonson, 1683), pp. 40–1.
[17] Heywood, *Gynaikeion*, p. 222.
[18] Mandeville *The Voyages and Trauailes of Sir John Maundeuile*, sig. L3r.
[19] Walter Raleigh, *Discovery of the Large, Rich, and Beautiful Empire of Guiana, by Sir W. Ralegh: With a Relation of the Great and Golden City of Manoa (Which the Spaniards Call El Dorado), Etc. (1596)* (London: Hakluyt Society, 1848), pp. 27–9.

I do not finde to be true', most other accounts disagreed.[20] Mandeville specified that Amazon girls of noble birth had the left breast removed by cautery to allow them to better bear a shield, while ordinary girls had the right breast removed to befit them for a bow and arrow.[21] Heywood asserted that 'the right brest they burne off, that with the more facilitie they may draw a Bowe, thrill a Dart, or charge a Launce'.[22] Meanwhile, Bulwer argued that there existed a number of different Amazonian tribes, among whom breast removal was a common practice:

> The Ancient *Amazones*, of whom we read so oft in learned Authors, were wont to seare off their right breasts, which was then the archers fashion. *Porta* saies, the Amazons sear off their right paps, that more nourishment going into the hand next to it, might increase the strength of that which was but weake by nature. Others say, that the Amazons much helping themselves in the wars with bows and arrows, and finding that in this and other exercises of armes their dugs or breasts were a very great hinderance to them, they used to burne off the right pap, both of themselves and their daughters, and thereupon they were called Amazons, which signifieth in the Greeke tongue, No Breasts.

> The chiefe of the guard of the King of Congo are lefthanded Amazons, who seare off their left paps with a hot iron, because it should be no hinderance to them in their shooting.[23]

All these reports had in common a fascination with the anomalous body of the Amazon, akin to that which characterised reports of castrato bodies. Here, as there, bodily difference was bound up with racial Otherness, and both had potential to titillate. It was no coincidence that Bulwer's and Mandeville's texts both contained pictures of Amazon women with their chests partially or fully exposed. Heywood's text similarly teased readers with its description of Amazon dress: 'Their garments cover not their bodies round; their right side is still bare towards their brest; their upper roabe which is buckled or buttoned above, descends no lower than the knee.'[24] In such discourse, Amazons were both objects of lust and causes for fear. While procreative, they evaded the structures of marriage and patriarchy, and engaged in sex for pleasure as well as for reproduction. Moreover, unlike other sexually promiscuous female figures, the Amazon could not be stereotyped as a prostitute; as Simon Shepherd acknowledges, '[t]he propertied Amazon cannot be cast aside, as would a whore. And she

[20] Ibid.   [21] Mandeville, *The Voyages and Trauailes of Sir John Maundeuile*, sig. l2v.
[22] Heywood, *Gynaikeion*, p. 223.   [23] Bulwer, *Anthropometamorphosis*, pp. 321–2.
[24] Heywood, *Gynaikeion*, p. 223.

imitates men in using social power for sexual exploitation. Hence the nightmarish turning of the tables.'[25] Instead, Amazon women were understood to use their bodies and exercise their sexuality in ways which were not easily defined. In Kathryn Schwarz's insightful *Tough Love: Amazon Encounters in the English Renaissance*, she shows how Amazon stories influenced representations of contemporary femininity, including depictions of Elizabeth I. Often, argues Schwarz, stories about Amazons envision them becoming domesticated, turned into obedient wives and mothers. Yet their attraction remains in their 'queerness', an alterity of desire which reveals rigid heterosexual and homosocial structures as cultural rather than natural.

> 'Amazon' cannot signify in any singular or straightforward way . . . Bringing them close to home invites chaos: as separatists they are a threat, but as mothers and lovers and wives and queens they are a disaster, participating in and altering the structures that should work to keep them out. Yet even as texts from this period locate the alien within the familiar, they suggest the sense in which that process is already redundant: in representations of Amazons as in representations of women and men, challenges to conventional identities and hierarchies are at least as familiar as conventions themselves. The imaginative power of domestic Amazons lies not only in the inherent perversity of the term, but in its exposure of the incongruities that underlie social and sexual acts.[26]

As Schwarz shows, the underdetermination of Amazons in terms of location and origins allowed them to embody a range of anxieties around homosociality, gender roles, and sexual desire. Looking at the Amazon body through the lens of early modern surgery raises other questions – namely, can we also consider these bodies as doing cultural work which extended to early modern survivors of mastectomy? The repudiation of heteronormative structures and of traditional motherhood implicit in the Amazons' self-alteration speaks in unexpected ways to discourses about cancer and mastectomy, in which images of maternity were omnipresent. As I have described elsewhere, cancer was believed to be far more common in women than in men, with diagnoses of breast cancer far outstripping all others. The language in which cancerous growth was described often mirrored that used about foetuses: each drew nourishment from the woman's body, and was 'delivered' with much pain and hazard. In practical terms too, maternity and cancer were close companions. Cancer was

[25] Simon Shepherd, *Amazons and Warrior Women: Varieties of Feminism in Seventeenth-Century Drama* (Brighton: Prentice Hall/Harvester Wheatsheaf, 1981), pp. 16–17.
[26] Kathryn Schwarz, *Tough Love: Amazon Encounters in the English Renaissance* (Fordham: Duke University Press, 2000), p. 23.

often believed to have its origins in 'burnt' humours concocted in the womb, particularly when the menses were stopped.[27] This was thought to be a decisive factor in the high incidence of cancers in post-menopausal women. Even more commonly, tumours were thought to start with mastitis, which in turn could be caused by problems with breastfeeding, or by not breastfeeding.[28]

The possible extent of linkage between Amazonian and medical mastectomy is apparent in pictorial representations of both phenomena. Figure 2.1, for instance, shows Amazons as they are represented in Bulwer's *Anthropometamorphosis*. The images are remarkable in several respects. They pointedly show the healthy breast alongside the missing one, and relegate the wound left by amputation to a linear scar. Attention is further diverted from this scar by the figures' lavishly draped clothing, jewellery, and weaponry, all of which attest to the Amazons' status as at once warlike and feminine. Moreover, the images are double: both the removal of the left and of the right breast are shown, despite the limited educational utility of this repetition. We may usefully compare these images to Figure 2.2, an illustration from a 1674 translation of Johannes Scultetus' *The Chyrurgeon's Store-House* (originally *Armamentarium Chirurgiae*, 1655), in which the images marked I to IV show the mastectomy operation. While the styles of these two representations are markedly different, certain aspects of their presentation are strikingly similar. In Scultetus' image as in Bulwer's, the intact breast is revealed, with the figure's clothing draped suggestively around the waist as if in the act of disrobing, though in Scultetus' image the flowing locks and jewellery which suggest a continuing feminine identity are absent. The faces of these figures, like those of Bulwer's Amazons, are blank despite the pain which is evidently being inflicted in Scultetus' image. The repetition of the figure in Scultetus' image has more explanatory value than in Bulwer's, but the urge to itemise the body is the same, even to the extent of showing the amputated breast. Correspondingly, the quasi-divine power of the disembodied hands descending into the scene, as if from heaven, describes a surgical power of remaking which is akin to the classificatory power of the ethnographer. As I will discuss below, people living with one-breasted bodies were under-represented on stage and in text. However, when such bodies could be viewed at a remove – within the confines of an

---

[27] Alanna Skuse, 'Wombs, Worms and Wolves: Constructing Cancer in Early Modern England', *Social History of Medicine* 27:4 (2014): 632–48.
[28] On the gendering of cancer, see Skuse, *Constructions of Cancer in Early Modern England*, pp. 40–60.

Amazons that feare off their Left Paps &c.

322   *Man Transform'd : O*R,

that the *Amazons* much helping themselves in the wars with Bows and Arrows, and finding that in this and other exercises of Armes their Dugs or Breasts were a very great hinderance to them, they used to burne off the right Pap, both of themselves and their Daughters, and thereupon they were called *Amazons*, which signifieth in the Greeke Tongue, No Breasts.

Purch. Ngr.3. lib.7.

Pigafetta in his relation of Gongo.

The chiefe of the Guard of the King of *Congo* are left-handed *Amazons*, who feare off their left Paps with a hot Iron, because it should be no hinderance to them in their shooting. *Pigafetta* in his reports of the Kingdome of *Congo*, makes the like mention of these

---

Figure 2.1   Detail from John Bulwer's *Anthropometamorphosis: = Man Transform'd: Or, the Artificiall Changling* (London, 1653).

Image produced by ProQuest as part of Early English Books Online (EEBO) www.proquest.com

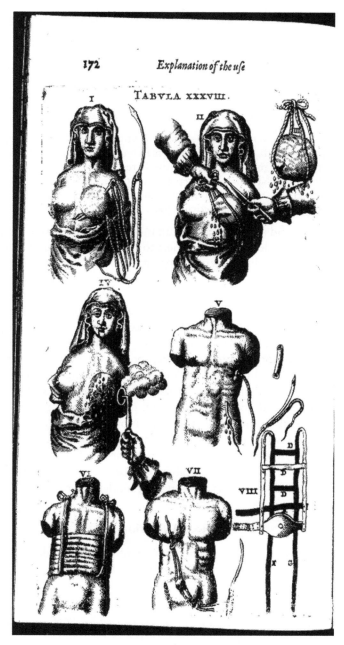

Figure 2.2   Detail from Johannes Scultetus, *The Chyrurgeons Store-House* (London, 1674).
Image produced by ProQuest as part of Early English Books Online (EEBO) www.proquest.com

ethnographic or medical text – they drew on a shared visual language in which the altered female body was both a desirable and a fearful object.

We might then read the unimammarian Amazon body and the body of the mastectomy survivor in parallel. In Amazons, one-breastedness was an effect of a society in which maternity took a back seat to martial valour; it was, as Bulwer asserted, the physical means of 'discarding the tendernesse of their Sexe'.[29] Gail Kern Paster similarly recognises,

> Mastectomy ... implies the Amazon's crucial bodily heresy at least by comparison with the many claims, material and symbolic, on womb and breast in early modern culture – the heresy visibly to control their own bodies, to regulate their own reproductivity, and to offer a model of self-government in which reproduction and nurture are only two of several forms of service and productive activity.[30]

While Amazons did not necessarily shun motherhood, they were commonly said to give their male children to others to raise. The Amazon's willingness to relinquish some of her maternal capacity, and some of her children, may have resonated with critics of wet-nursing, who saw the practice as indicating an unnatural paucity of maternal instinct.[31] Meanwhile, the survivor of medical mastectomy was an unwilling participant in 'gestating' the tumour which might kill her, and which she attempted to expel through the painful and life-threatening experience of surgery. This sinister inversion of the process of pregnancy and birth was often bound up with perceived failure in or unwillingness to breastfeed one's child, though writers stopped short of blaming women for their illness. Whether early modern people perceived these similarities, and how that perception might have affected the experiences of mastectomy survivors, is opaque. No accounts of cancer surgery, medical or otherwise, make the link between the altered body of the mastectomy survivor and the Amazon. Nonetheless, I shall argue that this absence may itself say something about the way in which altered female bodies were placed – or displaced – in early modern culture.

Abject Alteration

As I have described, early modern ethnographic texts usually highlighted the Amazons' altered bodies. Amazon one-breastedness was strongly

[29] Bulwer, *Anthropometamorphosis*, p. 323.
[30] Gail Kern Paster, *The Body Embarrassed: Drama and the Disciplines of Shame in Early Modern England* (New York: Cornell University Press, 1993), p. 237.
[31] Jacques Guillemeau, *Childbirth, or, the Happy Delivery of Women* (London, 1612).

indexed to sexual freedom and a gynocentric way of living. The anxieties over maternity and sexuality Amazons provoked were also relevant to the bodies of early modern mastectomy survivors, though their exact relationship was unclear. In order to understand more about how images of the Amazon body might have impacted on the lived experiences of mastectomy survivors, I argue that one needs to look not only at those texts in which Amazon one-breastedness is present, but at those in which it is curiously and conspicuously absent.

Sexually altered female bodies were automatically excluded from many of the literary forms in which altered male bodies appeared. Unimammarian bodies were not deemed aesthetically useful in the same way as gelded male bodies. Hence, while castrati dominated the pages of newspapers and periodicals, Amazons were largely forgotten. Amazons did appear, however, in several seventeenth-century dramas, and in these plays, the missing breast is just that – missing. The absence is particularly striking when one considers early modern audiences' love of stage effects such as crutches, limps, and what Farah Karim-Cooper describes as 'the spectacle of dismemberment'.[32] The image of a one-breasted woman, with the site of her mastectomy bared, would seem at first to be a gift to cross-dressing boy actors, who might utilise their naturally flat chests in the service of theatrical realism. One would imagine, too, that the missing breast would be a boon to playwrights, who so keenly played on the ideas of missing parts and no-thingness implied by the Amazon's correlate, the eunuch. Yet neither of these possibilities is realised. Shakespeare's Hippolyta, for instance, makes no mention of bodily difference, and neither does her husband-to-be, Theseus.[33] John Weston's 1667 *The Amazon Queen* makes much of the Amazons' sexual freedom, but neither the women nor their lovers mention their having one breast.[34] Moreover, John Fletcher and Philip Massinger's *The Sea Voyage* (1622) features an unspecified desert island populated by 'Amazons' who fulfil their ethnographic stereotypes by eschewing male authority while taking the play's shipwrecked male protagonists as temporary lovers. These women are said to be 'shaped like Amazons' in their social and sexual habits, but again, there is nothing in

---

[32] Farah Karim-Cooper, *The Hand on the Shakespearean Stage: Gesture, Touch and the Spectacle of Dismemberment* (London: Bloomsbury, 2016) pp. 197–241. On the cultural and religious significance of dismemberment, see Chapters 4 and 5, below.

[33] For a perceptive discussion of Hippolyta's narrative functions, see Schwarz, *Tough Love*, pp. 205–10.

[34] John Weston, *The Amazon Queen, or, The Amours of Thalestris to Alexander the Great* (London: printed for Hen[ry] Harrington, 1667).

the text to suggest that they are one-breasted (5.4.44).[35] Furthermore, by the end of this play, the 'Amazons' are reunited with the husbands they thought had been lost at sea, and traditional – that is, patriarchal – domesticity is restored.

These are all dramas in which the unimammarian body supposedly associated with Amazon women is quietly sidelined. On occasion, however, the omission of one-breastedness from representations of the Amazon on stage becomes positively conspicuous. In Jasper Maynes' 1648 *The Amorous Warre*, which features supposedly historical Amazons including the queen Thalestris, the play's protagonists sleep with what they believe are Amazons, only to later discover that they have in fact been tricked into 'cheating' with their own wives. The men have explicitly *evaded* an encounter with unimammarian women, and their response highlights the distinct lack of such bodies on stage:

> Theag[ines]: In my opinion, my Lord, these are
> The strangest Amazons that ever left
> Their female countrey for the use of men.
> How did you find yours? Mine had *breasts*.
> Mel[eager]: Troth mine, I thinke hath scap't the rasour too; I had
> No leisure to examine parts. I found
> No defects in her; But methought she was
> To me a whole and perfect woman; I'm sure
> She found me an entire and perfect man.[36]

Meleager's assurance that his bed partner found him 'entire' again hints at the possibility of male castration as an equivalent to female mastectomy, a threat which is raised by the thought of an anomalous female body and must be dismissed along with it. The invocation of the razor here as the instrument of mastectomy is perhaps significant, since this device was associated with both surgical procedures and with the removal of that masculine appendage, the beard. However, the integrity of the male protagonists' partners is stressed – they assuredly *had* breasts, *had* escaped the razor, and were whole and perfect. It appears that while missing arms and legs may be staged, and missing testicles may be heard of, if not seen, missing breasts are outside the realms of dramatic possibility.

The reluctance of early modern playwrights to stage the Amazon unimammarian body may be partly a facet of the general absence of

---

[35] John Fletcher and Philip Massinger, 'The Sea Voyage', in *Three Renaissance Travel Plays*, ed. Anthony Parr (Manchester: Manchester University Press, 1995), pp. 135–216.

[36] Jasper Mayne, *The Amorous Warre* (London: S.N., 1648), pt. 5.1.

America and its peoples from the early modern stage which has been observed by Gavin Hollis. In his book on the subject, Hollis notes that early modern plays rarely discuss the possibilities offered by European colonisation of America, and even less frequently frame those possibilities in positive terms, despite the concerted efforts of the Virginia Company's 'promotional machine'.[37] Since Amazons were often believed to hail from Guiana, they came under the 'American' umbrella, and as elsewhere in this book, issues of gender, disability, and race intersect to render the body Other along multiple registers. Nonetheless, I contend that the determined inattention paid to Amazon one-breastedness on stage also reflects discomfort about altered female bodies in general. Viewed alongside the refusal of medical writers to discuss the anomalous bodies of mastectomy survivors, these Amazon absences indicate that early modern audiences had a problem with viewing sexually altered women 'in the flesh'. Ethnographic accounts of Amazons benefited from the conceptual distance imposed between readers and people who were clearly racial and social Others, even to the extent of explicitly picturing the one-breasted body. However, to imagine the site of mastectomy was horrifying when it was closer to home, that is, when it was presented on stage, or related to 'real' cancer surgeries. Though other kinds of bodily difference were certainly underrepresented and misrepresented in early modern texts, this reluctance to picture the results of surgical alteration was particular to breast amputation. Moreover, the effect of such omission was to deny the subjectivity and continued narrative of the mastectomy survivor. As Sarah Covington notes of early modern ex-soldiers, 'scars ... were corporal evidence of healing as well as damage – a memorializing faultline on the body that reminded the veteran of the "before" and "after" that his life had taken upon the injury he suffered'.[38] The denial of the mastectomy scar precludes any possibility of 'memorializing' the female experience in the same way.

What made these altered bodies so different from others? Modern 'psycho-oncological' studies tracing women's experiences of cancer recognise that removing the breast has unique social significance. Mastectomy, it is argued, excludes women from a patriarchal culture in which their participation is always contingent and fragile:

---

[37] Gavin Hollis, *The Absence of America: the London Stage, 1576–1642* (Oxford: Oxford University Press, 2015), p. 4.

[38] Sarah Covington, *Wounds, Flesh, and Metaphor in Seventeenth-Century England* (Basingstoke: Palgrave Macmillan, 2009), p. 86.

> Women's bodies occupy culturally liminal positions as part of cultural
> contexts that value women for their bodily appearances and their sexual
> desirability to men. In the present study, the liminal position of the
> women's bodies was demonstrated through accounts of the abject postcan-
> cer body, demonstrating difficulties in making meaning and 'placing'
> women's bodies within the symbolic order, as well as experiences of horror
> and repulsion toward the body ... Many of the women reported ...
> becoming invisible to the male gaze and having less value in terms of sexual
> attractiveness and beauty.[39]

In other words, there is no clear place for the non-breasted or one-breasted
woman in a culture which commonly deems that feature unattractive, and
which indexes attractiveness to social value. Early modern and modern
perceptions of beauty do not always correlate, and as I have detailed
elsewhere, the early modern breast signified in culturally specific ways.[40]
Arguably, the close physiological connection between lactation and menstruation which was prevalent in early modern medicine made breasts a
somewhat problematic site of eroticism.[41] Nonetheless, mastectomied
Amazonian bodies might likewise have been excluded from view because
it was simply too difficult to square the sexual titillation offered by exotic
half-naked women with the perceived unattractiveness of a missing breast.

   While this observation goes some way to explaining the absence of one-
breasted Amazons on stage, it does not fully account for the silence that
surrounds recovery from mastectomy in other kinds of early modern text.
To do so, we need to consider again the subject/object status of the body.
Early modern lived experience, as this book will demonstrate, entailed
intersubjectivity.[42] However, it also required as its ground a distinct 'self'
which could be said to act, sense, and have experiences; in other words, to

---

[39] Chloe M. Parton, Jane M. Ussher, and Janette Perz, 'Women's Construction of Embodiment and
the Abject Sexual Body after Cancer', *Qualitative Health Research* 26:4 (2016): 500, https://doi.org/
10.1177/1049732315570130. See also Dennis D. Waskul and Pamela van der Riet, 'The Abject
Embodiment of Cancer Patients: Dignity, Selfhood, and the Grotesque Body', *Symbolic Interaction*
25:4 (2002): 487–513, https://doi.org/10.1525/si.2002.25.4.487. For an overview of work on
disability and feminism, see Anita Silvers, 'Feminism and Disability', in *The Blackwell Guide to
Feminist Philosophy*, ed. Linda Martín Alcoff and Eva Feder Kittay (Oxford: Blackwell, 2007),
pp. 131–42, https://doi.org/10.1002/9780470696961.ch7.
[40] Skuse, *Constructions of Cancer in Early Modern England*, pp. 45–53.   [41] Ibid., pp. 45–7.
[42] There has been much work on the importance of relationships and communities in constituting
early modern identities: see, for example, Margreta de Grazia, Maureen Quilligan, and Peter
Stallybrass, eds., *Subject and Object in Renaissance Culture* (Cambridge: Cambridge University
Press, 1996); James Kuzner, *Open Subjects: English Renaissance Republicans, Modern Selfhoods, and
the Virtue of Vulnerability* (Edinburgh: Edinburgh University Press, 2011); Christopher Tilmouth,
'Passion and Intersubjectivity in Early Modern Literature', in *Passions and Subjectivity in Early
Modern Culture*, ed. Freya Sierhuis and Brian Cummings (Farnham: Ashgate, 2013), pp. 13–32.

relate to the 'outside world' requires an 'inside' identity, even when that identity is itself materially grounded. To understand why the self–other distinction may be threatened by mastectomy, it is useful to turn to Julia Kristeva's *Powers of Horror* (1980). Drawing on Lacanian psychoanalysis, Kristeva identifies as 'abject' those things or phenomena which undermine our sense of physical and psychic integrity. The abject is that which 'disturbs identity, system, order. What does not respect borders, positions, rules. The in-between, the ambiguous, the composite.'[43] Witnessing the permeability of the bodily envelope through the abject is profoundly disturbing to one's sense of one's own subjectivity, as Josh Dohmen summarises:

> Kristeva introduces the concept of abjection to offer a pre-Oedipal account of splitting that must occur before the formation of a stable subject and its stable objects. Whereas an object reveals the subject's detachment and autonomy, '[t]he abject has only one quality of the object – that of being opposed to I' ... The abject is a nonobject splitting from (but never completely split from) the subject-to-be.[44]

Read in this way, the mastectomied body is 'abject' along multiple registers. Like any wounded body, the body after mastectomy displays to viewers the fragility of the boundary between life and death, and between the interior of the body and the outside world. On the most basic level, the mastectomy operation brought life and death into uncomfortably close proximity; it was arguably even more dangerous than a limb amputation, so much so that many surgeons shunned the operation in favour of palliative care.[45] Moreover, the unimammarian body is abject not only because it is hurt but also because it makes visible the material relations between one body and another. That is, by removing one breast, attention is drawn to the nutritive function of the remaining breast, and thus to the state of infancy in which mother and child are imperfectly separated. As Ashley Denham Busse explains:

> in Kristeva's analysis the maternal function comes to stand in not only for the subject's pre-Symbolic existence in its imagined wholeness but also for all that which must be cast aside continually in order for the subject to exist, that is, any reminder of one's material origins or mortality. What results is

[43] Julia Kristeva, *Powers of Horror: An Essay on Abjection*, trans. Leon S. Roudiez (1980; New York: Columbia University Press, 1982), p. 4.
[44] Josh Dohmen, 'Disability as Abject: Kristeva, Disability, and Resistance', *Hypatia* 31:4 (2016): 768, https://doi.org/10.1111/hypa.12266.
[45] Skuse, *Constructions of Cancer in Early Modern England*, p. 127.

an erotic ambivalence, a desire and fascination for the (maternal) body as well as a fear of its power to annihilate.[46]

The positioning of the altered female body as abject is recognised by modern psycho-oncology, with Parton et al. describing how women after mastectomy felt 'outside normality', such that 'discursive resources were limited for capturing embodied experiences, and . . . the women's subject positioning subsequently became unsettled and fragile'.[47] In an early modern context, this effect is heightened by the longstanding association of women's bodies (healthy or otherwise) with abjection. While they do not employ Kristeva's overtly psychoanalytic methodology, historicist readings of early modern drama have broadly agreed that the functions of the lactating, menstruating, *leaky* female body persistently troubled playwrights and authors.[48] The illimitability of the female body was suspected to pervade everyday life, from the effects of maternal imagination on a growing foetus to the menstruating woman's ability to curdle milk with a glance.[49] Furthermore, the classification of anomalous female bodies as abject follows what Schwarz describes as the 'familiar pattern of abjection, which consolidates the center by exacting its price from the margins'.[50] Making the anomalous female body marginal repositions maleness and able-bodiedness as normal, makes male sexual desire the criterion for social acceptability, and quells perceived threats to this 'normality' posed by Amazon women who elude heteronormative social structures and accepted definitions of 'ability'.[51] This is, as Schwarz observes of Shakespeare's dead female characters, an easier project to fulfil when the troublesome women in question are deceased, since 'death might

---

[46] Ashley Denham Busse, '"Quod Me Nutrit Me Destruit": Discovering the Abject on the Early Modern Stage', *Journal of Medieval and Early Modern Studies* 43:1 (2013): 73, https://doi.org/10 .1215/10829636-1902549.

[47] Parton et al., 'Women's Construction of Embodiment and the Abject Sexual Body after Cancer', 493. On abjection as a means for theorising disability (including the limitations of such an approach), see Bill Hughes, 'Wounded/Monstrous/Abject: A Critique of the Disabled Body in the Sociological Imaginary', *Disability and Society* 24:4 (2009): 399–410, https://doi.org/10.1080/ 09687590902876144.

[48] Paster, *The Body Embarrassed*.

[49] Mary Elizabeth Fissell, *Vernacular Bodies: The Politics of Reproduction in Early Modern England* (Oxford: Oxford University Press, 2004), p. 208; Patricia Crawford, 'Attitudes to Menstruation in Seventeenth-Century England', *Past and Present* 91 (1981): 46–73.

[50] Kathryn Schwarz, 'Death and Theory: Or, the Problem of Counterfactual Sex', in *Sex before Sex: Figuring the Act in Early Modern England*, ed. James M. Bromley and Will Stockton (Minneapolis: University of Minnesota Press, 2013), p. 58.

[51] For an interesting discussion of abjection and the male subject, see Catherine Bates, *Masculinity, Gender and Identity in the English Renaissance Lyric* (Cambridge: Cambridge University Press, 2007), especially pp. 136–73.

fix a particular condition of worth; whether necrophilic or necrophobic, history digests its victims in the service of its authors'.[52] While not necessarily dead, the abjection of one-breasted women seems to follow the same principle: marginalising and repudiating bodies works better when those bodies are not around to assert themselves as subjects. Nonetheless, the very need for repudiation implies a continuing blurring of boundaries; as Schwarz argues, 'Attempts to fix a particular condition of worth collide with the polyvalence of that counterfactual "what if?"'[53] The threat posed by abjection is never extinguished because the project of repudiating the abject is always incomplete. Thoughts of mastectomy crept into early modern plays even as the characters insisted that their partners *'had breasts'*, revealing a fascination with the twin qualities of maternity and death evoked by the one-breasted body.

When the maternal body met the altered body, then, the result was more unpalatable than intriguing, since to look upon this body was to risk a collapse of personal identities. Jokes could not be made about mastectomy as they were about castration or limb loss. Amazons might be imagined as vocal and powerful on stage, but only if the matter of their altered body was suppressed. Furthermore, in this respect art imitated life. While numerous medical texts gave instructions for mastectomy operations, and a few supplied accounts thereof, details about the lives of women after mastectomy are, remarkably, entirely absent from early modern writing of all kinds. This book will show early modern texts populated by amputees, prosthesis users, and people with 'altered bodies' of all kinds. Mastectomy survivors are not in those texts.

Conclusion

In 1734, a letter written to the editor of *The Prompter*, complaining about castrati, suggested an extraordinary means of resolving the 'opera problem':

> Mr *Prompter*, if all your Attempts to pull down Operas, and get rid of these Monsters [castrati], should prove ineffectual, I have a Thought come into my Head, that I believe will not fail. Indeed, I scarce dare communicate it, but when the publick Good is in View, nothing shou'd hinder a Man. It is this then, for I must tell you; Suppose we should castrate, or qualify, our Women, as they do their Men in Italy ... 'Tis plain, that in this way those Shoals of Females that wander about the Town, quite useless for want of Husbands or Lovers, might be made very serviceable to the *Publick*, by so

---

[52] Schwarz, 'Death and Theory', p. 58.   [53] Ibid., p. 59.

considerable an Improvement of Operas. But I find I am got a little beside my Purpose. For I propose the thing, because I am assured it clears the Voices of *Girls*, as well as *Boys*. And since Women have naturally shriller and sweeter Pipes than Men, if the artificial Improvement shou'd be but equal, it will be an angelical Charm to hear them.[54]

Clearly, this letter-writer was not in earnest. *The Prompter* was a publication whose main concern was satirising and gossiping about the theatre and its inhabitants, not proposing experimental surgeries.[55] Yet, the outraged author had not pulled their suggestion from thin air. The sterilisation of women had been mooted before, in the same texts in which Amazonian mastectomy was described, and like this practice (and like some kinds of eunuchism), female sterilisation was believed to have originated in Africa and the Middle East. The 1658 *Rare Verities*, for instance, attested that

> It's a far harder matter to Eunuchize women [than men], yet in former and latter times it hath been accomplished. *Antonius Ulmus* saith it may be done by cutting the Nympha, which is the throne of love and lust. Thus many of the Egyptian women have been used by reason of their untamed lust. Now properly to castrate a woman, is to take out her womb, for the doing of which, since it is so hard and dangerous, I dare not give any directions.[56]

The *Oxford English Dictionary* suggests that 'nympha' in this period referred to labia minora; this author clearly believed that their removal would impede female sexual pleasure, though an internal operation was required to truly sterilise the female patient. John Bulwer's *Anthropometamorphosis* (1653) and Nicholas Venette's *Mysteries of Conjugal Love* (1707) both similarly suggested that female castration might have been undertaken in the ancient world or more recently in Africa and the Middle East.[57] Again, both questioned how the operation could have been completed without killing the patient. Venette suggested that the 'castration' had in fact been a kind of chastity belt, or perhaps the stitching up of the women's 'privities'. Bulwer, however, took a more credulous view:

[54] 'Letter to the Editor', *Prompter*, 19 December 1735.
[55] Kalman A. Burnim, 'Aaron Hill's "The Prompter": An Eighteenth-Century Theatrical Paper', *Educational Theatre Journal* 13:2 (1961): 73–81.
[56] Giovanni Benedetto Sinibaldi, *Rare Verities* (London: P. Briggs, 1658), pp. 50–1.
[57] Bulwer, *Anthropometamorphosis*, pp. 363–4; Nicholas Venette, *The Mysteries of Conjugal Love Reveal'd Written in French by Nicholas de Venette, … The 8th Edition. Done into English by a Gentleman*, 2nd edition (London, 1707), pp. 495–6.

For he must necessarily cut both the flankes who would castrate a woman, a worke full of desperate hazzard; yet it may be done with little or no danger, if it be attempted with an artfull hand. And a Friend of mine told me he knew a maid in Northampton-shire that was thus spaded by a sow-gelder, and escaping the danger grew very fat.[58]

Stories about the sterilisation of women were exceedingly rare, much rarer than those about Amazons. Nonetheless, the terms in which such tales were framed underline how ethnography functioned as a way of thinking about different kinds of bodily change, whilst keeping the physical and social implications of bodily alterity safely at arm's length. They also demonstrate how sex-specific alterations to the female body were consistently indexed to the illimitability of female desire. By forcing a comparison between castrati and neutered women, the *Prompter's* letter-writer actually demonstrated their non-equivalence. Despite his feigned naivety, the author knows that spayed women cannot have an instrumental value like that of castrati. Eliminating the risk of pregnancy for women who wander the streets creates a different kind of commodified body: not opera stars, but prostitutes.

'Spayed' and unimammarian female bodies functioned similarly to provoke conflicted reactions in the (overwhelmingly male) authors by whom they were described. On one hand, it is clear that such bodies were a source of fascination, and sometimes of titillation. On the other, surgical changes to the female body – especially when focussed on sexual characteristics – were a cause for anxiety. Wounds, even when healed, showed the permeability and impermanency of the bodily envelope. Female bodies likewise threatened illimitability and unboundedness. The combination of the two was therefore experienced as a threat to personal identity. Furthermore, this threat was experienced more profoundly because, as the following chapters will show, early modern models of embodiment were unfixed, often dwelling on indeterminacy and change. In this climate, stories of surgically altered bodies were almost always stories of *male* bodies. The phenomenological experiences of surgically altered women were obfuscated and ignored in order to maintain the distinction between 'self' and 'other' on which authors' and audiences' sense of subjective identity depended.

---

[58] Bulwer, *Anthropometamorphosis*, p. 364.

CHAPTER 3

Second-Hand Faces: Aesthetic Surgery

That none may complain for want of timely Notice; Be it known to all men, by these presents, that this summer, at Temple-Oge, there will be a vast collection of fair hands, brilliant eyes, rosy cheeks, nimble tongues, ivory teeth, ruby lips, dimpled chins, high fronts, long necks; together with snowy breasts, handsome legs, and other valuable commodities, which, for weighty reasons, are determined to be concealed 'till the merchandizes before-mentioned are first disposed of and sold: There will be large quantities of kind glances, studied courtesies, languishing looks, sighs piping hot from the heart, and scornful sneers, that are only copies of the countenance; likewise ogles of all kinds, from a side leer to a full stare. . . . And, that people, even in the most forlorn of circumstances, may not fail of proper accommodations, special care is intended to be taken, that there shall, likewise, be some second-hand faces, stale reputations, and broken constitutions, for the use and behoof of battered beaux, maimed debauchees, old batchelors, and other helpless persons, who have not money, or merit, enough to supply themselves more conveniently.[1]

Purposely or otherwise, most early modern surgical interventions left their mark. The aesthetic results of mastectomy and amputation were profound, but more or less readily concealed by clothing. Childhood castration, as we have seen, created bodies which were profoundly aesthetically different and had a sexual value to match. Surgery on the face, however, posed unique challenges. As the above passage from the *Universal Weekly Pamphlet* makes clear, one's face could be one's fortune in the early modern marriage market, particularly for women. The face was not only the site of much sensory perception; it was also something to be itemised and anatomised, assessed and found wanting. It was a mark of, and criterion for, social and

---

[1] Eustace Budgell, ed., 'Notice of a Sale of Beauties, at Temple-Oge.', *Bee, or Universal Weekly Pamphlet Revived, May 1733–June 1733* 2:17 (16 June 1733): 738–40.

economic capital. Beauty and agreeableness might, as this author suggested, be feigned, with 'studied courtesies' in which one's face was an
instrument of deception; faces supplied only imperfect clues to the more
'valuable commodities' of virginity and fertility. However, faces also gave
the game away, revealing the true characters of 'battered beaux' and
'maimed debauchees'.

This chapter examines the topic of those 'second-hand faces' which
were, by one means or another, medically 'put on' – the result of prostheses, elaborate dentistry, or ground-breaking surgery. The potential of
medicine to change appearances in this way once again raised the question
of whether the body was 'me' or 'mine', subject or object. Did one own a
face as one owned an item of clothing, to be augmented or transformed at
will? Or was the face an intrinsic part of selfhood, such that changes to
one's countenance were changes to one's very identity? A series of surprisingly bold innovations in facial prosthetics and surgery brought these
questions to the fore for early modern audiences. The implantation of
human teeth from one mouth to another, or the use of human teeth in
dentures, might be viewed as forward-thinking or as exploitation.
Meanwhile, allografting – the transfer of flesh from one body to another –
fired the imagination of satirists and scientists alike. In each instance of
remaking the face, questions of bodily integrity and morality, the personal
and social significance of the face, loomed large.[2]

Saving Face

If the face was important in early modern culture, it was also imperilled.
Longstanding dangers to the face remained, including accidents resulting
from handling livestock and horses, hazards from dangerous manual
trades, and diseases such as cancers and syphilis. Added to these, the
prevalence of armed conflict, and the nature of that conflict, inevitably
produced a large number of serious facial injuries. Charles Carlton, for
instance, claims that during the reign of Elizabeth I, around 55 per cent of
all men aged between eighteen and thirty-nine would have served in the
armed forces in one form or another.[3] In the Nine Years War (1688-97),

---

[2] Certain material in this chapter is also treated in Emily Cock, *Rhinoplasty and the Nose in Early
Modern British Medicine and Culture* (Manchester: Manchester University Press, 2019), which was
published as final editing of this book was taking place. I have tried to provide references to
Rhinoplasty and the Nose where it is appropriate; our respective works on this subject may be read
as two ways of approaching the same problem.

[3] Charles Carlton, *This Seat of Mars: War and the British Isles, 1485–1746* (New Haven: Yale University
Press, 2011), p. 37.

one in seven Englishmen served in the military.[4] During long campaigns, these men were exposed to infectious disease and loss of extremities from frostbite, as well as from traditional close combat. They were also, more than ever, vulnerable to firearms and artillery. Cannon posed a particular threat when aimed at ships, where they produced shrapnel and could trigger devastating fires and explosions. The 'weight, softness, and slow trajectory' of musket balls could easily eviscerate their targets.[5] Moreover, such wounds were particularly likely to become gangrenous, as fragments of cloth, dirt, and wood were carried deep into the flesh. It is unsurprising, therefore, that numerous eminent surgeons included detailed instructions for facial surgery and prostheses in their textbooks. Most remarkable among these was Ambroise Paré's *Workes*, in which he suggested modes of restoring the ears, eyes, nose, and soft palate among other parts of the face. As a military surgeon, he had clearly encountered many such cases of catastrophic but survivable damage.

The first duty of facial prostheses was, wherever possible, to restore the function of the damaged part. More than any other contemporary surgeon, Paré supplied innovative methods of doing just that. For instance, he prescribed a remedy for holes in the palate which he hoped would allow the afflicted person to eat and speak. The patient was to put into their mouth a slightly dished piece of gold or silver, to which was attached a small sponge. Inserted into the cavity of the palate, the sponge would, Paré explained, soak up the moisture 'distilling from the brain' and swell so that the metal piece would sit firmly in the mouth. Such a recourse was typical of Paré's inventiveness in prosthesis design, and it was apparently effective: the surgeon attested that 'I have observed [this method] not by once or twice, but by manifold trial.'[6] Paré, and later Johannes van Horne, also wrote of having seen men who had lost part of their tongue inserting a small piece of wood in their mouth to allow them to speak.[7] In these cases, utility, sensory function, and sociability went hand in hand: Paré recorded that, having discovered this expedient, the man with the tongue-piece

[4] Ibid., p. 227.
[5] Sarah Covington, *Wounds, Flesh, and Metaphor in Seventeenth-Century England* (Basingstoke: Palgrave Macmillan, 2009), p. 85.
[6] Ambroise Paré, *The Workes of That Famous Chirurgion Ambrose Parey Translated out of Latine and Compared with the French. by Th: Johnson* (London: printed by Th. Cotes and R. Young, 1634), p. 873.
[7] Ibid.; Johannes van Horne, *Micro-Techne; or, a Methodical Introduction to the Art of Chirurgery* (London: printed by J. Darby, for T. Varnam and J. Osborne, and J. and B. Sprint, 1717), pp. 61–2.

'always carried [it] hanging at his neck, as the onely interpreter of his mind, and the key of his speech'.[8]

Of course, for many people with facial injuries, full restoration of function was impossible. Nobody could restore sight or hearing in people who had lost an eye or ear, and many mouth and palate injuries were to be imperfectly managed rather than fully cured. Nonetheless, it is clear that in such cases, Paré considered that the surgeon still had a job to do – specifically, allowing the injured person to pass in able-bodied society as more or less aesthetically 'normal'. His recommendations for patients who had lost an eye exemplified this project. First he suggested the obvious expedient of an artificial eye, which might be 'counterfeited and enamelled, so that it may seem to have the brightnesse, or gemmie decencie of the naturall eye, into the place of the eye that is so lost'.[9] If the patient was unable or unwilling to insert such an eye, however, Paré had another suggestion:

> You must have a string or wiar, like unto womens eare-wiars, made to bind the head harder or looser as it pleaseth the patient, from the lower part of the head behind above the eare, unto the greater corner of the eye, this rod or wiar must be covered with silke, and it must also be somewhat broade at both ends, lest that the sharpnesse thereof should pierce or pricke any part ... But the end wherewith the empty hollownesse must be covered, ought to bee broader than the other, and covered with a thin piece of leather, that thereon the colours of the eye that is lost may be shadowed or counterfeited.[10]

Paré's idea of a painted piece of leather attached with a system of thin wires around the head seems, at best, precarious. Nonetheless, it shows the lengths to which this surgeon was prepared to go to spare his patients the ignominy of wearing an eyepatch, as well as the possible discomfort and expense those patients were willing to endure in order to pass as able-bodied. The importance of having a 'normal' face recurred throughout Paré's work. On people who had suffered facial cancers or burns, he commented that 'Such persons must be so trimmed and ordered, that they may come in a seemely manner into the company of others.'[11] Specifying the details of a good artificial nose, he advised that it should 'not want any thing that may adorne or beautifie the face'.[12] As the father of military surgery, Paré's advice was repeated in numerous surgical texts throughout the seventeenth and eighteenth centuries. In 1717, for

---

[8] Paré, *The Workes*, p. 873.   [9] Ibid., p. 869.   [10] Ibid., p. 870.   [11] Ibid., p. 874.
[12] Ibid., p. 871.

instance, van Horne's *Micro-techne; or, a Methodical Introduction to the Art of Chirurgery* followed Paré in observing that

> we supply the want of an Eye with a Glass or golden one colour'd: and the loss of an Ear by thick Paper or Parchment painted; we repair the want of a Nose by Silver Plates: and though we are not so happy as to imitate the famous Taliacotius … yet we can restore lost Teeth, if the speech be deficient, by factitious ones of Ivory; and we fix a Silver Lamina or Plate, when a Portion of the Palate is eaten away.[13]

In this text he referred directly to Paré as an exemplar, as well as to the more contested Tagliacotian operation which I explore below. As in Paré's *Workes*, van Horne framed such interventions as 'Prosthesis, or a *supplying by Art what is deficient*', which 'conduces not a little to the Beauty of a human Body'.[14]

In all these examples, aesthetics and function are hardly separable. Restoring the damaged face is not a matter of vanity, or of enhancement. Rather, it is a restitution to basic social acceptability – the ability to be in company or to walk the streets without provoking horror. As Simon Dickie has explored, it was widely considered acceptable to mock and torment people with facial disfigurements during the seventeenth and eighteenth centuries, even among the so-called better sort.[15] Furthermore, early modern medical practitioners and natural philosophers understood well the centrality of non-verbal expression to communication. John Bulwer's *Chirologia* (1648) dwelt on hand gestures, but included many facial expressions under that banner (for example, kissing the fingers). *Chirologia's* sister text, *Philocophus, or, the Deaf and Dumb Man's Friend* (1648) instructed its readers in lip reading among other skills.[16] As Elizabeth Bearden has noted, Bulwer's texts promulgated an 'inclusive

[13] Horne, *Micro-Techne; or, a Methodical Introduction to the Art of Chirurgery*, pp. 61–2.
[14] Ibid., p. 61.
[15] Simon Dickie, *Cruelty and Laughter: Forgotten Comic Literature and the Unsentimental Eighteenth Century* (Chicago: University of Chicago Press, 2011), p. 110.
[16] John Bulwer, *Chirologia, or, The Naturall Language of the Hand Composed of the Speaking Motions, and Discoursing Gestures Thereof: Whereunto Is Added Chironomia, or, The Art of Manuall Rhetoricke, Consisting of the Naturall Expressions, Digested by Art in the Hand, as the Chiefest Instrument of Eloquence, by Historicall Manifesto's Exemplified out of the Authentique Registers of Common Life and Civill Conversation: With Types, or Chyrograms, a Long-Wish'd for Illustration of This Argument* (London: Tho[mas] Harper, sold by R. Whitaker, 1644); John Bulwer, *Philocophus, or, The Deafe and Dumbe Mans Friend Exhibiting the Philosophicall Verity of That Subtile Art, Which May Inable One with an Observant Eie, to Heare What Any Man Speaks by the Moving of His Lips: Upon the Same Ground … That a Man Borne Deafe and Dumbe, May Be Taught to Heare the Sound of Words with His Eie, & Thence Learne to Speake with His Tongue* (London: printed for Humphrey Moseley, 1648).

view of nature' in which one sense (sight) could stand in for another (hearing), thus de-stigmatizing sensory difference.[17] Nonetheless, facial difference remained a special case: facial injury could impede one's own senses *and* offend the senses of those who looked upon it. In recognition of this fact, by 1687, Parliament had passed an act specifically against maiming, and injuries to the face were treated particularly seriously, such that in 1722, two men were executed for having slit the nose of an acquaintance.[18] As Alexander Read explained, 'without doubt a Maim in the Face must be the principal: for it disfigures the best favoured part'.[19]

'Hypocrisy of Countenance'

Supplying prostheses to fill in gaps on the face – lost palates, ears, eyes, and noses – was thus viewed as a matter of medical necessity, of the same order as bandaging a wounded arm or splinting a broken leg. As the century progressed, however, medical practitioners of various kinds started to offer kinds of prostheses which aimed not only to restore faces damaged by trauma and disease, but to improve a patient's overall appearance. Of these, probably the most ubiquitous were teeth. Dentures and tooth transplants had been available in one guise or another since ancient Egypt, but in the seventeenth century, the demand for – and consequently, innovation in – false teeth expanded as never before. In the words of Charles Allen, author of the pre-eminent English dentistry text of this period:

> When our decay'd Teeth are so far gone before we think of any Remedy for their preservation, that whatever we can do, proves but fruitless . . . or that some intolerable pain has made us to draw them: we are not yet to despair, and esteem ourselves toothless for all the rest of our life: the loss indeed is great, but not irreparable; there is still some help for it, the natural want may be supplied artificially, and herein Art imitates Nature so *naifly* [naturally], that when the succedaneous [permanent] Teeth . . . are well set in, they cannot be distinguished from the natural ones.[20]

[17] Elizabeth B. Bearden, 'Before Normal, There Was Natural: John Bulwer, Disability, and Natural Signing in Early Modern England and Beyond', *PMLA* 132:1 (2017): 45.

[18] Anon, *The Tryal and Condemnation of Arundel Coke Alias Cooke Esq; and of John Woodburne Labourer, for Felony, in Slitting the Nose of Edward Crispe* (London: printed for John Darby and Daniel Midwinter, 1722).

[19] Alexander Read, *Chirurgorum Comes; or, The Whole Practice of Chirurgery* (London: Edw. Jones, for Christopher Wilkinson, 1687), p. 460.

[20] Charles Allen, *Curious Observations on the Teeth* (1687), ed. L. Lindsay (London: John Bale, Sons & Danielsson, 1924), p. 12.

Artificial and implanted teeth offered patients the chance to eat and speak normally, as well as to look younger and healthier. As a consequence, both kinds of dentistry became very popular. A. S. Hargreaves finds the incidence of tooth transplantation to have increased substantially from the later sixteenth century to the late eighteenth century, at which point ceramic alternatives became commonplace.[21] Donor teeth might come from corpses, or from those still living, who found that strong, white teeth proved a saleable commodity in times of need. Moreover, Mark Blackwell contends that in the eighteenth century, dentistry was 'riven by commercialism and fashion'.[22] New teeth were less a medical procedure than a luxury commodity.

In eighteenth-century newspapers, the advantages of the new dentistry were eagerly described. In 1707, for instance, John Watts promised that

> [he] sets in Artificial Teeth so firm as to eat with them, and so exact as not to be discover'd from Natural: They are an Ornament to the mouth, and a very great help to Speech, and not to be taken out every Night, as is by some falsely suggested, but may be worn Years together.[23]

The theme of undetectability was common among such advertisements, with other proprietors claiming to set in teeth 'so even, neat, and firm, that they need not be removed for seven Years, and [patients] may eat with them as well as with their former, and cannot be distinguish'd from their natural ones'.[24] Like the commodification of the castrato body discussed in Chapter 1, the commodification of teeth was indexed to the rise of newspapers and periodicals. As with castrati, however, the alliance between bodily alteration and commercial interest provoked unease in many observers. In her article on wigs in the eighteenth century, Lynn Festa notes that the 'shuttl[ing] between different individuals' of such objects 'erodes the boundaries that set the individual subject off from the world', creating both disputes over the ethics of harvesting hair from the heads of the poor and concerns over personal integrity:

> the liberal idea of the subject as an individual jostles against the notion of the self as the possessor of detachable parts. If the individual is

---

[21] A. S. Hargreaves, *White as Whales Bone: Dental Services in Early Modern England* (Leeds: Northern Universities Press, 1998).

[22] Mark Blackwell, '"Extraneous Bodies": the Contagion of Live-Tooth Transplantation in Late-Eighteenth-Century England', *Eighteenth-Century Life* 28:1 (2004): 21–68.

[23] *Flying Post or The Post Master*, 7–10 June 1707.

[24] *Weekly Journal or British Gazetteer*, 16 March 1717. See also *Daily Courant*, 11 December 1719.

composed of removable and detachable layers that it owns, what exactly is doing the owning?[25]

As a rarer commodity (and one irreplaceable for the donor), dentures and implants made from real teeth heightened these concerns, and medical practitioners, moralists, and satirists alike questioned the ethics of putting teeth from one human being into another. Allen, for instance, stated that

> I do not like that method of drawing Teeth out of some folks heads, to put them into others, both for its being too inhumane, and attended with too many difficulties; and then neither could this be called the restauration of Teeth, since the reparation of one, is the ruine of another; it is only robbing Peter to pay Paul.[26]

Allen's objection was based explicitly on the ethics of removing teeth from human beings for transplantation, since elsewhere he suggested that one might usefully implant teeth from dogs, sheep, or baboons into humans: 'In such case I do not only approve of it as lawful and facile, but so also esteem it as very profitable and advantageous.'[27] Baboons aside, however, human tooth transplantation almost inevitably involved the exploitation of the young and poor by the old and rich. John Ward, for instance, recorded in his diary hearing of 'a Lady [who] having a rotten tooth drawn caused a sound tooth at the same time to bee drawn from her waiting maid, which was substituted and in time so rooted that shee could make use of itt as well as of any other'.[28] Such tales were unsurprisingly distasteful to many observers. Blackwell notes, 'This age disparity was exploited to good effect by writers and artists who imply that the beauty of the old can be maintained only by disfiguring the young ... on an unmannerly species of consumption that involves the nation's harvesting its young stock, cannibalizing its own progeny.'[29]

Notably, neither Allen nor Ward seems to have viewed tooth implantation – either from humans or from animals – as a possible source of contagion. This is in contrast to discourses about grafted noses (below) and transplanted limbs (Chapter 4) in which differences of race and class figured prominently, with 'foreign' additions perceived as threatening the integrity of the 'original' body. This may have been because implanted

[25] Lynn M. Festa, 'Personal Effects: Wigs and Possessive Individualism in the Long Eighteenth Century', *Eighteenth-Century Life* 29:2 (2005): 48.
[26] Allen, *Curious Observations on the Teeth*, p. 13.   [27] Ibid.
[28] John Ward, 'Notebook of John Ward, Vol. 1' (*c.* 1650–70), Folger Shakespeare Library, v.a. 284–299, p. 211.
[29] Blackwell, 'Extraneous Bodies', 38.

teeth were usually viewed as senseless. Thus in Pierre Fauchard's 1746 *Treatise on the Teeth*, he observed that 'I could not imagine that a tooth transferred from one mouth to another could be susceptible of pain, in view of the fact that its nerve and the membranes had been cut off.'[30] Instead, objections to false and implanted teeth usually approached the subject from the angle of social morality. As Farah Karim-Cooper has identified, and as I discuss below, the lines between prostheses and cosmetics were often blurred. Both entailed the 'systematic assemblage of material goods' to supplement elements of the body that were lacking.[31] Given that some prostheses such as false eyes were clearly non-functional in sensory terms, the perceived difference between bodily additions that were cosmetic and those that were deemed medically necessary depended on numerous factors, including the nature of the supplier, the circum-stances of the original 'lack', and the intentions of the user-wearer.

   This tension between bodily additions as acts of vanity or acceptable restorations was recognised in 1656, when John Gauden framed a fictional discourse between 'Two Ladies' arguing over the morality of cosmetics. Against cosmetics, one lady argues:

> while we disguise and alter our face ... we are not what we seem to be to *our selves* ... Whereas the wise *Creator* hath by *nature* impressed on every face of man and woman, such *Characters,* either of *beauty,* or *Majesty,* or at least of *distinction,* as he sees sufficient for his own honor, our content, and others sociall discerning or *difference,* whereby to avoyd confusions or mistakes.[32]

However, Gauden's second lady, arguing in favour of cosmetics, points out the hypocrisy inherent in sharp distinctions between redressing bodily faults and augmenting beauty:

> Who ever is so impertinent a bigot, as to find fault, when the hills and dales of crooked and unequall bodies, are made to meet without a miracle, by some iron bodies, or some benign bolsterings? Who fears to set straight or hide the unhandsom warpings of bow legs and baker feet? What is there as to any defect in nature, whereof ingenuous art, as a diligent handmaid waiting on its mistresse, doth not study some supply or other? So farre as to

---

[30] Pierre Fauchard, *The Surgeon Dentist, or, Treatise on the Teeth*, trans. Lillian Lindsay, 2nd edition (Pound Ridge, NY: Milford House, 1969), p. 143. Fauchard noted one case in which the new tooth had gained sensation, but this was the exception, not the rule.

[31] Farah Karim-Cooper, *Cosmetics in Shakespearean and Renaissance Drama* (Edinburgh: Edinburgh University Press, 2006), p. 114.

[32] John Gauden, *A Discourse of Auxiliary Beauty. Or Artificiall Hansomnesse. In Point of Conscience between Two Ladies* (London: printed for R. Royston, 1656), p. 34.

graff in silver plates to crackt sculls, to furnish cropt faces with artificiall noses, to fill up the broken ranks and routed files of the teeth with ivory adjutants or lieutenants.[33]

Overall, Gauden suggested that cosmetics were not qualitatively different from prosthetics. The use of cosmetics was therefore not morally reprehensible, provided that they were employed sparingly, and not used to entice or entrap men. It is clear, however, that many early modern people drew different conclusions about the continuity of prostheses and cosmetics. Positioned at the boundary between medicine and beautification, false and implanted teeth became vulnerable to the sort of misgivings which Gauden's first disputant identified about cosmetics: that they disguised the face, and impeded the discernment of rich from poor, young from old. The judgements casually levelled against users of false teeth could be vitriolic. Samuel Pepys, for example, recorded in his diary that

> Sir William Batten doth rail still against Mr Turner and his wife (telling me he is a false fellow, and his wife a false woman and hath rotten teeth and false, set in with wire) and as I know they are so, I am glad he finds it so.[34]

For Pepys, Mrs Turner's rotten teeth were a physical expression of her rotten character, and *should* be visible to others on that basis. She and her husband were, as Pepys stresses, 'false' both in body and in behaviour. Similarly, Robert Herrick's *Hesperides*, published in 1648, included an epigram on 'Glasco':

> Glasco had none, but now some teeth has got,
> Which though they furre, will neither ake, or rot.
> Six teeth he has, whereof twice two are known
> Made of a Haft, that was a mutton-bone.
> Which not for use, but meerly for the sight,
> He wears all day, and drawes those teeth at night.[35]

For both authors, false teeth seemed an unfair advantage in the social game. Their subjects had not the face they deserved, but the one they had bought. The fact that Glasco's teeth are made from a haft, or knife handle, aptly represents the technologisation of the body offered by such procedures, in which the natural and artificial meet. 'Haft' may also underline the duplicity Herrick sees as inherent in this set-up: the

---

[33] Ibid., pp. 59–60.

[34] 'Monday 10 October 1664', *The Diary of Samuel Pepys*, accessed 6 April 2018, www.pepysdiary .com/diary/1664/10/10.

[35] Robert Herrick, 'Upon Glasco. Epig.' in *Robert Herrick*, ed. Stephen Romer (London: Faber and Faber, 2010), n.p.

word was also employed as a verb meaning 'to use subtlety or deceit, to use shifts or dodges'.[36]

False teeth – in particular, implanted teeth – raised questions about the interface between one body and another, between bodies and technology, and between bodies and the people who 'read' them. We might thus consider false teeth as prostheses within the 'free-ranging' definition of that word advanced by Will Fisher in his 2006 *Materializing Gender*.[37] Discussing items such as beards, codpieces, and handkerchiefs, Fisher argues that such accoutrements functioned as 'supplementary' to the early modern body in a Derridean sense, that is, both an addition to one's 'natural' self and a necessary part of it.[38] Fisher's particular interest is in those items that acted dually as contributors to and markers of the assignment of gender, which he argues was based on a number of differently 'weighted' signs. While genitalia were the most heavily weighted indicators of masculine or feminine identity, clothing, voice, and manners all had a role to play. Facial prostheses in general, and false teeth in particular, seem likewise to have functioned as 'weighted' signs – this time, of (dis)ability and socio-economic status. Whilst they may not have been part of the 'natural' material body, they were intrinsic to the lived experience of the embodied subject, altering both their social and sensory worlds.

The early modern period possessed dynamic paradigms for thinking about these problems of appearance and identity, particularly in relation to social class. As Alexandra Shepard has shown, it was held in the sixteenth and seventeenth centuries that virtues such as chivalry, honesty, and bravery could be found 'in' the nobility in a physiological sense. Indeed, 'aspirations to the temperate [bodily] ideal were restricted to an elite minority variously distinguished by their moral, religious, and, more implicitly, their social superiority'.[39] This was not a quaint tradition, but a live and important issue. As we have seen in the case of castrati, the fast-changing economic climate of the early modern period had the potential both to undermine and to render sacrosanct the perceived connection between bodily qualities and social standing. Mark Breitenberg has

---

[36] '† Haft, v.2', in *OED Online* (Oxford University Press), accessed 1 February 2018, www.oed.com/view/Entry/83190.

[37] Will Fisher, *Materializing Gender in Early Modern English Literature and Culture* (Cambridge: Cambridge University Press, 2006), p. 29.

[38] Ibid., p. 27.

[39] Alexandra Shepard, *Meanings of Manhood in Early Modern England* (Oxford: Oxford University Press, 2006), p. 49.

observed how 'the term "aristocratic body" denotes not a readily distin-
guishable rank in early modern England ... but rather an ideal to which
various degrees of the gentry might aspire, or a symbol that might
legitimate newly acquired status as if it were inherent'.[40] Accordingly,
the body might function to bridge the gap between economic status,
which was changeable, and 'rank', which was generally inherited.
Equally, it might prevent the *nouveau riche* (that is, those who attained
wealth through commerce rather than by birth) from truly assimilating
into aristocratic society. Thus attributes such as height potentially functioned, in Fisher's terms, as 'weighted signs' of socio-economic status. As
so often in such discourses, the body imagined as noble or otherwise was
paradigmatically male, partly because the male seed was commonly understood as that which shaped the gross matter supplied by females in the
generative process.[41]

While seductive, however, notions of the naturalness of noble bodies
were not uncomplicated. Many physical assessments of nobility were more
or less founded on physiognomy, the notion that character could be read
in a person's facial features. Physiognomy had a long history, reaching back
to Greek classicism, and bolstered by the Galenic notion that bodily
temperature might govern characterological temperament.[42] Mixing
pseudo-science and scurrility, it proved immensely popular for much of
the early modern period: Martin Porter estimates that there were around
300,000 copies of texts on physiognomy circulating in England during the
period 1470–1780.[43] Nonetheless, physiognomy seemed to lose much of
its authority in the early eighteenth century, shifting from a fairly respect-
able branch of natural philosophy to a 'vulgarised' parlour game (though
later to be revived by Johann Caspar Lavater's 1775 *Essays on Physiognomy*).
Among the chief factors in this decline was a rise in the use of cosmetics,
which, just as Gauden's *Discourse of Auxiliary Beauty* had predicted, went
hand-in-hand with an increasing emphasis on fashion and personal self-
fashioning.[44] As Roy Porter points out, this necessarily undermined the

---

[40] Mark Breitenberg, *Anxious Masculinity in Early Modern England* (Cambridge: Cambridge
   University Press, 1996), p. 73.
[41] See Matthew Cobb, *Generation: the Seventeenth-Century Scientists Who Unraveled the Secrets of Sex,
   Life, and Growth* (New York: Bloomsbury Publishing USA, 2008), pp. 210–20.
[42] Roy Porter, *Flesh in the Age of Reason* (London: Allen Lane, 2003), pp. 245–46; Bernadette
   Wegenstein, *The Cosmetic Gaze: Body Modification and the Construction of Beauty* (Cambridge:
   MIT Press, 2012), pp. 5–8.
[43] Martin Porter, *Windows of the Soul: Physiognomy in European Culture, 1470–1780* (Oxford:
   Clarendon Press, 2005), p. 96.
[44] Porter, *Flesh in the Age of Reason*, pp. 244–57.

'universal sign-grammar of good and bad'[45] promised by physiognomic reading:

> It had always been acknowledged, of course, that reading character might present difficulties, rather like peering through a glass darkly; but what if looks were actually designed to lie? How could physiognomy cope with systematic hypocrisy of countenance?[46]

However it was generated, 'hypocrisy of countenance' undermined the trust on which relationships were based and threatened the very assumptions upon which social order was based. Nowhere was this hypocrisy demonstrated more clearly, and more outrageously, than in early modern nose grafting.

Reputation and Rhinoplasty

In 1704, gentlewoman Sarah Cowper recorded in her diary her encounter with an acquaintance whose nose had collapsed as a result of venereal disease. Cowper did not seem particularly perturbed that the woman had contracted the disease, nor that it had damaged her face to such an extent. She was, however, a little surprised by the woman's response to this misfortune:

> The Lady Millbank whose husband (tis said) gave her the disease of St Job, to that degree as her nose fell flatt, yet was afterwards so well cured that she bore Sr [Millbank] eight children that are handsome, sound, and well. This Lady was in Health but five days since and now is dead of the small pox. I was commending her for she seemed well assured, content, and easie with so unfortunate a disaster. A La[dy] made answer that moreover she was airy, brisk, and a great Dancer. *Methought that was more than enough, for by no means shou'd any Woman dance without a nose, tho' never so innocently lost.*[47]

Cowper's cutting understatement was rather typical of her diaries, in which most of her acquaintances, as well as her family and servants, are judged and found wanting. Lady Millbank's fate, however, also tells us something of the importance of the nose in early modern culture, and the ignominy which accompanied losing it. Within the physiognomic tradition described above, the nose was a particularly important feature, the size and shape of which was believed to denote personal qualities including

---

[45] Ibid., p. 249.   [46] Ibid., p. 251.
[47] Sarah Cowper, 'Diary, Volume 1, 1700–1702' (*Defining Gender, 1450–1910*, n.d.), p. 219, www .gender.amdigital.co.uk (emphasis added).

'straitnesse of heart and indignation of thought'.[48] In privileging this organ, physiognomists shared something with more informal, but long-standing adages about the significance of the nose. In the popular imagination, the size of a man's nose might correspond with that of his penis, while, as Peter Berek has shown, comedically oversized noses were often used to denote Jewishness on the early modern stage.[49] The mutilated, slit, or amputated nose, meanwhile, was 'situated within the idiom of insult', marking out the bearer as deceitful, roguish, or seditious, and being closely associated with castration.[50] This logic underlay both extrajudicial and judicial maiming, both aimed at 'exacerbating the risk of dishonour'.[51] As Cowper's account demonstrates, the collapsed or missing nose was most strongly associated with venereal disease, such that – especially for women – this feature was instantly readable to any onlooker. In her extensive work on rhinoplasty, Emily Cock describes how the physiognomic tradition of viewing long noses as sexual intersected with readings of the missing nose as indicating pox, such that 'texts focussed on bawds and whores repeatedly feature women who have lost long noses, or authorial surprise that they should still have one'.[52] In this hostile environment, it is unsurprising that those with missing or collapsed noses sought to remedy the lack. Attempts to palliate the physical and social effects of a lost nose usually consisted of artificial noses made of metal, paper, or leather. These devices were often painted or enamelled to resemble the original as closely as possible, though the effect was probably unconvincing at close quarters.[53] Moreover, prosthetic noses brought their own problems. Holly Dugan points out that prosthetic noses hindered rather than helped one's ability to smell, and functioned as a 'visible reminder' of the dangers of pox.[54] In the absence of a better solution, prosthetic noses at least covered

---

[48] Thomas Vicary, *The Surgion's Directorie, for Young Practitioners, in Anatomie, Wounds, and Cures, &c. Shewing, the Excellencie of Divers Secrets Belonging to That Noble Art and Mysterie. Very Usefull in These Times upon Any Sodaine Accidents. And May Well Serve, as a Noble Exercise for Gentlewomen and Others; Who Desire Science in Medicine and Surgery, for a Generall Good* (London: printed by T. Fawcett, 1651), p. 37.

[49] Garthine Walker, *Crime, Gender and Social Order in Early Modern England* (Cambridge: Cambridge University Press, 2003), p. 92; Peter Berek, '"Looking Jewish" on the Early Modern Stage', in *Religion and Drama in Early Modern England: the Performance of Religion on the Renaissance Stage*, ed. Jane Hwang Degenhardt and Elizabeth Williamson (Farnham: Ashgate, 2011), pp. 55–70.

[50] Walker, *Crime, Gender and Social Order in Early Modern England*, p. 92; Patricia Skinner, 'The Gendered Nose and Its Lack: "Medieval" Nose-Cutting and Its Modern Manifestations', *Journal of Women's History* 26:1 (2014): 45–67; Cock, *Rhinoplasty and the Nose*, p. 31.

[51] Cock, *Rhinoplasty and the Nose*, p. 32.   [52] Ibid., p. 27.   [53] Ibid., pp. 38–42.

[54] Holly Dugan, *The Ephemeral History of Perfume: Scent and Sense in Early Modern England* (Baltimore: Johns Hopkins University Press, 2011), p. 96.

the facial bones exposed by tissue loss, which allowed one to venture
outdoors without causing horror. For a few individuals, however, the effect
of losing their nose was such that they were prepared to undergo a
dangerous and pioneering form of reconstruction.

In one form or another, reconstructive rhinoplasty has been a fixture of
the medical profession for more than two thousand years. Jerome Webster
and Martha Teach Gnudi find nose reconstruction operations to have
been first detailed in the ancient Hindu surgical writings of Susrata.[55]
Though its history thereafter is murky, at some point, probably by the
tenth century AD, this text's secrets travelled westward to the
Mediterranean.[56] The first detailed account of the nose-reconstruction
operation being practised in Europe comes from the fifteenth-century
Italian historian Bartholommeo Fazio, describing the work of father-and-
son surgeons Branca the Elder and Antonio Branca.[57] In the sixteenth
century, a Bolognese surgeon, Gaspare Tagliacozzi, is believed to have
learned his craft from the Brancas. He became synonymous with the nasal
graft, with which he could apparently craft a nose 'so resembling nature's
pattern, so perfect in every respect that it was [the patients'] considered
opinion that they like these better than the original ones which they had
received from nature'.[58]

Tagliacozzi's seminal text on nasal grafting, *De Curtorum Chirurgia per
Institionem,* was first published in Venice in 1596–7. It contained pains-
takingly detailed instructions for this operation which suggested that the
author had undertaken the procedure many times, despite the fact that it
appears to have been a long, risky, and painful process. To craft the new
nose, a portion of the skin of the upper arm first had to be lifted up with
forceps and cut on two sides, before lint was placed underneath to prevent
the skin reuniting with the flesh.[59] When the swelling from this wound
had died down, one was to cut the third edge of the skin flap, fold it
backwards, and bandage it.[60] After two weeks or so, one could consider
suturing the flap – still attached at one end to the arm – to the mutilated

[55] Martha Teach Gnudi and Jerome Pierce Webster, *The Life and Times of Gaspare Tagliacozzi,
Surgeon of Bologna, 1545–1599. With a Documented Study of the Scientific and Cultural Life of
Bologna in the Sixteenth Century* (New York: H. Reichner, 1950), p. 106.
[56] Ibid., pp. 107–8.   [57] Ibid., p. 110.
[58] Gaspare Tagliacozzi, 'Letter to Hieronymus Mercurialis', in Gnudi and Webster, *The Life and
Times of Gaspare Tagliacozzi*, pp. 136–9. For a detailed examination of the circulation of rhinoplasty
texts in early modern Europe, see Cock, *Rhinoplasty and the Nose*, pp. 112–49.
[59] Gaspare Tagliacozzi, *De Curtorum Chirurgia per Institionem*, ed. Robert M. Goldwyn, trans. Joan
H. Thomas (New York: Gryphon Edition, 1996), pp. 133–5.
[60] Ibid., pp. 150–7.

nose, binding the area with specially made bandages.[61] For the first week, it was essential that the patient avoid any movement, even talking, if the skin was to have a chance of adhering. Three weeks later, one might fully detach the skin from the arm and continue shaping the nose. However, it would be a further six to nine weeks before the surgeon could form the nose's columella, and two more weeks before the nostrils could be formed.[62] Tagliacozzi himself pointed out difficulties which attended every step of the operation. For instance, patients were required to have their heads shaved prior to the procedure – not because of infection risk, but because the movement of scratching one's lice-ridden head would ruin the shape of the finished nose.[63] The new nose needed to be made considerably larger than eventually required, since the skin could be expected to contract over the first year of adhesion. Moreover, it was an inescapable fact that hair might grow on the new nose 'so luxuriant that it must be shaved'.[64] The result was certainly better than the 'horrendous and abominable sight' of a missing nose, with the internal bones and flesh of the face exposed.[65] Still, Tagliacozzi admitted, 'The grafted nose differs from the normal nose in its color, softness, sensitivity, size, and hirsuteness, as well as in the magnitude of the nostrils.'[66]

Partly because of the difficulties Tagliacozzi described, and partly because of misinterpretations and corruptions of his instructions, it has been widely believed that his operation fell out of favour in the later sixteenth century, leaving plastic surgery to stagnate until the First World War revived the craft.[67] However, Cock has shown that copies of *De Curtorum Chirurgia* were circulated among British surgeons of the seventeenth and eighteenth centuries.[68] Moreover Alexander Read, who had long taken an interest in Paré's techniques for facial reconstruction, became strongly associated with the promulgation of Tagliacozzi's work. Cock notes that 'A translation of book two of Tagliacozzi *De curtorum chirurgia* outlining the rhinoplasty procedure was attached to a posthumous selection of Read's works', titled *Chirurgorum comes* and possibly edited by James II's physician Francis Bernard.[69] It is unclear if Read or his

---

[61] Ibid., pp. 170–7.   [62] Ibid., pp. 200–2.   [63] Ibid., pp. 12–13.   [64] Ibid., p. 111.
[65] Ibid., p. 25.   [66] Ibid., p. 110.
[67] On the revival of Tagliacotian rhinoplasty from 1800 onward, see Cock, *Rhinoplasty and the Nose*, pp. 91–105.
[68] See Emily Cock, '"Lead[ing] 'em by the Nose into Publick Shame and Derision": Gaspare Tagliacozzi, Alexander Read and the Lost History of Plastic Surgery, 1600–1800', *Social History of Medicine* 28:1 (2015): 1–21, https://doi.org/10.1093/shm/hku070; Cock, *Rhinoplasty and the Nose*, pp. 112–49.
[69] Cock, *Rhinoplasty and the Nose*, p. 112.

contemporaries actually carried out the operation described in this text. What is clear, however, is that public and medical interest in the nose reconstruction operation continued unabated throughout the seventeenth century.[70] Moreover, in the latter half of the seventeenth century, this interest became increasingly coloured by the idea that the operator might take the skin or flesh of another person to supply the graft material for nose reconstruction. This idea had no basis in Tagliacozzi's *Curtorum*. Indeed, he explicitly dismissed the possibility of inter-personal grafts on the grounds that 'the danger to the patient would be considerable and the outcome dubious, if not hopeless'.[71] Nevertheless, later writers showed themselves either unaware of Tagliacozzi's statement or simply disinclined to let the truth get in the way of a good story. Jean-Baptiste van Helmont, for instance, attested that

> A certain inhabitant of *Bruxels*, in a combat had his nose mowed off, addressed himself to *Tagliacozzus* a famous Chirurgeon ... that he might procure a new one; and when he feared the incision of his own arm, he hired a Porter to admit it, out of whose arm, having first given the reward agreed upon, at length he dig'd a new nose. About thirteen months after his return to his own Countrey, on a sudden the ingrafted nose grew cold, putrified, and within a few days, dropt off. To those of his friends, that were curious in the exploration of the cause of this unexpected misfortune, it was discovered, that the Porter expired, neer about the same punctilio of time, wherein the nose grew frigid and cadaverous.[72]

This account, like others, touched on the doctrine of sympathy which I discuss below. The grafted flesh, they suggested, would die at the same time as its original owner, and thus had to be sourced wisely. In 1662, James Cooke's *Mellificum Chirurgiae* provided readers with a brief description of the operation, adding that the grafted tissue 'may be either from their own bodies or some others: if they choose anothers [*sic*], let them be sure they are longer lived than themselves, lest they lose their Nose again before they die'.[73] M. de la Vauguion likewise asserted that 'the Ancients

---

[70] Cock, '"Lead[ing] 'em by the Nose"', 8–12; Gnudi and Webster, *The Life and Times of Gaspare Tagliacozzi*, pp. 273–80, 303–7.

[71] Tagliacozzi, *De Curtorum Chirurgia per Institionem*, pp. 76–7.

[72] Johan [Jean] Baptiste van Helmont, *A Ternary of Paradoxes. The Magnetick Cure of Wounds*, trans. Walter Charleston, 2nd edition (London, 1650), pp. 13–14.

[73] James Cooke, *Mellificium Chirurgia, or the Marrow of Many Good Authors Enlarged: Wherein Is Briefly, Fully, and Faithfully Handled the Art of Chirurgery in Its Four Parts, with All the Several Diseases unto Them Belonging: Their Definitions, Causes, Signes, Prognosticks, and Cures, Both General and Particular* (London: printed by T.R. for John Sherley, 1662), p. 374.

repaired the loss of parts, as a Nose cut off or the like, by inoculating Flesh out of the Arms or Buttocks of their Slaves'.[74]

That these stories began to circulate widely from the middle of the seventeenth century was no coincidence. In the 1660s, members of the Royal Society were testing the limits of biological experimentation. Primarily using dogs, they made blood transfusions and skin grafts, first between different parts of the same animal, and then between one animal and another.[75] Moreover, some experiments tested the boundaries between one species and another.[76] In 1667–8, blood transfusions between animals and humans were undertaken in France and England, and were eagerly documented in the Royal Society's *Philosophical Transactions*. The procedure's pioneer, Jean-Baptiste Denis, claimed to have cured several patients of madness by infusing them with lamb's or calf's blood, and in 1667, Edmund King and some colleagues transfused blood from a sheep to a clergyman.[77] The aim of these transfusion experiments was not to prevent death through blood loss, but to ascertain the role of blood in determining bodily processes and behaviours. Writing on dog-to-dog transfusions in 1666, for instance, Robert Boyle pondered

> Whether by this way of Transfusing Blood, the disposition of individual Animals of the same kind, may not be much altered (As whether a *fierce* Dog, by being often quite new stocked with the blood of a *cowardly* Dog, may not become more tame; & *vice versa*, &c.?)[78]

Tellingly, Boyle also wondered whether dogs which received transfusions would retain their characters and abilities. Would they, for example, 'fawn

---

[74] M. de la Vauguion, *A Compleat Body of Chirurgical Operations, Containing the Whole Practice of Surgery. With Observations and Remarks on Each Case. Amongst Which Are Inserted, the Several Ways of Delivering Women in Natural and Unnatural Labours. The Whole Illustrated with Copper Plates, Explaining the Several Bandages, Sutures, and Divers Useful Instruments.* (London: printed for Henry Bonwick, T. Goodwin, M. Wotton, B. Took, and S. Manship, 1699), p. 355.

[75] David Hamilton, *A History of Organ Transplantation: Ancient Legends to Modern Practice* (Pittsburgh: University of Pittsburgh Press, 2012), pp. 25–6; Anita Guerrini, 'The Ethics of Animal Experimentation in Seventeenth-Century England', *Journal of the History of Ideas* 50:3 (1989): 391–407.

[76] Paolo Savoia's *Gaspare Tagliacozzi and Early Modern Surgery*, published as this book was going to press, also explores the connection between Tagliacozzi's work and horticultural grafting. See *Gaspare Tagliacozzi and Early Modern Surgery: Faces, Men and Pain* (London: Routledge, 2019), pp. 140–82.

[77] Holly Tucker, *Blood Work: a Tale of Medicine and Murder in the Scientific Revolution* (New York: W. W. Norton, 2012), pp. 163–70; Guerrini, 'The Ethics of Animal Experimentation in Seventeenth-Century England', 401.

[78] Robert Boyle, 'Tryals Proposed by Mr Boyle to Dr Lower, to Be Made by Him, for the Improvement of Transfusing Blood out of One Live Animal into Another', *Philosophical Transactions*, 11 February 1666. Folger Shakespeare Library.

upon' their owners? Would retrieving dogs continue to retrieve and bloodhounds to follow scents?[79]

Though discussants of Tagliacozzi did not explicitly link his nose grafts to these blood transfusions, it was not a great leap to see that both procedures raised questions about the relations between the 'stuff' of the body, the subjective experience of the body, and selfhood as a whole. These queries were likewise provoked by the doctrine of sympathy, which acquired a scientific gloss in the later seventeenth century. Influenced by Paracelsus and Van Helmont, adherents to this doctrine contended that all physical bodies shared a connection with one another, either mystically or (in later iterations of the doctrine) via material qualities.[80] Whilst some dismissed the theory as quackery, work by Seth Lobis has convincingly demonstrated that sympathy remained a topic of discussion throughout the seventeenth and into the eighteenth century, being reworked into new forms rather than wholly rejected.[81] Among the most influential writers on sympathy were Sir Kenelm Digby and Robert Fludd, both of whom defended the idea of curing by sympathy, with 'sympatheticall powder' and 'weapon-salve' respectively.[82] Using sympathetic connection between a weapon and the wound it had created, or between a drop of blood and the whole body, the authors asserted that even serious injuries might be cured without so much as seeing the patient.[83] Sympathy was the supposed force behind the Anodyne Necklace, a device discussed earlier in this book. Moreover, unlike the Royal Society's experiments, the doctrine of sympathy was explicitly connected to the Tagliacotian operation, and even took anecdotes about that operation as proof of theory. Fludd, for instance, told the story of an Italian nobleman who had, after losing his

---

[79] Ibid.

[80] Seth Lobis, *The Virtue of Sympathy: Magic, Philosophy, and Literature in Seventeenth-Century England*, Yale Studies in English (New Haven: Yale University Press, 2015), pp. 9–13.

[81] Cock, *Rhinoplasty and the Nose*, pp. 158–69.

[82] Kenelm Digby, *A Late Discourse, Made in a Solmne Assembly of Nobles and Learned Men at Montepellier in France: By Sr Kenelme Digby, Knight, &c. Touching the Cure of Wounds by the Powder of Sympathy; With Instructions How to Make the Said Powders; Whereby Many Other Secrets of Nature Are Unfolded*, trans. R. White (London: printed for R. Lownes and T. Davies, 1658); Robert Fludd, *Doctor Fludds Answer Vnto M· Foster or, The Squeesing of Parson Fosters Sponge, Ordained by Him for the Wiping Away of the Weapon-Salve Wherein the Sponge-Bearers Immodest Carriage and Behauiour towards His Bretheren Is Detected; the Bitter Flames of His Slanderous Reports, Are by the Sharpe Vineger of Truth Corrected and Quite Extinguished: And Lastly, the Verrtuous Validity of His Sponge, in Wiping Away of the Weapon-Salve, Is Crushed out and Cleane Abolished* (London: printed for Nathaneal Butter, 1631).

[83] Lobis, *The Virtue of Sympathy*, pp. 45–50.

nose, persuaded his slave to provide the flesh needed to make another. Afterwards, he reported,

> The slave being healed and rewarded, was manumitted, or set at liberty, and away he went to Naples. It happened, that the slave fell sicke and dyed, at which instant, the Lords nose did gangrenate and rot; whereupon, the part of the nose which hee had of the dead man, was by the Doctors advice cut away.[84]

Fludd insisted that this phenomenon should be attributed not to the 'trumpery of the divell' but rather to 'God's vivifying spirit', which operated so remarkably that despite the distance between the nose's original owner and its new possessor, 'neither the tall Hills of Hetruria; nor yet the tall Appenine mountaines could stop the concourse and motion of these two spirits, or rather one spirit continuated in two bodies'.[85] Less hyperbolically, Digby posited that 'artificiall noses that are made of the flesh of other men ... do putrifie as soon as those persons out of whose substance they were taken come to die, as if that small parcell of flesh ingrafted upon the face did live by the spirits it drew from its first root, and source'.[86] While some discussions of sympathetic cure were decidedly mystical in emphasis, Digby in particular viewed this phenomenon as a mechanistic one, in which atoms were attracted like to like.[87]

What was the effect of all this scientific speculation on men and women with collapsed or missing noses? It seems clear that the scientific interest in sympathy and Tagliacozzi did not cause surgeons to actually start engrafting new noses. As had long been the case, people who lost their noses had to rely on false ones of various kinds. Nonetheless, medical and scientific speculation on the possibility of allografting (that is, grafting from one individual to another) had an impact on the ways in which bodily integrity and partition could be imagined. My own 2018 article on homoplastics, sympathy, and the noble body in the *Tatler* examines in detail a piece by

---

[84] Fludd, *Doctors Fludds Answer*, p. 132.   [85] Ibid., p. 133.
[86] Digby, *A Late Discourse*, pp. 115–16.
[87] The exact workings of sympathetic cure remained confused, but Lobis explains that in the case of a man cured by applying sympathetic powder to his bloodied garter: 'The blood atoms on the garter are attracted to those of the wound, where they are more plentiful. When the powder is added to the garter, light, which enables the cure, carries both the blood atoms and those of the vitriol in the powder and diffuses them in the air, where they are borne directly to the wound ... The aeration of the vitriol concentrates [its] virtue, and so the powder is more effective when applied at a distance than when it is administered directly' (Lobis, *The Virtue of Sympathy*, pp. 49–50).

Joseph Addison, in which he satirises the Tagliacotian operation.[88]
Imagining a slew of petty nobility receiving new noses, he goes on to
envisage the disruptive possibilities of sympathy between noble noses and
ignoble buttocks. Addison's piece takes its departure from Samuel Butler's
Hudibras (1674–8):

> So learned Talicotius from
> The brawny part of Porter's bum
> Cut supplemental noses, which
> Lasted as long as parent breech:
> But when the date of nock was out,
> Off drop'd the sympathetic snout.[89]

It shows how allografting might undermine the association between noble
characters and noble bodies, between one's face and one's deeds.
Moreover, Addison draws from a contemporary culture seemingly
obsessed with uncovering the disjuncture between appearances and reality,
from Jonathan Swift's vision of Celia at her toilet to Edward Ward's gleeful
description of 'Ugly' and 'No-Nose' Clubs.[90]

Both *Hudibras* and the *Tatler*, however, were preceded by a lesser-
known depiction of Tagliacotian rhinoplasty in which the socio-politics
of the body were sharply apparent. In the 1630s, William Davenant, poet
laureate, lost his nose to syphilis. In the 1640s or '50s, Hester Pulter,
whom Marcus Nevitt affirms had never met Davenant, wrote a poem in
which she humorously proposed to donate some of her own flesh to
replace the missing member.[91] She would, she argues, give her nose, were
it not for the fact that she would then be supposed to have suffered the
effects of venereal disease:

> For who but that bright Eye above
> Would know 'twere *charity*, not *love*?
> Then Sir, your pardon must I beg –
> Excuse my nose: accept my leg!

---

[88] Alanna Skuse, '"Keep your Face out of my Way or I'll Bite off your Nose": Homoplastics,
Sympathy, and the Noble Body in the *Tatler*, 1710', *Journal for Early Modern Cultural Studies*
17:4 (2018): 113–32.

[89] Samuel Butler, *Hudibras* (London: John Murray, 1835).

[90] Jonathan Swift, *The Complete Poems*, ed. Pat Rogers (London: Penguin, 1983), p. 448; Edward
Ward, *The Second Part of the London Clubs; Containing, the No-Nose Club, the Beaus Club, the
Farting Club, the Sodomites, or Mollies Club, The Quacks Club* (London: printed by
J. Dutton, 1709).

[91] As I describe below, there is some confusion around the date of this poem's composition (Marcus
Nevitt, 'The Insults of Defeat: Royalist Responses to Sir William Davenant's *Gondibert* [1651]',
The Seventeenth Century 24:2 [October 2009]: 287).

> But yet, be sure, both night and day,
> For me as for yourself you pray.
> For if I first should chance to go
> To visit those sad shades below
> As my frail flesh there putrifies,
> Your nose, no doubt, will sympathize.[92]

Pulter's poem demonstrates that the humorous potential of the Tagliacotian operation was recognised long before *Hudibras*. Furthermore, this humour assumed that the poem's audience had at least some notion of physiological sympathy and why it might cause a grafted nose to drop off with the original owner's death. The image Pulter presents of offering up her flesh, which may later die on the face of the recipient, is both grotesque and bizarrely erotic. Any man, Pulter asserts, 'Would give his nose, to have yo' wit'. However, Pulter is self-evidently already a witty woman, and the imagined donation is more visceral than cerebral, tying the fates of their two bodies together.

The picture is complicated further by the sensory implications of receiving a new nose. Given that the olfactory bulb is located within the skull, recipients of a nose graft (as well as those with missing noses) could presumably still smell. Thus in Addison's satire on nose transplantation and sympathy, he imagined that 'if anything went amiss with the nose, the porter felt the effects of it', such that if the recipient should 'smell pepper, or eat mustard . . . the [donor] part where the incision had been made was seized with unspeakable twinges and prickings'.[93] Where one portion of flesh can stand in for another, so haptic sensations (pricking) can 'anagrammatise' for olfactory ones, just as Bulwer later proposed when he extolled the usefulness of sign language for the deaf.[94] It is unclear whether Pulter similarly envisions a tactile kick-back from Davenant's sense of smell, but the sympathetic link between the two parties now entwines their sensory landscapes. Thus, the speaker's concern about the social inadvisability of sacrificing her own nose deliberately misses the point: joining the flesh of one person to that of another is an innately intimate act, which is the more easily read as sexual because Davenant is already marked by sexual vice. Neither are Davenant's indiscretions assumed to be behind him. If and when Cupid strikes again, warns Pulter, 'Then the next

---

[92] Hester Pulter, 'To Sir W.D. upon the Unspeakable Loss of the Most Conspicuous and Chief Ornament of His Frontispiece', in *Women's Works: 1625–1650*, ed. Donald W. Foster and Tobian Banton, 1st edition (New York: Wicked Good Books, 2013), pp. 160–1.

[93] Joseph Addison, 'Non Cuicunque Datum Est Habere Nasum', *Tatler*, 1710.

[94] Bearden, 'Before Normal, There Was Natural'.

loss will be your brain'. To lose one nose, it seems, is unfortunate; to lose another implies a level of carelessness which even this sympathetic author cannot excuse:

> Prodigious the *knight* remains,
> Without or nose, or fame, or brains.
> Then a bold ordnance struck the title off!
> Thus the proud Parcae sit and at us scoff.
> What now remains – the *man*, at least?
> No, surely: nothing left, but *beast*.
> Then royal favour glued it on again,
> And now the knight is bow-dyed and in grain.
> Then trample not that honor in the dust
> In being slaves to those are slaves to lust.[95]

Pulter's tone is relatively gentle here. As a confirmed Royalist, she and Davenant were – politically at least – on the same side. Cock thus reads this poem principally as an exercise in aristocratic beneficence 'bequeathed from a position of privilege', albeit one with strings attached.[96] In imagining a sympathetic bond between their two bodies, Pulter places herself in the thick of the Royalist campaign by proxy: 'through the logic of the transplant, Pulter's private body is brought into public politics and the masculine spaces of war'.[97] Moreover, Pulter's argument reveals something about the way in which bodily integrity became particularly important in periods of socio-political unrest. There is much uncertainty about the dates of Davenant's losing his nose and of Pulter's composing the above poem. The editors of *Women's Works: 1625–1650* put the former at 1638 and the latter soon after in 1643. Mary Edmond believes Davenant to have contracted syphilis in 1630 and to have become disfigured by 1634.[98] Nevitt argues that Davenant lost his nose sometime in the 1630s and Pulter wrote about it in the 1650s.[99] Despite these differences, it is apparent that Pulter was not alone in drawing attention to Davenant's altered face; indeed, her rhetoric had much in common with Davenant's Cromwellian detractors. Nevitt has described how Davenant's missing nose became for his enemies 'synecdochic of the vanishing pleasures

---

[95] Pulter, 'To Sir W.D. upon the Unspeakable Loss of the Most Conspicuous and Chief Ornament of His Frontispiece'.

[96] Cock, *Rhinoplasty and the Nose*, p. 220.   [97] Ibid., p. 222.

[98] Mary Edmond, *Rare Sir William Davenant: Poet Laureate, Playwright, Civil War General, Restoration Theatre Manager* (Manchester: Manchester University Press, 1987), pp. 44–5.

[99] Nevitt, 'The Insults of Defeat', 287.

(riotously convivial, unashamedly sexual) of Caroline England'.[100] Such jibes had particular bite because, as Covington describes, some Royalists embraced facial wounds as signs of valorous conduct, attained in face-to-face combat.[101] Davenant's facial difference suffered even more by comparison, and may have undercut the chivalric ideals of his unfinished epic *Gondibert* (1650–2). For Pulter, Davenant's loss threatens the idea of the noble body. Without the redeeming factor of gentility, Davenant's sexual appetites render him positively sub-human, a 'beast' or 'slave'. 'Royal favour' – that is, the knighthood Davenant received in 1643 – may transform the way in which Davenant's past indiscretions are viewed, giving them a new 'dye'. In order for the dye to prove itself truly 'in grain', however, it is necessary that the newly ennobled Davenant *perform* nobility with his body, despite its shortcomings.

Read in this context, Pulter's treatment of Davenant's nose is entirely consistent with Alice Eardley's contention that 'Pulter holds men primarily responsible for the nation's political disintegration and for the widespread social and moral collapse with which that disintegration is associated.'[102] Moreover, Pulter's emphasis on Davenant's moral shortcomings and her strangely salacious suggestion of a sympathetic graft between their bodies need not be discordant. Well acquainted with the latest scientific developments, Pulter saw that allografting and other transformative surgeries called into doubt the connection between body, character, and innate abilities. In so doing, new science had the potential to undermine the naturalness of the noble body, a belief upon which the King's right to rule was partly based. Pulter's exhortation to Davenant is thus timely. If one's claim to socio-political superiority is based upon a monist conception of self of which the body is an intrinsic part, it is perilous to undermine that conception by making one's body look decidedly *ig*noble. Rather, the connection must go both ways: as one's rank ennobles one's body, so one's body, and its appetites and behaviours, must come into line with one's social responsibilities.

---

[100] Ibid., 297. Conversely, Cock notes that Cromwell's large red nose was a common target of ridicule among his enemies, and the nose was torn off his funeral effigy during its lying in state at Somerset House (Cock, *Rhinoplasty and the Nose*, p. 218).

[101] Covington, *Wounds, Flesh and Metaphor*, pp. 96–7.

[102] Hester Pulter, *Poems, Emblems, and The Unfortunate Florinda*, ed. Alice Eardley (Toronto: Iter, 2014), p. 3.

Conclusion

At the beginning of this chapter, we saw how one's face might be one's fortune in early modern society. It was also the part of the body on which misfortunes were most clearly displayed – maims associated with illness and injury, teeth lost through age and poverty or regained through wealth, and, most shamefully, noses sacrificed to venereal disease. The face was likewise the location of many sensory organs, and damage to the face thus affected the texture of one's everyday life in a profound way, influencing what one did or did not taste, smell, see, and feel.

For these reasons, medical and cosmetic interventions to the face captured the imagination of medical practitioners, writers, and thinkers. The possibilities offered by transplanted teeth and grafted noses were an imaginatively stimulating means of thinking about the question of how intrinsically one's own flesh 'belonged' to oneself. Was it possible, for example, that a transplanted piece of flesh would react to the illnesses and injuries of its original owner, as proponents of sympathy suggested? This idea may have seemed as far-fetched to most early modern people as it does to modern readers. However, its popularity as a tool for thought reiterates how far authors and readers of the seventeenth and eighteenth centuries were interested in considering the nature of embodiment, from both philosophical and scientific perspectives. In some respects, scientific exercises such as allografting and blood transfusions implied that the flesh was merely matter, to be exchanged and manipulated as it suited the person 'inside'. At the same time, however, even satirical representations of these fleshly additions recognised that there was nothing superficial about changing the exterior of a person. To alter the face in particular was to reshape a person's social and sensory encounters with the world, and thus to alter their lived experience.

CHAPTER 4

Acting the Part: Prosthetic Limbs

Act 4 of *Titus Andronicus* opens with Lavinia, tongueless and handless, running after Lucius' son as he carries a bundle of books under his arm. Using her stumps to turn to the page of Ovid's *Metamorphoses* which describes the rape of Philomel, she is for the first time able to communicate something of the rape and mutilation enacted upon her. In an iconic sequence, Marcus sees an opportunity for Lavinia to reveal the names of her attackers:

MARCUS: My lord, look here. Look here, Lavinia,
This sandy plot is plain. Guide if thou canst
This after me.
        He writes his name with his staff, and guides it with feet and mouth.
I here have writ my name
Without the help of any hand at all.
Cursed be that heart that forced us to this shift!
Write thou, good niece, and here display at last
What god will have discovered for revenge.
Heaven guide thy pen to print thy sorrows plain,
That we may know the traitors and the truth
        She takes the staff in her mouth, and guides it with her stumps, and writes.
O, do ye read, my lord, what she hath writ?
[*Titus*] 'Stuprum – Chiron – Demetrius.'(4.1.67–88)[1]

Lavinia's taking up of the staff between mouth and hands is an imitation of Marcus' demonstration made with mouth and feet. Marcus' actions make sense. One cannot hold the stick between one's feet sufficiently securely to write, and he cannot show a means to use the stick 'without the

---

[1] I cite here from *The Oxford Shakespeare: Complete Works*, ed. John Jowett, William Montgomery, Gary Taylor, and Stanley Wells, 2nd edition (Oxford: Clarendon Press, 2005). However, the stage directions in this scene are remarkably stable. They appear identically, albeit with unmodernised spelling, in the First Folio (1623), Second Folio (1632), and First Quarto (1594), and are adopted without substantial differences by most modern editions.

help of any hand' otherwise, since his own hands are intact. When Lavinia takes up the staff, she understandably adapts the method Marcus has shown her, and instead of using her feet, she uses her stumps to guide the stick. However, Lavinia too takes up the staff in her mouth, and in her case, I argue that this action is *not* a simple case of utility. Wielding Marcus' staff in this way is a struggle. It is easier – or at least, no more difficult – to write in the sand with a stick held between one's stumps than one held in the mouth, particularly since this is not a mere twig but a large 'staff', perhaps hardly fitting in the mouth of the boy actor playing this role. Indeed, the whole action of the stick and stumps is somewhat curious, since there are other ways in which Lavinia might express herself. Before Marcus intervenes, Titus has begun to list possible assailants, a list to which Lavinia might nod or shake her head. Even writing with her toe in the sand would seem easier than using an implement. But if the stick in Lavinia's mouth is as much a hindrance as a help to the scene's action, why does Shakespeare place it there?

Titus is one of the most studied plays in the English canon, and generations of scholars have pored over the discursive significance of the drama's profusion of disembodied parts, gore, and horror. It is not my aim to attempt another analysis of *Titus'* violence in general. However, I will argue that Lavinia's experience – particularly her use of the staff – may be illuminated in new ways by a closer appreciation of the practical and ideological aspects of limb prostheses in early modern England. Such items were of social and economic as well as personal significance. Artificial arms and legs clearly performed a necessary function. Their use was widespread, and for most users, their 'meaning' seems to have been little thought of. In the discourses which circulate around the period's most sophisticated prostheses, however, one can trace the functions – and therefore the bodily attributes – which were of most concern to artificial limb users and makers. Prostheses, I will argue, may thus be thought of in terms of 'drag', as that word is used by Judith Butler to denote stylisations that make visible the performativity underpinning the 'natural' and 'normal' gendered (or in this case, able) body.[2] While the artificial limb is not a costume assumed willingly, those features which are exaggerated in prosthesis illuminate

---

[2] 'Disability drag' is discussed in the early modern context by Coker-Durso and Row-Heyveld. Lauren G. Coker-Durso, 'Metatheatricality and Disability Drag: Performing Bodily Difference on the Early Modern English Stage' Ph.D. (Saint Louis University, 2014); Lindsey Row-Heyveld, *Dissembling Disability in Early Modern English Drama* (Basingstoke: Palgrave, 2018). The issue of able-bodied actors 'cripping up' to play disabled parts is increasingly a topic of debate in contemporary theatre and film: see Mat Fraser, 'Cripping It Up', *Journal of Visual Art Practice* 12:3 (2013): 245–8; Frances

what are seen as the most valuable, most heavily reinscribed attributes of the able body. Thus, as we see clearly in Lavinia's case, properties and prostheses overlap. As prosthesis, an artificial leg, arm, hand, or foot can allow the user to avoid the stigmatisation associated with disability and reassert themselves as an agential subject. As prop, however, such items have a significatory life of their own, threatening to erase, as well as enable, the subject-user.

The Prosthetic in Society

Lavinia loses her limbs by force. Her attackers sever her hands and cut out her tongue so that she may not speak or write of their crime, but also so that she must live with the humiliation associated with rape and disability. While Lavinia's ordeal is grotesquely extreme, however, to lose a limb in early modern England may have been less unusual than it is today. The audience of *Titus* would likely have included people lacking fingers, hands, arms, or legs, or people who knew those people well. Moreover, while many amputations were the result of violence, and hastily undertaken on the battlefield or at sea, there is ample evidence of civilian cases in which the excision of a limb was a considered decision. In these cases, patients consented to a radical operation knowing that excruciating pain and risk of death lay ahead.

How did one make the decision to undergo an amputation while fully conscious? Clearly, only serious debility and disease can have warranted such a step. Patients who took this course did so as a last resort, to avoid imminent death by blood poisoning or spreading disease. In such circumstances, both surgeons and patients seem to have reconciled themselves to the horror of what lay ahead by framing the part to be excised as no longer belonging to their body. When the surgeon Hugh Ryder encountered a young patient afflicted with multiple fistulas and ulcers as the result of a poorly treated leg injury, for instance, he found the boy philosophical about his chances:

> I told his Father, I had considered, the circumstances he lay under, were so severe, that I thought, there was no likelyhood of his recovery, nor possibility of Cure; to which the Boy very heartily replied, he knew he should be

Ryan, 'We Wouldn't Accept Actors Blacking up, so Why Applaud "Cripping up"?', *The Guardian*, 13 January 2015.

well, if I would cut off his Thigh; and that if I would lend him a Knife, he would cut it off himself.[3]

Ryder agreed to undertake the amputation, and the boy was soon cured and 'very lively'. Though Ryder's account may smack of self-promotion, his description of the terrible sufferings which led his patient to this juncture is all too believable. Weeks of diarrhoea had left the boy a 'skeleton', and his leg was covered in ulcers 'stinking beyond all comparison, his Heel stuck to his Buttock, and his Knee disjointed ... the Ligaments being all eaten asunder'.[4]

This extreme example demonstrates the way in which patients with long-term afflictions might experience the ill parts of their body as alien. Limbs which failed to move, which perceptibly rotted, stank, or seemed to threaten healthy adjacent parts – all of which were features of advanced gangrene, cancers, and other diseases – might be regarded in hostile terms. In John Woodall's *A Treatise of Gangraena*, for instance, the part of the body to be amputated was represented as having committed a 'fault' or 'error':

> [I]t is just, that so much be amputated as deserveth expulsion, and not, as is said, to take away a sound and blamelesse legge, when it is innocent and free from fault, errour, or disease: for the noblenesse of each member of mans body, and namely of the legge, is highly even in humanitie to be tendred and regarded.[5]

Woodall's point was that one ought not to amputate further up the leg than necessary, but rather preserve as much as possible. Nonetheless, he focused on the parts which 'deserveth expulsion', implying that diseased limbs were somehow morally reprehensible and divorced from the rest of the 'noble' body. This tactic allowed Woodall to frame his surgeries as necessary and even heroic; elsewhere, he described a diseased limb as like the 'dead bowes' of a tree, which were to be 'pruned off' to save the plant.[6] The localised dysfunction effected by gangrene was particularly apt to encourage both sufferers and physicians to regard the diseased part as somehow foreign or hostile to the body proper. Alexander Read's *Somatographia Anthropine*, for instance, asserted that 'the rage and

[3] Hugh Ryder, *New Practical Observations in Surgery* (London: printed for James Partridge, 1685), pp. 54–5.
[4] Ibid., p. 54.
[5] John Woodall, 'A Treatise of Gangraena', in *The Surgeons Mate, or, Military & Domestique Surgery: Discouering Faithfully & Plainly [the] Method and Order of [the] Surgeons Chest, [the] Vses of the Instruments, the Vertues and Operations of [the] Medicines, Wth [the] Exact Cures of Wounds Made by Gun-Shott; and Otherwise* (London: printed by Rob. Young, for Nicholas Bourne, 1639), p. 386.
[6] Ibid., pp. 389–90.

malignity of [gangrene] is so great, that it will out of hand, not onely kill the part affected, but by contagion also sease upon the neighbour parts, and in time upon the whole body'.[7] With a curious turn of phrase, it advised the amputating surgeon to 'gather up the sound parts of [the patient's] body' before applying a ligature above the gangrenous area.[8]

The apparent facility of both patients and surgeons for imagining diseased limbs as separate from the rest of the body was in part a cultural phenomenon. As I have discussed elsewhere in relation to cancer, the image of post-mortem consumption by worms which ran through early modern Christian texts crossed over into medical language when cancers were described as worms eating living flesh.[9] Gangrenous limbs generally provoked less colourful language, but their wounds could, if untended, breed maggots, and this propensity can only have enhanced patients' sense of their infected limb as more corpse than animated flesh. In addition, early modern patients arguably experienced their sick limbs as 'estranged' simply because they were strange, in the several senses of that word. Limbs affected by gangrene could progressively turn yellow or black, marking them apart from the neighbouring flesh. Gangrenous parts might also lose sensation. In so doing, they lost an aspect of what set them apart from other kinds of matter. In phenomenological terms, the fact that when one touches one's arm or leg, one also *feels* that touch, is crucial to the body's unique status as 'lived' matter, both object and subject.

Drew Leder's theory of bodily 'dys-appearance' usefully expands this notion of bodily estrangement. Under normal circumstances, argues Leder, we do not much notice our bodies functioning. In everyday actions – walking, seeing, eating – they recede from our consciousness, and may be said to dis-appear. We 'exist' our bodies, he argues, as a perceptual vanishing point, from which all experience seems to take place.[10] Of necessity, '[m]y being-in-the-world depends upon my body's self-effacing transitivity'; one hardly notices one's legs while casually strolling.[11] By contrast, when we become aware of our bodies, it is generally because they 'dys-appear'. That is, they become prominent because they

---

[7] Alexander Read, *Somatographia Anthropine, or, a Description of the Body of Man. With the Practise of Chirurgery, and the Use of Three and Fifty Instrument.* (London: printed by Thomas Cotes, and sold by Michael Sparke, 1634), p. 105.

[8] Ibid., p. 104.

[9] Alanna Skuse, *Constructions of Cancer in Early Modern England: Ravenous Natures* (Basingstoke: Palgrave Macmillan, 2015), pp. 61–73.

[10] Drew Leder, *The Absent Body* (Chicago: University of Chicago Press, 1990), pp. 12–13.

[11] Ibid., p. 15.

are in pain, or because they do not function as we expect. Dys-appearance, as Chapter 1 discussed, can also occur when the gazes or actions of others cause us to think closely about our bodies, whether because they are non-normative (the wheelchair user attracting whispers and stares) or otherwise deemed remarkable (the woman walking down the street to catcalls). Central to dys-appearance is the sense of alienation from one's own body, in part or whole, and the sense that a dysfunctional body part might be working against 'oneself'. Leder explains:

> Whenever our body becomes an object of perception, even though it perceives itself, an element of distance is introduced. I no longer simply 'am' my body, the set of unthematized powers from which I exist. Now I 'have' a body, a perceived object in the world.[12]

Leder's description of the dysfunctional body emphasises how the 'object-ness' of the body may take over when illness takes hold. The subject may no longer feel themselves to be co-extensive with their flesh, but rather imagine their mind as somehow inhabiting that flesh as an occupant inhabits a house. As we have seen elsewhere in this book, material and cultural circumstances might cause the pendulum to swing between a vision of body, soul, and mind as fully integrated, and one in which the 'Complexion of the body ... many times puts Yokes and Manacles upon the Soul; so that (at the best) it is but as a close Prison'.[13]

There were, of course, some limits to this mental flexibility. However dispassionately one might regard one's sickly limb, and however heartily one might wish to be rid of it, the realities of amputation were sobering. Patients rightly feared the procedure, and they were often distrustful of the motives and capabilities of the surgeons who carried it out. Predictably, given the number of amputations that took place in wartime, operators were often characterised as bloodthirsty sawbones, who severed limbs because they lacked the skill to heal them by other means. In 1703, for instance, 'T.D.' angrily denounced an over-eager surgeon as a 'Butcher', who thought no more of removing a body part 'than some Persons do to pair [pare] their Nails'.[14] Tobias Smollet's 1748 *Roderick Random*

---

[12] Ibid., p. 77.
[13] Thomas Case, *Movnt Pisgah, or, A Prospect of Heaven Being an Exposition on the Fourth Chapter of the First Epistle of St Paul to the Thessalonians, from the 13th Verse, to the End of the Chapter, Divided into Three Parts* (London: Thomas Milbourn, for Dorman Newman, 1670), p. 94.
[14] T.D., *The Present State of Chyrurgery, with Some Short Remarks on the Abuses Committed under a Pretence to the Practice. And Reasons Offer'd for Regulating the Same* (London, 1703), p. 19.

capitalised on this perception in its depiction of the saw-happy surgeon, Mackshane:

> the patient ... pronounced with a woful countenance, 'What! Is there no remedy, doctor? Must I be dock'd? can't you splice it?'– 'Assuredly, doctor Mackshane (said the first mate) with submission, and deference ... I do apprehend, and conjecture, and aver, that there is no occasion nor necessity to smite off the poor man's leg.' ... Mackshane, very much incensed at his mate's differing in opinion from him so openly, answered, that he was not bound to give an account of his practice to him; and in a peremptory tone, ordered him to apply the tourniquet.[15]

Smollet's account probably rang true at sea and on the battlefield, where time and resources were scarce. In a civilian context, however, there is evidence not only that surgeons suffered from the 'sad schreeking' of their patients, but that they made a concerted effort to amputate in ways that preserved as much post-operative function as possible.[16] In effect, this usually meant ensuring that the stump could be readily fitted with a prosthesis. Thus, in contrast to Woodall's exhortations to preserve as much of the limb as possible, surgeons commonly advocated amputating closer to the knee or elbow, even taking off healthy flesh. Joseph de la Charriére, for instance, advised in 1695 that

> If it be the Leg, though only the Foot should be concern'd, you must Amputate 3 Fingers below the Knee ... because of the long suppuration which rots the Tendons, and other accidents that may happen; and to put on an Artificial one more easily.[17]

His counsel was echoed in the 1699 *Compleat Body of Chirurgical Operations*, in which the author suggested: 'The Leg must be cut off as near the Knee as possible ... for the more commodious carrying a Wooden Legg ... On the contrary cut as little as may be off the Arm, because it serves as an Ornament and Counterpoise to the Body, and an Artificial Hand may be made to be useful in some cases.'[18]

---

[15] Tobias Smollet, *The Adventures of Roderick Random, in Two Volumes*, vol. 1 (London: John Osborn, 1748), pp. 256–7.

[16] John Moyle, *Abstractum Chirurgiae Marinae, or, An Abstract of Sea Chirurgery* (London: printed by J. Richardson for Tho. Passinger, 1686), p. 25.

[17] Joseph de la Charriére, *A Treatise of the Operations of Surgery. Wherein Are Mechanically Explain'd the Causes of the Diseases in Which They Are Needful, ... To Which Is Added, a Treatise of Wounds, ... Translated from the Third Edition of the French, Enlarg'd, Corrected and Revis'd by the Author, Joseph de La Charriere* (London: printed by R. Brugis, for D. Brown and W. Mears; and T. Ballard, 1712), pp. 283–4.

[18] M. de la Vauguion, *A Compleat Body of Chirurgical Operations, Containing the Whole Practice of Surgery. With Observations and Remarks on Each Case. Amongst Which Are Inserted, the Several Ways of Delivering Women in Natural and Unnatural Labours. The Whole Illustrated with Copper Plates,*

Such advice suggests that prosthetic use was seen as the natural and desirable endpoint of amputation, at its best, offering a partial restoration to aesthetic and functional normality. This is borne out by hospital records which show prosthetic limbs being produced in large numbers for the use of wounded soldiers and sailors. In his work on Ely House military hospital during the civil war and interregnum, Eric Gruber von Arni finds that

> In January 1653 an order was placed for, 144 crutches, 72 long and 72 short, at a total cost of £5 2s ... The work of William Bradley, the hospital carpenter, who was frequently required to provide wooden legs and the associated attachments for them, is illustrated in the bills that he submitted for his work. For example, on 12 February 1654, a soldier named Fisher was provided with a wooden hand costing 5s. On 15 May 1654 he fitted Thomas Swain with a pair of legs with straps and buckles, adjusted the wooden legs of seven residents and supplied two spare pins for another.[19]

As Arni's research indicates, the vast majority of prosthesis users were equipped with simple peg legs and crutches, which were rudimentary but affordable. They were ubiquitous enough that the wooden-legged ex-soldier or -sailor became a trope which proliferated in early modern drama. In the 1599 *A Larum for London*, for instance, the protagonist 'Stump' describes his wooden leg as his 'passport', showing he has 'known the wars' (6.771–8).[20] Patricia Cahill observes that during this period of intense conflict, 'bodies like that of the play's lame soldier may have been a common sight in London'.[21] Nearly a hundred years later, a fictional piece in the *Observator* periodical showed that dismemberment was still regarded as an occupational hazard for seamen. Two civilians are discussing the merits of a naval career. Explaining his reluctance to go to sea, one asserts:

> I shou'd return Home like an Old Woman cut shorter ... a poor Dismember'd Wretch, a meer hop-Frog; and suppose I should make good the Deficiencies of Nature by Art, and get a couple of Wooden Supporters,

---

Explaining the Several Bandages, Sutures, and Divers Useful Instruments (London: printed for Henry Bonwick, T. Goodwin, M. Wotton, B. Took, and S. Manship, 1699), p. 291.

[19] Eric Gruber von Arni, *Justice to the Maimed Soldier: Nursing, Medical Care and Welfare for Sick and Wounded Soldiers and their Families during the English Civil Wars and Interregnum* (Aldershot: Routledge, 2001), p. 185.

[20] On the institution of 'passports' for ex-servicemen, which allowed the bearers to travel freely through different parishes and receive aid on their journey to their home parish, see Audrey Eccles, *Vagrancy in Law and Practice under the Old Poor Law* (Farnham: Ashgate, 2012).

[21] Patricia A. Cahill, *Unto the Breach: Martial Formations, Historical Trauma, and the Early Modern Stage* (Oxford: Oxford University Press, 2008), p. 190.

and Stump it about like the Devil upon two Sticks, how would the Country Fellows Laugh at me.[22]

His concerns reflect not only the dangers of naval life, but the ignominy of visible disability and the helplessness associated therewith – a factor which, as I shall argue, drove innovation in prosthetics. As Chapter 3 detailed, huge numbers of early modern men served in the military, and the connection between military service and limb loss was well known.[23] This connection could have pragmatic use in marking out the bearer as among the 'deserving poor': Sarah Covington observes how 'Veterans who found themselves vagrant . . . relied upon their wounds as the sole currency with which they could be brought over to the category of worthiness.'[24] The dark side to this 'currency' was that it could be employed fraudulently, as when Shakespeare's Falstaff determines that his 'haulting' gait (brought on by gout, or pox, or both) will easily pass for a war wound, and 'my pension shall seeme the more reasonable'. (*2 Henry IV*, 1.2.245–50). Lindsey Row-Heyveld discusses how itinerant beggars, claiming to have been maimed in the wars, were frequently described in rogue literature as hobbling around on one natural leg and one wooden, their other healthy limb being bent double inside their clothes.[25] As these renderings show, the possession of a wooden leg was partly pragmatic, partly performative. For the genuinely impaired, it allowed movement and garnered sympathy, but it also signalled the (male) user's interpellation into the role of 'maimed soldier', with all the varied connotations that role entailed.[26]

Despite their ubiquity, we know little about how wooden legs or hands were bought and fitted, or how they benefited the user. Instead, the written record tells us much more about the small subset of amputees who were able to afford more sophisticated artificial limbs. These items were, as the Ely House records suggest, far more expensive than their simpler counterparts. Von Arni relates how at Ely hospital, 'George Matheson, who had suffered an above-knee amputation, was supplied with a prosthetic limb described as "a new artificial leg with a leather box, plated all over with iron, complete with swivels and pins" at a cost of

[22] *Observator*, 13 January 1705.
[23] Geoffrey L. Hudson, 'Disabled Veterans and the State in Early Modern England', in *Disabled Veterans in History*, ed. David A. Gerber (Ann Arbor: University of Michigan Press, 2012), pp. 117–44; Arni, *Justice to the Maimed Soldier*.
[24] Sarah Covington, *Wounds, Flesh, and Metaphor in Seventeenth-Century England* (Basingstoke: Palgrave Macmillan 2009), p. 113.
[25] Row-Heyveld, *Dissembling Disability in Early Modern English Drama*, especially pp. 2–5.
[26] Alanna Skuse, 'Missing Parts in *The Shoemaker's Holiday*', *Renaissance Drama* 45:2 (2017): 161–79.

£3 3s 11d.'[27] This single limb cost the same as around one hundred crutches from the same supplier. Nevertheless, articulated prostheses captured the imaginations of medical writers, who described them in fascinated detail. Ambroise Paré had been among the first to design such items in the late sixteenth century, including in his *Workes* drawings of mobile hands, arms, and legs that are extraordinary in their complexity. His design for an artificial hand, for instance, contains a series of tiny cogs and wheels which allow each finger to move individually. A blueprint for an artificial leg, while simpler, includes a pulley which moves the foot from a pointed to a flat position (see Figure 4.1). Paré's prostheses were, he argued, 'not onely profitable for the necessity of the body, but also for the decency and comelinesse thereof', facilitating 'the functions of going, standing and handling'.[28]

When other medical practitioners advised on artificial limbs, they drew on Paré's work, presenting complicated articulate limbs as the ideal even when they recognised that such items might be unattainable. In 1662, for instance, James Cooke's *Mellificium Chirurgiæ* revealed its author's struggle between medical idealism and practicality. The surgeon affirmed 'Artificial [hands] must be framed, as also Legs', but immediately admitted that 'the former are seldom in use'.[29] Backtracking again, he then suggested 'Artificial armes and hands must of necessity be fram'd with many Scrues and Wheeles for to procure some kind of motion when set on work.'[30] Interestingly, Cooke did not appear to have the same high ideals when it came to artificial legs. Though he noted that legs might be made 'in form of a natural Leg' or 'all small downward' (i.e. a peg leg), the only real requirements were that they could be securely tied to the thigh, and that they contained a pillow for the stump to rest on.[31] Just as Cooke had been inspired by Paré, he in turn influenced future writers. In 1698, William Salmon's *Ars Chirurgica* borrowed some phrasing – including that of being 'all small downward' – directly from Cooke's work, with other snippets culled from Paré himself. He, however, set aside financial concerns, and described with wonderment the full scope of prosthetic limbs:

[27] Arni, *Justice to the Maimed Soldier*, p. 185.
[28] Ambroise Paré, *The Workes of That Famous Chirurgion Ambrose Parey Translated out of Latine and Compared with the French. by Th: Johnson* (London: Th. Cotes and R. Young, 1634), p. 880.
[29] James Cooke, *Mellificium Chirurgiæ, or the Marrow of Many Good Authors Enlarged: Wherein Is Briefly, Fully, and Faithfully Handled the Art of Chirurgery in Its Four Parts, with All the Several Diseases unto Them Belonging: Their Definitions, Causes, Signes, Prognosticks, and Cures, Both General and Particular* (London: printed by T.R. for John Sherley, 1662), pp. 378–9.
[30] Ibid.   [31] Ibid.

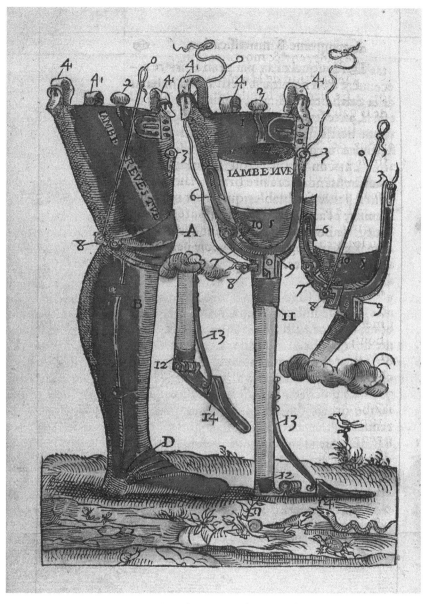

Figure 4.1   A. Paré, 'La maniere de traicter les plaies'.
Credit: Wellcome Collection. CC BY

it is necessity which investigates the means whereby we may help and imitate nature, and supply the defects of members, which are perished and lost; which in the case of arms or legs may well be done with silver, latten [copper alloy, e.g. brass], steel, copper, wood, or some other fit matter.

II. And some have been made by ingenious smiths, or other artificers, with which the party which wore them, have performed the proper functions of going, standing, and handling; and with their artificial legs, feet, arms and hands, have done other necessary flexions and extensions, beyond what can possibly be imagined, by any but such as have seen them ...

IV. Arms, hands and fingers must be made of iron, or latten, with many wheels and screws, to make the required motion, that they may be the more useful when applied to the intention; and they are to be conveniently fixed to the shoulder, elbow or wrist, and be tied on with strings.

V. Legs, feet and toes are more frequently made use of, especially the first; some being made in the forms of natural legs, others all small downwards, with a seat, wherein are put small pillows or bolsters for the knee to rest on; which also are to be fastned with strings to the thigh.[32]

The 'ideal' prostheses described by Paré, Salmon, and others all have in common that they are articulated, complex, and moveable. They allow the user to perform 'motion' and 'intention', that is, they allow them to perform able-bodiedness. In so doing, these descriptions reflect the abiding tendency of surgical texts to frame recovery from amputation in terms of a return to movement. In Paré's *Apologie*, for instance, he describes how one patient 'was happily cured without the application of hot irons, and walketh lustily on a woodden legge'.[33] Another amputee was 'at this present cured and in health, walking with a woodden Leg'.[34] In Woodall's idealistic description of an artificial leg, he expanded this idea, to paint the amputee as supremely capable:

[It is] a great honour and comfort to the man, when, if without a foot, by the helpe of Art, namely, of an hollow Case or the like, with an artificial foot adjoyned, a man may decently and comely walke, and ride, goe over a style, yea, and runne, and sit streight, and behave himselfe man-like in Bed, and at Boord, and doe good service for the defence of his countrey, or of himselfe: In regard whereof, I would esteeme that Artist a very unworthy, unwise, and wilfull person, who by any good

---

[32] William Salmon, *Ars Chirurgica* (London, 1698), p. 125.
[33] Ambroise Paré, *The Apologie and Treatise of Ambroise Paré, Containing the Voyages Made into Divers Places, with Many of His Writings upon Surgery*, ed. Geoffrey Keynes (London: Falcon Educational Books, 1951), p. 10.
[34] Ibid., p. 11.

meanes could keepe a profitable part of any member untaken off, and would presume to take it away.[35]

In Woodall's depiction, an artificial leg enables a level of bodily functionality which is unavailable to even many able-bodied people, involving physical skill (at riding and fighting) as well as deportment (sitting up straight). It is also markedly gendered: this restored man can behave himself 'man-like' in diverse situations including the bedroom.[36]

Woodall's description does not invoke any particular disabled person, and he does not seem to have a specific prosthesis in mind. Indeed, he conspicuously ignores the problems of fit and balance which must have attended many artificial limbs. His vision, and that of Paré and Salmon, is of a classically ideal body, complete and proportionate. This body is, as Bakhtin describes, diametrically opposite to the unbounded and changeable disabled body.[37] Where the Bakhtinian classical body is primarily an aesthetic construct, however, the 'ideal' prostheticised body is a body in motion, capable of economic and social activity. Woodall, for example, made clear the continuity between 'polite' and useful bodies when he recalled his treatment of a dying patient at St Bartholomew's hospital. After amputation of the leg, he wrote,

> my poore patient grew more and more lusty and cheerefull; and to conclude, in the space of 10 weekes, he was perfectly healed, and being then sound and lusty, gave thanks to the Governour of the Hospitall, in full payment of his cure, and so departed from the Hospitall upon a legge of wood, he then being faire and fat, and very formall.[38]

Woodall's patient had not only escaped death; he was restored to the polite world, capable of being 'lusty' and 'formall'. Notably, this patient was also solvent, able to pay his fee in full. He cuts a figure very different from the destitute 'cripples' which populate many early modern discussions of disability.

The social and economic importance of maintaining one's mobility was further underlined in a 1710 advertisement for John Sewers, an artificial limb-maker from London. After refuting some malicious

---

[35] Woodall, 'A Treatise of Gangraena', p. 396.
[36] On limb loss and male sexuality, see Skuse, 'Missing Parts in *The Shoemaker's Holiday*'.
[37] Mikhail Bakhtin, *Rabelais and His World*, trans. Helene Iswolsky (Bloomington: Indiana University Press, 1984). See especially 'The Grotesque Image of the Body and Its Sources', pp. 303–67.
[38] Woodall, 'A Treatise of Gangraena', pp. 389–90.

reports that he is dead, Sewers' advertisement assures readers that he still makes false legs on which

> the Party may walk with the greatest Ease and Safety, and take as firm and large Steps as ever. They are so *Exact* as hardly to be discern'd, and so *Light* as in the whole proportion not to weigh more than Three Pound and half. Women may walk in Pattens [protective overshoes] with them.[39]

Moreover, Sewers promised that he could provide prostheses even for people with short stumps, or unhealed stumps, on which they might walk 'safe and easy'. Repeatedly, Sewers stressed his ability to restore a normal gait, concluding that 'He undertakes to make the patient walk with such a Leg in Three or Four Hours time, without a Crutch.'[40]

Sewers' conviction that one could learn to use an artificial leg in the course of an afternoon is evidently a marketing strategy.[41] Nonetheless, it highlights the movement from conspicuous dys-appearance to unremarkable dis-appearance implicit in idealised visions of prostheses. What is promised here is not merely a transition from one kind of bodily difference to another, less debilitating kind. Rather, the use of one's false limb becomes so easy that it recedes from the notice of both user and onlookers – especially given that one's legs would always be clothed when in public. Leder views such 'incorporation' of prostheses, or of other broadly assistive technologies such as canes and telephones, as a remapping of the boundaries of the body, such that the item one relies upon becomes a part of one's phenomenological experience. By expanding one's possibilities for action – the possibility of walking further, or of communicating over distances – the use of tools can 'redesign one's extended body until the extremities expressly mesh with the world'.[42] To become fully enmeshed or 'incorporated', however, the prosthetic should interact seamlessly with the natural body. Vivian Sobchack, herself a prosthesis user, describes how she experiences her artificial leg in this way: 'not "into" or "on" but "as" the subject, the prosthetic becomes an object only when a mechanical or social problem pushes it obtrusively into the foreground of

---

[39] John Sewers, 'Advertisement' (printed by John Cluer in Twelve-Bell-Court in Bow Church-Yard, Cheapside, 1710), EPH 528:3, Wellcome Library.
[40] Ibid.
[41] As a twenty-first-century comparison, the Amputee Coalition (USA) estimates that learning to use a modern prosthetic leg may take anything from several weeks to six months or more ('Prosthetic FAQs for the New Amputee', *Amputee Coalition* (blog), accessed 11 May 2018, www.amputee-coalition.org/resources/prosthetic-faqs-for-the-new-amputee/.)
[42] Leder, *The Absent Body*, p. 34.

the user's consciousness'.[43] In the early modern context it is important to remember that, as I shall discuss, discourses about prostheses also include discussion of their engineered properties, their abiding difference as well as their assimilation. Nevertheless, it is evident that consumers and medical writers prized limbs which *worked*.

This emphasis seems natural – after all, we might think it self-evident that the greatest good of a prosthesis would be viewed as being the restoration of the user to motion and function. However, the fact that this was not necessarily the case is demonstrated by the rhetoric attached to other kinds of prosthetic. As Chapter 3 explored, facial prostheses were explicitly designed to recreate as closely as possible a natural appearance. They might also confer functional advantages, but these tended to be secondary. Likewise, in their 'Technologies of the Body', David Turner and Alun Withey describe how truss manufacture and promotion advanced in the eighteenth century such that a truss became not only a medical object but a consumer good. Trusses were, they argue, a means for 'passing' as able-bodied and attaining the straightness associated with 'polite', aristocratic bodies. As such,

> a striking characteristic of advertisements was their use of the language of polite commerce, selling items such as prosthetics not merely as a means of alleviating suffering, but also as objects of taste and technological innova-tion that in turn defined the consumer in terms that went beyond the medicalized 'patient' . . . Products were sold as offering an aspirational ideal, of a body well trained and capable of pleasing (or at least not frightening) others, its defects smoothed out.[44]

As Turner and Withey acknowledge, the market for prosthetic limbs also expanded during this period, with an eventual focus on undetectability that mirrored that surrounding trusses. However, it appears that this shift took place later in the eighteenth century, and that for the previous 150 years, surgeons' ideas about limb replacement had remained fairly stable. By contrast, trusses and other orthopaedic devices had from the seven-teenth century been associated with bodily aesthetics for both sexes.

Prosthetic limbs, therefore, were imaginatively distinct in the privileging of movement over all other concerns, including weight, comfort, and

---

[43] Vivian Sobchack, 'A Leg to Stand On: Prosthetics, Metaphor, and Materiality', in *The Prosthetic Impulse: From a Posthuman Present to a Biocultural Future*, ed. Marquard Smith and Joanne Morra (Cambridge: MIT Press, 2006), p. 22.

[44] David Turner and Alun Withey, 'Technologies of the Body: Polite Consumption and the Correction of Deformity in Eighteenth-Century England', *History* 99: 338 (2014): 777, https://doi.org/10.1111/1468-229X.12087.

appearance. Indeed, early modern descriptions of artificial limbs rarely mention their appearance, though some would have been rendered more lifelike by being covered in leather or painted. Rather – and in addition to being markedly masculine – the vision of bodily functionality invoked by prosthesis narratives was distinctly mechanistic in emphasis. It is instructive that in the advertisement above, Sewers the prosthesis-maker declares that he will *make* the patient walk rather than *allow* them to do so. His project is thus framed as one which creates as well as restores the body. Other writers were more direct about the mechanical nature of their work. Salmon, for instance, imagined the amputee as potentially augmented by the work of 'artificers', with the prosthetic limb showing a range of movement which exceeded that of a natural limb.[45] Cooke likewise spoke of 'Scrues and Wheeles', while Paré's blueprints for articulated hands and feet have as much in common with architectural plans as with medical illustrations.[46] This commonality partly bears out Jonathan Sawday's contention that, following Descartes, mechanistic conceptions of the body tended to focus on its utility above all else; the 'modern' body, he argues, was 'a body which worked rather than existed'.[47] However, it is equally evident that Cartesian dualist models were merely part of the milieu which promoted functionality as the highest value of the body. As we have seen in Chapter 3, the experimental splicing and dicing of bodies conducted by members of the Royal Society in the 1740s contributed to a vision of the body in which parts could be removed and replaced. Equally important (and themselves influenced by philosophical concerns) were the material circumstances in which prostheses were produced. As Reed Benhamou identifies, the most sophisticated articulated prostheses were marvels of engineering, requiring specialist manufacture:

> It is no coincidence that these [materials used in prosthesis] are the same materials used in 18th-century automatons, for several of the clockmakers, locksmiths, and *mécaniciens* who used the lightweight materials and miniaturization techniques required by these devices also produced artificial limbs. Indeed, some 18th-century prostheses may be called spin-offs of this technology.[48]

---

[45] Salmon, *Ars Chirurgica*, p. 125.   [46] Cooke, *Mellificium Chirurgiæ*, pp. 378–9; Paré, *The Workes*.
[47] Jonathan Sawday, *The Body Emblazoned: Dissection and the Human Body in Renaissance Culture* (Abingdon: Routledge, 2013), p. 32.
[48] Reed Benhamou, 'The Artifical Limb in Preindustrial France', *Technology and Culture* 35:4 (1994): 844.

To be associated with automata meant that the prostheticised body became associated with the man-made and precise – particularly in the later seventeenth century, when Wendy Beth Hyman argues that 'mechanistic and even deterministic theories of natural phenomena ... put the body, simply, back in its inanimate place'.[49] Certain functions of complex prostheses also recalled the tricks of which automata were capable. Benhamou describes how in 1732, the French clockmaker Kreigseissen was commissioned to make a limb for an amputee who had lost his arm below the elbow:

> According to the meticulous description, the device, made from sheets of copper, bent at the wrist and at the first and second knuckle joints. The thumb moved only in a lateral direction (a palmar pinch). The mechanism consisted of pulleys turned by catgut cords that were activated by bending the elbow, one moving the palm and thumb, the other moving the fingers. Leaf springs mounted on the index finger permitted this digit to move at all joints. Bending the elbow brought the hand toward the body, causing the fingers to flex and the thumb to oppose the fingers. Straightening the elbow released the tension on the cords, and returned the hand to its original position.[50]

It is unclear if such feats crossed the Channel. Nonetheless, even if marvels such as those Benhamou describes were not produced in Britain, they must have appeared as the gold standard of bodily restoration, just as Parisian surgery was esteemed among the best in the world. The effect of these rare creations, coupled with the ideal prostheses imagined in contemporary medical texts, was to reify a particular vision of how a 'whole' body ought to look and move. That is, they ideally allowed the user to perform able-bodiedness – to avoid looking disabled, and thus avoid the associations of economic and social exclusion which often accompanied disability. It is striking, for instance, that one specially commissioned arm from the early eighteenth century reportedly allowed the wearer to 'raise his hand to his hat, remove it, and put it back'.[51] This action can hardly have been the most pragmatic use of prosthetic technology, but it allowed the bearer to 'pass' as bodily normative. It also demonstrates how prostheses might become conducive to viewing the body as either/both object and/or subject. As a curious and wondrous device, the hat-raising arm made its user something like an automaton, a spectacular but empty vessel.

[49] Wendy Beth Hyman, 'Introduction', in *The Automaton in English Renaissance Literature*, ed. Wendy Beth Hyman (Farnham: Ashgate, 2011), p. 12.
[50] Benhamou, 'The Artifical Limb in Preindustrial France', 840.   [51] Ibid., 838.

On the other hand, the fact of being able to tip one's hat allowed the user to perform their normal social role, assuring onlookers that the same subject remained 'inside' their altered body.

Frustratingly, there is virtually no record of how early modern amputees felt about their own prostheses. The fact that complicated metal limbs were so rare may suggest that practical as well as financial considerations drove most amputees towards simpler devices. Wooden arms and legs did not have the same capabilities, but they were lighter, more comfortable, and probably as useful for many tasks. Texts *about* these people, however, show that onlookers believed that the strongest desire of the amputee was (or ought to be) to perform able-ness – to look like one's bodily alteration did not affect one's capability to act in socially prescribed ways. Unlike with naturalistic prostheses, one's dys-appearance might not vanish through the use of these items, but it could dis-appear – that is, it could cease to be constitutive of one's place in the world.

Titus Andronicus and the Point of the Staff

The technologically advanced world of early modern artificial limbs may appear at first glance to have little to do with Lavinia's use of a simple staff to scrawl in the dirt. However, the extreme experience of this amputee character addresses issues of bodily normativity and anomaly in ways difficult to access in medical and commercial texts, emphasising the vexed relationship between sexuality, embodiment, and sociability. It may thus help to fill in some of the manifold gaps in our understanding of what limb loss *felt* like, both for the amputee and for those around them. Moreover, the driving force behind prosthetic innovation in the early modern period – that is, war – is also the context underlying Lavinia's rape and mutilation. While Lavinia's staff is the most rudimentary from of prosthesis, it, like the articulate arms and legs described above, shows how prosthetics revealed what was felt to be important about human agency in a given historical moment. Lavinia's rape and dismemberment is a horrific reminder of the prevalence of sexual violence in armed conflict. Her identity as *more* than a rape victim inheres in the ability to express herself, and her use of the staff becomes a symbolic and pragmatic reclamation of that capacity.

We have seen that the early modern period was one in which armed conflict affected a substantial portion of the male population. Consequently, women were also exposed to the hardships and cruelties associated with war. Barbara Donagan notes how in the sixteenth and seventeenth centuries, legislation surrounding conduct in wartime became

increasingly secular in tone, and increasingly detailed.[52] These laws officially forbade 'ravishing of women' by soldiers, on pain of death. However,
contemporary literature – including that by Shakespeare – demonstrates
that rape was frequently understood as 'a predictable side-effect of armed
conflict'.[53] Written in 1599, *Henry V* dwells repeatedly on the possibility
of rape being committed by besieging soldiers:

> *King Harry*: The gates of mercy shall be all shut up,
> And the fleshed soldier, rough and hard of heart,
> In liberty of bloody hand shall range
> With conscience wide as hell, mowing like grass
> Your fresh fair virgins and your flow'ring infants.
> . . .
>
> What is't to me, when you yourselves are cause,
> If your pure maidens fall into the hand
> Of hot and forcing violation?
> What rein can hold licentious wickedness
> When down the hill he holds his fierce career?
>
> (3.3.93–106)

As Jordi Coral observes of this passage, rape is here imagined exclusively in
terms of the violation of virgins, as in *Titus Andronicus*. As in that play, it is
also presented as potentially titillating. Moreover, Henry implicates potential rape victims in their own assault by protesting that he cannot control
invading soldiers in the heat of battle. The women and girls under attack
have apparently brought their misfortune on themselves by happening to
live in a town which elects not to surrender to Henry's siege. This notion
that rape occurred during the frenzy of victory was widespread, becoming
particularly strong in accounts of the Hundred Years War and Thirty Years
War.[54] In *Titus*, however, Lavinia's rape and dismemberment is framed
differently: not as the spoils of war, but as a covert act of revenge by the
defeated party, and a tactical means of striking at a more powerful captor.
Violent rapes carried out by victorious soldiers were not sanctioned, but
they were understood as a corollary of the blood-lust and hatred for the
enemy necessary to conduct a successful campaign. By contrast, the
extremes of violence Chiron and Demetrius inflict on Lavinia are inversely

---

[52] Barbara Donagan, 'Law, War and Women in Seventeenth-Century England', in *Sexual Violence in Conflict Zones: From the Ancient World to the Era of Human Rights*, ed. Elizabeth D. Heineman (Philadelphia: University of Pennsylvania Press, 2011), p. 189.

[53] Jordi Coral, '"Maiden Walls That War Hath Never Entered": Rape and Post-Chivalric Military Culture in Shakespeare's *Henry V*, *College Literature* 44:3 (2017): 410.

[54] Donagan, 'Law, War and Women in Seventeenth-Century England', pp. 190–1.

proportional to their martial power. It is thus necessary, in symbolic terms, that Chiron and Demetrius both rape and mutilate Lavinia. Where rape is imagined as dishonouring the family name, the attackers' decision to disable Lavinia is not only a pragmatic means of avoiding detection, but a symbolic retribution for the loss they have suffered at the hands and voice of her father.

Ironically, this treatment of Lavinia as a symbol or proxy repeats in horrific terms the objectification which Lavinia experiences from members of her family, both before and especially after her rape. Scholarship on *Titus* has frequently pointed out the fact that Lavinia begins as well as ends the play in a state of voicelessness – first, as a facet of her ideally submissive and compliant role, and later by dint of physical impairment. Lavinia begins the play as an object with exchange value, to be swapped between potential husbands as it becomes politically expedient (1.1). When she reappears ravished, tongueless, and handless, Lavinia's body is an object that provokes speech from others, prompting Marcus to make the play's longest speech and one of its most eloquent (2.4.11–57). Lavinia's body melds with the world of things as it is variously taken to evoke Philomel and Titan, a tree, a fountain, a Thracian poet. At the same time as it signifies so abundantly for onlookers, however, this body is unable to make aural or written signs, and therefore to bespeak Lavinia's own, subjective, presence.

After her mutilation, then, Lavinia's material and objective substance seems to exist apart from her lived body as an interactive and perceptive subject. Indeed, Marcus concludes as much when he tells Titus that 'this was thy daughter' (3.1.61). Lavinia, to outside eyes, seems no longer to 'live her body', no longer to be present 'inside' her mutilated flesh. Since she cannot be anywhere *but* her body, she is effectively non-existent. Marcus' conclusion, of course, is one which relies on his own perception of 'Lavinia-ness' as an identity which exists primarily in terms of relational object value. The things that make Lavinia, Lavinia, in Marcus' eyes, are her beauty and chastity, passive aspects of her selfhood which are identity-forming inasmuch as they mediate her relationship to other people. As Sallie Anglin argues, 'She can no longer play the part of maid or wife and retains no social or economic power as a widow because her mutilation makes her undesirable . . . She is a dead girl walking – a visible reminder of a life that no longer exists.'[55] Having lost the identity that made her 'Rome's rich ornament' and become something animal,

---

[55] Sallie J. Anglin, 'Generative Space: Embodiment and Identity at the Margins on the Early Modern Stage', Ph.D. (University of Mississippi, 2013), p. 133.

Lavinia is both still Lavinia and no longer Lavinia. For the characters, her body cannot represent the maid, the wife, the body of Rome, or the woman. Lavinia is a kind of memento mori, but in this case she is a visual reminder and harbinger of her own death, a death that is still in progress.[56]

Marcus' view is, of course, partial: there is more involved in 'living a body' than he realises, and it is left to Titus to remind the assembled mourners that Lavinia remains his daughter. Nonetheless, Lavinia's spectacularly altered body speaks of its trauma so loudly that it drowns out all alternative narratives, including the narrative thread which links ornament-of-Rome Lavinia to victim-Lavinia to potential-future-Lavinia. This present state is so visually and emotionally arresting that it seems to sever ties to past identity and truncate the possibility of a future one. Marcus, Titus, and Lucius all seek to speak for Lavinia, interpreting her tears and claiming to 'understand her signs' (3.1.143). She is effectively ventriloquised by men who wish to speak through and about her body. In their speeches, however, they rehearse her muteness, such that their interventions only emphasise her erasure as a subject and her status as a readable object:

> Titus: . . . What shall I do
> Now I behold thy lively body so?
> Thou hast no hands to wipe away thy tears,
> Nor tongue to tell me who hath martyred thee . . .
> Look Marcus, ah, son Lucius, look on her!
>
> (3.1.105–10)

The symbolic meanings ascribed to Lavinia in this discourse recollect that which 'naturally' belongs to the play's racial Other, Aaron the Moor. As Lavinia's bodily difference motivates the slew of killings which follow, Aaron's blackness is understood as the driving force behind his Machiavellianism, imbuing him with the desire to do 'a thousand dreadful things' (5.1.141). His qualitative difference from other characters is identified by Jennifer Feathers as recollecting the concern with personal boundaries and interpersonal 'contagion' which permeates *Titus* as a whole.[57] Where blackness is singular in its alliance with devilishness, however, there remains potential for Lavinia's body to signify in different ways. To escape her status as a spectacle of woe requires Lavinia to reclaim

---

[56] Ibid., p. 138.

[57] Jennifer Feather, 'Contagious Pity: Cultural Difference and the Language of Contagion in *Titus Andronicus*', in *Contagion and the Shakespearean Stage*, ed. Darryl Chalk and Mary Floyd-Wilson, Palgrave Studies in Literature, Science and Medicine (Basingstoke: Palgrave Macmillan, 2019), pp. 169–87, especially 176–82, https://doi.org/10.1007/978-3-030-14428-9.

her body as not only a sign in itself, but a vehicle for *making* meaning, something which perceptibly looks upon the world as well as being looked at. This ability to make meaning is what is offered by Lavinia's use of the staff as prosthetic, and it is no accident that this comes in the form of reading and writing. As Mary Laughlin Fawcett contends, 'Words are embodied and disembodied throughout this work. One person becomes the text for another's explication, a challenge for interpretation.'[58] In her detailed work on the significance of hands on the early modern stage, Farah Karim-Cooper traces the connection between Lavinia's 'scrawl', which requires the already-written text of the *Metamorphosis* for its explication, and the nature of hand-writing in early modern culture.[59] One's 'hand', she argues, conveys one's character in all senses of that word, and the proliferation of pointing hands (manicules) in early modern texts serves as a visual reminder of the link between writing and thinking, body and text.[60] The agential significance of hands has also been emphasised by Katherine Rowe, who argues that the hand represents the juncture between mechanistic and analogical understandings of human intention and action. Early modern anatomies, she observes, privileged the hand as the pre-eminent example of divine design; 'the hand becomes the prominent vehicle for integrating sacred mystery with corporeal mechanism'.[61] Severing Lavinia's hands is therefore a symbolic as well as pragmatic act of disempowerment – replacing them, however crudely, is equally significant.

How does this solve the problem of the staff? In light of the above, I argue that including the staff in Act 4 Scene 1 reiterates both possibilities of response to Lavinia's body: as a sign to be read, and as a sign-maker. That is, the scene highlights Lavinia's status as both object and subject. Lavinia's mutilated body has been the text which others attempt to read. With the acquisition of the book and stick, however, she becomes able to make signs, and thus to demarcate herself as a subject with an interior life. Karim-Cooper describes how 'The act of writing produces [Lavinia's] "hand". Here she is re-membered properly through her script, her "character".'[62] Immediately after she writes on the sand, Lavinia is invited by

[58] Mary Laughlin Fawcett, 'Arms/Words/Tears: Language and the Body in Titus Andronicus', *ELH* 50:2 (1983): 263.
[59] Farah Karim-Cooper, *The Hand on the Shakespearean Stage: Gesture, Touch and the Spectacle of Dismemberment* (London: Bloomsbury, 2016), pp. 226–32.
[60] Ibid., p. 35.
[61] Katherine Rowe, 'God's Handy Worke', in *The Body in Parts: Fantasies of Corporeality in Early Modern Europe*, ed. David A. Hillman and Carla Mazzio (New York: Routledge, 1997), p. 287.
[62] Karim-Cooper, *The Hand on the Shakespearean Stage*, p. 233.

Marcus to kneel alongside him with young Lucius and her father to swear revenge. Though she has no voice to swear, it is now recognised that she is still 'inside' her mute body, and is capable of making a vow if not of uttering it. Titus' simple command at the end of the scene – 'Lavinia, come' – marks the end of the characters' dwelling on her alteration and the beginning of Lavinia's inclusion in the play's revenge plot. Admittedly, Titus' plan does not reach very far ahead, but it has intention and impetus, and sharing in it affords Lavinia some, albeit imperfect, agency.

Lavinia's staff redraws the limits of her phenomenological encounters with the world. In a limited way, therefore, the staff, the book, and Lavinia's body are 'incorporated', just as we have seen that more sophisticated artificial limbs could be incorporated with the natural bodies of their users. In criticism of *Titus*, much has been made of the potential melding of Lavinia's natural body with these man-made objects. Likening these items to 'phantom limbs', Shawn Huffman writes

> The *Metamorphosis* is her phantom limb … giving immaterial and fictional existence to the hands and to the tongue that Lavinia no longer has. As the scene [4.1] unfolds, she writes the names of her attackers on the sand with Marcus' wooden staff. When her entourage finally makes sense of the signs being produced through her phantom limbs, these limbs take on a material presence, yet always as an Ovidian textual ghost, the wooden staff literally a limb trimmed from the transformed Daphne, a phantom tongue through which Lavinia speaks the names of her rapists.[63]

Huffman is right to see how the *Metamorphosis* extends Lavinia's agential scope, and may thus be said to be imbued with her subjectivity despite its object status. The historical specificity of the phantom limb metaphor which he uses is discussed at length in Chapter 6 of this book. Nonetheless, I argue that it is equally important to consider the status of those prosthetic items as non-human and distinct from Lavinia's body. Lavinia uses the stick awkwardly; her powers of expression, and her utterance ('*Stuprum* – Chiron – Demetrius'), remain stunted. Though the interweaving of material goods and corporeal abilities is, as I have shown, crucial to narratives of prosthesis, Lavinia's stick is also significant because it is *not* her body. This means that when Lavinia makes meaning via those items – and is then able to discard them – she shifts the burden of object-hood on to these mute materials. Her body is thus able to be reinstated as a 'lived body', with the particular combination of subject- and

[63] Shawn Huffman, 'Amputation, Phantom Limbs, and Spectral Agency in Shakespeare's *Titus Andronicus* and Normand Chaurette's *Les Reines*', *Modern Drama* 47:1 (2004): 71.

object-hood that that entails. Her status as a thinking subject with an interior life can come to the fore only when she is able to direct the way in which her body 'speaks'.

This moment of reclaiming the voice is a powerful one. It is not, however, a straightforward rehabilitation. As we have seen, Lavinia's staff is a prosthetic, which enables some reclamation of subjecthood. Nonetheless, it is also a prop, which comes with its own significatory history, and the potential to make meaning in ways unintended by its user. Karim-Cooper and Caroline Lamb have both observed that Lavinia's attaining agency via material technologies has something in common with early modern narratives which show disabled people accomplishing 'normal' tasks by displaying incredible dexterity or tenacity. They read this connection as signalling the possibility of Lavinia's rehabilitation, even her emancipation. Karim-Cooper states: 'If the body is able to transcend manual dismemberment, an amputee might still be an active force expressing identity and intention,' and she indicates Paré's prosthesis writings as evidence of early modern people coping with limb loss.[64] Lamb similarly describes *Titus* as featuring 'a notable attentiveness to the personal and social negotiations disability engenders, especially in terms of how Titus and Lavinia face the potential of losing normative modes of corporeal expression (speech, gesture, writing)'.[65] The ability to physically adapt shown by Titus and Lavinia is, she argues, allied with 'a subject's ability to cultivate personal ability and agency'.[66]

However, if there is emancipatory potential here (and there is, albeit fleeting), there is also the potential for Lavinia's writing prowess to be read as a freak show, for the gaze to rest on the spectacle of a disabled body 'performing' rather than attending to the subjectivity of that body. This tendency is strongly evident in early modern renderings of the 'supercrip' trope of the very sort that Karim-Cooper cites. The 'supercrip' described in Paré's *Workes* displays amazing facility without his hands, as the surgeon relates:

> A few yeeres agone there was a man of forty yeeres old to be seene at *Paris*, who although he wanted his armes, notwithstanding did indifferently perform all those things which are usually done with the hands, for with the top of his shoulder, head and necke, hee would strike an Axe or Hatchet

---

[64] Karim-Cooper, *The Hand on the Shakespearean Stage*, pp. 229, 230–1.
[65] Caroline Lamb, 'Physical Trauma and (Adapt)Ability in *Titus Andronicus*', *Critical Survey* 22:1 (2010): 48.
[66] Ibid., 47.

with as sure and strong a blow into a poast, as any other man could doe with his hand; and hee would lash a coach-mans whip, that he would make it give a great crack ... but he ate, drunke, plaid at cardes, and such like, with his feet.[67]

This narrative, as Karim-Cooper argues, 'attests to the sense that the body, in spite of its disability or disfigurement, could somehow adapt itself to its new condition'.[68] However, there is also a sense that the tasks undertaken here – cracking a whip and wielding a hatchet – are performed for the gratification of the beholders rather than as a facet of normal life. Moreover, Paré concludes the tale with a twist: 'at last he was taken for a thiefe and murderer, was hanged and fastened to a wheele'.[69] Frequently in narratives about such 'supercrips', adaptability was matched by deviance, so that onlookers might feel themselves justified in staring at the adaptive body for signs of criminality or fakery. People with disabilities were often characterised as morally perverse, such that those who were capable of remarkable physical feats might also be capable of extraordinary crimes. This was, for example, the case when the disabled vagrant John Arthur was convicted in 1614 of having strangled his (also disabled) lover, despite being both 'lame and limblesse'.[70] The agency this man showed in attracting a lover and leading an itinerant lifestyle was understood as of a piece with the agency required to commit murder: 'The Cripple ... tooke the womans owne girdle, and putting the same slyly about her necke, where though nature had denied him strength and limbes, yet by the help of the divell ... he made meanes in her sleep to strangle her.'[71] 'Super-able' altered bodies were by no means regarded as unequivocally positive.

The visibly prostheticised person was thus always already an object of visual interest, an artefact signalling adaptability, ingenuity, and physical and economic limitation. However, Lavinia's prop-prosthetic has yet

---

[67] Paré, *The Workes*, p. 976.   [68] Karim-Cooper, *The Hand on the Shakespearean Stage*, p. 229.

[69] Paré, *The Workes*, p. 976.

[70] Anon., *Deeds against Nature, and Monsters by Kinde Tryed at the Goale Deliuerie of Newgate, at the Sessions in the Old Bayly, the 18. and 19. of Iuly Last, 1614. the One of a London Cripple Named Iohn Arthur, That to Hide His Shame and Lust, Strangled His Betrothed Wife. The Other of a Lasciuious Young Damsell Named Martha Scambler, Which Made Away the Fru[i]t of Her Own Womb, That the World Might Not See the Seed of Her Owne Shame: Which Two Persons with Diuers Others Vvere Executed at Tyburne the 21. o[f] Iuly Folowing. With Two Sorrowfull Ditties of These Two Aforesaid Persons, Made by Themselues in Newgate, the Night before Their Execution* (London: printed [by G. Eld] for Edward Wright, 1614), f. A2r

[71] Ibid., f. A3r

another significatory element which exceeds the control of its user. That
is, the temptation to gaze at Lavinia's supplemented body as an extraordinary object is exacerbated by the particular phallic potential of the stick
in her mouth. If the stick in this instance is a pen, it is also, as numerous
scholars have noted, a pen-is, and its use is implicated in the obsessive
rehashing of Lavinia's trauma that runs throughout the play. As King
describes,

> Lavinia's inability to bear witness becomes a pornographic fetish through
> the repeated invocation of her traumatized mouth. Even when Lavinia is
> granted limited agency ... the text demands an explicit and vulgar re-
> enactment of the offstage crime. In Lavinia's attempt to communicate, she
> takes the phallic staff into her mouth, mimicking not only an act of fellatio
> but gesturing towards the original trauma of rape with her wounded
> mouth/vagina.[72]

We may read this spectacle as a rehashing of the sexual objectification
which has dogged Lavinia since the play's beginning and culminated in
her rape and mutilation. This time, moreover, the audience is directly
implicated in Lavinia's ordeal; having seen only the spectacular effects of
the original rape, a symbolic version of that violation now mixes pity and
revulsion with fascination, even arousal. Imagining the staff as having an
'agenda' of its own, making meaning independently of the user, raises
further problems. To view objects as having an interactional 'life' of their
own, as proponents of object-oriented ontology advocate, is necessarily to
remove the distinction between 'subject' and 'object', such that subject–
object relations are replaced by object–object relations.[73] To place Lavinia
and her staff on the same plane, however, feels like reducing this
sympathetic character to an instrument, in the same way that Chiron
and Demetrius, Marcus, and even Titus have already attempted. The
audience who see Lavinia's staff acting with and upon her body are thus
complicit in her object-ification. If the body and the staff are the same
sort of *thing*, there is no reason why one may be used and abused and not
the other. Lavinia's prop-prosthesis may enable her to turn from a passive

---

[72] Emily King, 'The Female Muselmann: Desire, Violence and Spectatorship in *Titus Andronicus*', in
Titus out of Joint: Reading the Fragmented Titus Andronicus, ed. Liberty Stanavage and Paxton
Hehmeyer (Cambridge: Cambridge Scholars Publishing, 2012), p. 135; See also Kim Solga,
Violence against Women in Early Modern Performance: Invisible Acts (Basingstoke: Palgrave
Macmillan, 2009), p. 49.

[73] Andrew Cole, 'The Call of Things: a Critique of Object-Oriented Ontologies', *Minnesota Review*
no. 80 (2013): 106–18.

sign into an active sign-maker, from mute object to expressive subject. Inevitably, however, the meanings attached to such an item exceed the control of the character-user and even of the author. Lavinia's relationship to the 'thing' she exploits may thus turn out to be one of mutual manipulation.

Conclusion

In real life and on stage, people with altered bodies – including amputees – faced the problem of bodily dys-appearance. By looking and working differently, their bodies invited scrutiny as remarkable objects. The lived body was, as we have seen, always both object and subject. However, physical anomaly could obscure the 'subject' part of that equation, rendering the body alien to oneself, and merely a mute object in the eyes of others. Ideally, prostheses could turn this dys-appearance to disappearance, allowing the user to interact with the world as a feeling, thinking person, rather than being viewed principally as a curious, exotic, or pathetic *thing*. This was not necessarily a dis-appearance effected by covering up the anomalous part. We have seen how complex artificial limbs did not so much disguise disability as obviate it by promising a return to bodily functionality. Likewise, Lavinia's prosthetic staff does not hide her mutilation but only reminds her family that someone remains 'inside' that injured body. In both cases, prostheses showed what was deemed important about being human.

The irony of prosthesis use, however, was that these items could themselves attract the objectifying gaze. The engineering which made some early modern artificial limbs able to move and grasp objects also made them objects of wonder, to be verbally and visually anatomised in medical literature. Lavinia's unsophisticated writing aid attracts the gaze in a different way, as a freakish or sexual spectacle. Prosthetic limbs therefore amplify issues of subjectivity and objectivity which we have seen arise throughout this book. On one hand, depictions of prosthesis use seem to suggest that there is a person 'inside' the body, for whom a prosthesis – and the body in general – is an expressive tool. On the other, the matter of the body is viewed as integral to identity, such that the object-hood of the prosthesis, which includes its history and associations, only renders the user more open to objectification themselves. Indeed, it is only the observations made by able-bodied people about prostheses and their users which survive for modern analysis. The majority of people who used unremarkable wooden limbs have no voice in the historical record. Attempts by able-bodied authors to imagine how such voices might sound offer another perspective on attitudes towards the non-normative body, but one that nonetheless reflects an ableist bias. We may surmise that 'real' people with disabilities thought little about the relationship of their prosthetics to their natural body; but we cannot know for certain.

CHAPTER 5

'Recompact My Scattered Parts': the Altered Body after Death

In January 1720, the *London Journal* reported a very odd case of lost property:

> On Monday last part of the right Leg of a man was found in a Cellar Window in Bartholomew Close, which probably may have belonged to some Patient in the neighbouring Hospital, that has undergone an Amputation; some will have it otherwise, and to be a Limb of one that has been murdered. If the Owner be not living, the Flesh on it, shewed plainly that he has not been long dead.[1]

For readers of the *Journal*, this strange find must have raised many questions. How might the leg have found its way from the hospital to the cellar window? If it had come from a murder victim, where was the rest of the body? What had happened to the limb's 'owner'? Where was the leg now? For a twenty-first-century scholar, these questions may be joined by others. Did the hospital, or the amputee, care that the leg had gone astray? How was it treated after it was found? And if the limb clearly should not have been in the cellar window, where *should* it have been?

This chapter attempts to address the second set of questions, and investigates the afterlives of both removed body parts and altered bodies. As I shall show, the surgically changed body posed difficulties in religious as well as practical terms. It provoked questions about the nature of bodily identity and the specifics of bodily resurrection. The way in which early modern people asked and answered these questions was inflected by the subject/object status of the body, and in turn by its cultural, economic, and religious valences at any historical moment. It is worth noting that my analysis does not seek to provide anything like a comprehensive overview of the labyrinthine scholarly debate on bodily resurrection during the early modern period, or of the literary productions that arose from that debate. Most notably, I will omit discussion of Locke's *Essay on Human*

[1] *London Journal*, 27 January 1722, p. 2.

Understanding. Though all other contemporary theories might be seen as, in part at least, responses to that text, I am concerned with the very corporeality which Locke seeks to eschew. Proponents of bodily resurrection sought, as I will show, to keep the body and identity together. Instead, I will look to the competing theories of Robert Boyle, Humphrey Hody, and others. Their attempts to understand how the risen body might be at once newly perfect, *and* identical with the lived body, provide an illuminating context for the creative expressions of doubt and wonder about the resurrection of the body found in the work of John Donne, and in more slippery accounts of limb restoration miracles such as the Miracle of the Black Leg. Finally, I will return to consider the ways in which 'ordinary' people treated disembodied limbs or limbless bodies. By looking at scholarly, creative, and pragmatic expressions of beliefs about the body's afterlife, I argue that we can gain a more rounded picture of the complexity of this topic.

Scholarly Contexts

Almost all early modern Christian thinkers accepted the immortality of the soul, and most also accepted that the risen soul would be united with the same body that one had possessed in life. This belief was based both in scripture and in centuries of Church tradition.[2] Seemingly the most compelling piece of scripture for early modern theologians was 1 Corinthians 15, which described the perfection of the risen body:

> [35] But some man will say, How are the dead raised up? and with what body do they come?
>
> [36] Thou fool, that which thou sowest is not quickened, except it die:
>
> [37] And that which thou sowest, thou sowest not that body that shall be, but bare grain, it may chance of wheat, or of some other grain:
>
> [38] But God giveth it a body as it hath pleased him, and to every seed his own body.
>
> [39] All flesh is not the same flesh: but there is one kind of flesh of men, another flesh of beasts, another of fishes, and another of birds . . .[42] So also is the resurrection of the dead. It is sown in corruption; it is raised in incorruption:
>
> [43] It is sown in dishonour; it is raised in glory: it is sown in weakness; it is raised in power:
>
> [44] It is sown a natural body; it is raised a spiritual body. There is a natural body, and there is a spiritual body. (1 Cor. 15:35–44 KJV)

---

[2] See especially Matthew 27:52, Revelation 20:12–13, Philippians 3:20–1.

This passage, like others, promised a risen body which was diachronically identical with that which a person had had in life. Exactly what constituted 'identity', however, was a matter on which opinion was remarkably and consistently heterodox. The passage from Corinthians implied qualitative difference between the 'seed' lived body and the 'grain' resurrected state. By contrast, passages from Ezekiel and Revelations promised that the same bodies that were put in the grave would rise up, and the sea '[give] up the dead which were in it' (Ezekiel 37:13; Revelations 20:13). In his overview of the early modern debate on this topic, Lloyd Strickland identifies eight separate schools of thought about the way in which the body might be resurrected. At one end of the spectrum was the conviction (most favoured by the Church fathers) that the dead would rise with all and only the same matter as their bodies had had at the time of their death. At the other was the Lockean idea that identity consisted in continuing self-consciousness, and that the resurrected person did not therefore need to have their soul united with any of their lived material body in order to qualify as 'identical'.[3] Between these two points were a number of thinkers who held that, in one way or another, the body was to be resurrected with the same 'essential' matter intact as had been present in the body at its time of death, and the remainder supplied by other, undifferentiated matter. In the context of bodily alteration, this middle ground raises particularly interesting questions about bodily identity.

The interest of early modern people in matters of resurrection was far from merely scholarly naval-gazing. Churchgoers apparently pressed their clerics for answers about exactly *how* their souls and bodies were to be raised. In a sermon printed in 1636, for example, Martin Day admonished the 'foolish' people among his flock who asked such questions as:

> [W]hat *correspondence* shall there be, between man, and man? To *know* in what *kinde* of *stature* they shall *rise* in? What *colour* they shall have? What *imployment* shall they be *raised* for? Whether a *childe* shall rise as a *childe*? Whether an *old man* shall rise in his *old age*? Whether *crooked*, and *deformed* men, shall rise *crooked* and *deformed*? . . . It is an easier matter, to perswade a man of the *substance* of the *Resurrection*; then to perswade him of the *difference*, and of the *qualities* of men at the *Resurrection*.[4]

[3] Lloyd Strickland, 'The Doctrine of "the Resurrection of the Same Body" in Early Modern Thought', *Religious Studies* 46:2 (2010): 163–83.
[4] Martin Day, *Doomes-Day, or, a Treatise of the Resurrection of the Body* (London, 1636), p. 196.

Day felt that Christians ought not to trouble themselves with such matters, but his parishioners clearly felt differently; they wanted the gritty details about their next life. Moreover, these questions persisted over several centuries, through doctrinal, social, and political change. Ephraim Chambers in his 1728 *Cyclopaedia* noted that 'The Christians generally believe the Resurrection of the same identic Body', but struggled to answer questions such as 'Which of these many Bodies ... which the same Person has in the Course of his Life, is it that shall rise? Or does all the Matter that has ever belong'd to him, rise again? Or does only some particular System thereof?'[5] Caroline Walker Bynum has identified the same concerns in Peter Lombard's twelfth-century *Sentences*.[6] The minutiae of such questions has become famous (including, inevitably, whether the risen body would use the toilet). However, the examples with which such dilemmas were discussed were as important to the debate as the issues themselves. As Bynum argues for the medieval period:

> It is the examples to which the philosophers continually refer, rather than their abstract positions, that tell us how far we go toward assuming that material continuity is crucial for personal survival. It is in the examples also that we see reflected the extent to which popular culture has moved away from concern with mind/body dichotomies and turned instead to issues of integrity versus corruption or partition.[7]

Among the examples to which philosophers most continually referred in early modern debates were those which directly pertained to bodily alteration – in particular, the loss of body parts and bodily matter either before or after death. This concern is nowhere more evident than in the work of John Donne, who in his poetry and sermons combines detailed theological knowledge with an appreciation of the anxieties attending the resurrection of 'anomalous' bodies. A wedding sermon preached by Donne at the Earl of Bridgewater's house, for instance, dwells on the worrying possibility of being buried – and thus, perhaps, raised – without all one's body parts:

> What cohaereance, what sympathy, what dependence maintaines any relation, any correspondence, between that arm that was lost in Europe, and that legge that was lost in Afrique or Asia, scores of yeers between? One

---

[5] Ephraim Chambers, *Cyclopædia, or, An Universal Dictionary of Arts and Sciences* (London, 1728), pp. 1006–7, accessed 15 June 2018, https://uwdc.library.wisc.edu/collections/HistSciTech/.

[6] Caroline Walker Bynum, 'Material Continuity, Personal Survival, and the Resurrection of the Body: a Scholastic Discussion in its Medieval and Modern Contexts', *History of Religions* 30:1 (1990): 54.

[7] Ibid., 64.

humour of our dead body produces worms, and those worms suck and exhaust all other humour, and then all dies, and all dries, and molders into dust, and that dust is blowen into the River, and that puddled water tumbled into the sea, and that ebbs and flows in infinite revolutions, and still, still God knows in what Cabinet every seed-Pearle lies, in what part of the world every graine of every mans dust lies; and ... he whispers, he hisses, he beckons for the bodies of his Saints, and in the twinckling of an eye, that body that was scattered over all the elements, is sate down at the right hand of God, in a glorious resurrection.[8]

In Donne's rhetorical treatment of this topic, one sees him grappling with soteriology as both a cleric and a believer. Theologically, the scattering of body parts is an easy 'fix'. God's omnipotence, as Donne understands it, can readily solve the problem. As he turns the image of the dispersed body over in his mind, however, Donne aligns himself with the believer who *feels* that in losing the integrity of their body they are potentially losing spiritual integrity. Moreover, Donne's evocation of 'sympathy' in this passage shows him to have been in touch with the same scientific discourses in which we have seen animated discussions about allografting and Tagliacotian rhinoplasty. His theology is thus resolutely tied to the corporeal and the affective. The emotional pull of this image for Donne is confirmed by his return to the topic later the same year, 1627. In a sermon preached at Lincoln's Inn, he asked:

Shall I imagine a difficulty in my body, because I have lost an Arme in the East, and a leg in the West? Because I have left some bloud in the North, and some bones in the South? Doe but remember, with what ease you have sate in the chair, casting an account, and made a shilling on one hand, a pound on the other, or five shillings below, ten above, because all these lay easily within your reach. Consider how much lesse, all this earth is to him, that sits in heaven, and spans all this world, and reunites in an instant armes, and legs, bloud, and bones, in what corners so ever they be scattered.[9]

The partitioned body becomes both the topic about which Donne talks and a tool for thought which allows metaphysical speculation, both a means and an end. The utility of thinking through and with the body

[8] John Donne, 'A Sermon Preached at the Earl of Bridge-Waters House in London at the Marriage of His Daughter, the Lady Mary, to the Eldest Son of the Lord Herbert of Castle-Iland, November 19 1627' in *The Sermons of John Donne*, ed. Evelyn Simpson and George Potter, vol. VIII (of 10), no. 7 (Berkeley: University of California Press, 1956), pp. 4–5.
[9] John Donne, 'Preached at Lincolns Inne', in *The Sermons of John Donne*, ed. Simpson and Potter, vol. III (of 10), no. 3 (Berkeley: University of California Press, 1957), p. 19.

becomes evident as, via this image of dissolution, Donne reaches his emphatic conclusion:

> I, I the same body, and the same soul, shall be recompact again, and be identically, numerically, individually the same man. The same integrity of body, and soul, and the same integrity in the Organs of my body, and in the faculties of my soul too; I shall be all there, my body, and my soul, and all my body, and all my soul.[10]

As I shall discuss, Donne's tone here may betray anxiety as much as confidence; his repeated insistence that *all* his body is risen seems hyperbolic even for this habitually dramatic writer. Nonetheless, the mental image of God as a sort of giant caretaker gathering up the dispersed parts of bodies evidently appeals to Donne. It appears on his tomb, a statue of Donne standing on an urn, having been remade by God out of his ashes.[11] It is seen again in Donne's treatment of a notorious theological puzzle. The 'cannibal problem' was first posed by Augustine, and dogged virtually every discussion of bodily resurrection. In its most basic form, it posited that the flesh of one person might be eaten by another, either because the second person was a cannibal or because the flesh of the first person was consumed by an animal which was then eaten by the second person. The flesh of the second person would then have derived directly from that of the first, and that portion of flesh could not be restored to both parties at the resurrection. Donne frames the problem as one with a very similar solution to the 'scattered bodies' dilemma described above:

> And as if man feed on man's flesh, and so
> Part of his body to another owe,
> Yet at the last two perfect bodies rise,
> Because God knows where every atom lies.[12]

Donne seems to be bending the cannibal problem here to suit an image of which he had become fond, namely that of God in his counting house. This fondness was likely augmented by Donne's interest in atomism. As David Hirsch argues, '[T]he atom in its "immortality" provided the poet with a stabilizing center and limit to the dissolution of somatocentric

---

[10] Ibid., pp. 19–20.

[11] Donne famously posed for a portrait of himself in a funerary shroud whilst still very much alive, an act which says much about his preoccupation with the materiality of the body after death.

[12] 'Obsequies to the Lord Harrington, Brother to the Countess of Bedford', in *John Donne: the Major Works*, ed. John Carey (Oxford: Oxford University Press, 2000), ll. 47–56.

identity.'[13] *Where* every atom lay, however, was not the real crux of this problem, as Donne must have known. The issue was rather to whom every atom *belonged*, the cannibal or the cannibalised. Nonetheless, he employed the same sleight of hand in a sermon on Easter Day, 1626:

> [W]here mans buried flesh hath brought forth grasse, and that grasse fed beasts, and those beasts fed men, and those men fed other men, God that knowes in which Boxe of his Cabinet all this seed Pearle lies, in what corner of the world every atome, every graine of every mans dust sleeps, shall recollect that dust, and then recompact that body, and then re-inanimate that man, and that is the accomplishment of all.[14]

In insisting on God's omnipotence as a solution to the cannibal problem, Donne admitted and exalted his own ignorance, which he insisted reflected the general inability of the human mind to comprehend God's workings. In this sermon, however, he also allowed that resurrection might be conceived of in several different ways, and that it was not a sin to differ in opinion on this matter (though he insisted that bodily resurrection as a general idea was an article of faith).

Donne apparently took his own advice regarding doctrinal flexibility. Though he adhered to Church orthodoxy in his sermons, his poetry reveals an emotional connection to the idea of his own corpse, and a horror of bodily partition. In 'The Funeral', for instance, Donne imagines a bracelet of his lover's hair keeping his skeleton knit together in the same way that the spinal cord connects the bones of the living body, a motif which recurs in the 'Second Anniversary' (l. 211). In 'A Valediction of My Name in the Window', the importance of the non-atomised, non-cannibalised corpse is evident even as God's power to 'recompact' parts is asserted:

> Then, as all my souls be
> Emparadised in you, (in whom alone
> I understand, and grow and see,)
> The rafters of my body, bone
> Being still with you, the muscle, sinew, and vein,
> Which tile this house, will come again.
>
> Till my return repair
> And recompact my scattered body so,
> As all the virtuous powers which are

[13] David A. Hedrich Hirsch, 'Donne's Atomies and Anatomies: Deconstructed Bodies and the Resurrection of Atomic Theory', *Studies in English Literature, 1500–1900* 31:1 (1991): 70, https://doi.org/10.2307/450444.
[14] 'From a Sermon Preached on Easter Day, 1626', in *John Donne: the Major Works*, ed. Carey, p. 369.

Fixed in the stars, are said to flow
Into such characters, which graved be
When these stars had supremacy.[15]

Though Donne here imagines himself as preserved in memory and in text, it is clear that, as Hirsch argues, 'his conception of self is deeply rooted in the integrity of his personal body'.[16] As the stars act upon the earth, his soul will reanimate his body, but this is not a one-way affair: the nature of the stars is only fully expressed when their 'virtuous powers' flow outward, and the soul is not fully itself without the body.

Donne's particular emphasis on preserving his skeleton, the 'rafters' which hold up the house of his body, has much in common with a theory of bodily resurrection which I shall call 'essentials resurrection'. This theory – perhaps partly inspired by Donne – flourished in the later seventeenth century. Proponents of essentials resurrection were not satisfied with the vague 'God's omnipotence' solution to the cannibal problem which writers like Donne proffered. Clearly, they reasoned, some portion of matter from every person *would* probably be assimilated into other humans or otherwise lost. In addition, they speculated that it was not necessary for every atom of the material the body was composed of at death to be present in the risen body in order to proclaim that body 'identical'. So, what was necessary for continuing identity? Criticism has tended to focus on those thinkers – most notably Locke – who insisted that identity consisted in the soul, and that the same soul joined to a new body could be deemed diachronically identical. Others, however, tried to locate sameness in particular body parts, to which they believed that other, undifferentiated matter might be added to make up the whole body. Like Donne, they saw some parts of the body as 'rafters', essential to the structure of the whole, and other parts as replaceable 'tiles'. Robert Boyle's *Some Physico-Theological Considerations about the Possibility of the Resurrection* (1675) was one such text. In it, Boyle took up that concern with the partitioned body which had characterised Donne's work and gave it a newly mechanistic emphasis. It was in tune with Boyle's personal interests, but also with the ever-growing public interest in science and technology which we have seen at work elsewhere in this book.

In answer to the cannibal problem, Boyle drew on his chemical knowledge to argue that the body was constantly changing, producing over a

---

[15] 'A Valediction: Of My Name in the Window', in *John Donne: the Major Works*, ed. Carey, ll. 25–36.
[16] Hirsch, 'Donne's Atomies and Anatomies', 80.

lifetime much more material than was required to make up one adult body:

> I consider that a human body ... is in a perpetual flux or changing condition, since it grows in all its parts, and all its dimensions, from a corpusculum no bigger than an insect to the full stature of a man, which in many persons that are tall and fat may amount to a vast bulk, which could not happen but by a constant apposition and assimilation of new parts ... And since men, as other animals, grow but to a certain pitch and till a certain age (unless it be the crocodile, which some affirm to grow always until death), and therefore must discharge a great part of what they eat and drink by insensible transpiration ... it will follow that, in no very great compass of time, a great part of the human body must be changed; and yet it is considerable that the bones are of a stable and lasting texture, as I found not only by some chemical trials, but by the skulls and bones of men whom history records to have been killed an exceeding long time ago.[17]

In Boyle's view, it was therefore possible that God could unite the matter remaining in the (very durable) bones with other atoms which had been exhaled or otherwise shed from the person's body during their lifetime. As a chemist, Boyle was optimistic about the possibility of isolating these exhaled atoms from wherever they might have ended up. As he pointed out, pork from pigs fed on fish tasted fishy, and cows eating garlic produced garlicky milk. Atoms clearly retained their original properties even when they passed through the bodies of other creatures. Moreover, he, a mere mortal, was able to separate gold from other metals in a compound; God could do exponentially more.[18] Most importantly, Boyle accepted that these surviving atoms could be combined with other particles of unrelated but 'fit' matter, to 'restore or reproduce a body which, being united with the former soul, may, in a sense consonant to the expressions of scripture, recompose the same man whose soul and body were formerly disjoined by death'.[19] This was possible because diachronic identity persisted in spite of changes in the size and shape of the body, such that 'the same soul being united to a portion of duly organized matter is said to constitute the same man, notwithstanding the vast differences of

---

[17] Robert Boyle, 'Some Physico-Theological Considerations about the Possibility of the Resurrection (1675)', in *Selected Philosophical Papers of Robert Boyle*, ed. M. A. Stewart (Manchester: Manchester University Press, 1979), pp. 198–9.

[18] T.E. and Robert Boyle, *Some Considerations about the Reconcileableness of Reason and Religion. By T.E. a Lay-Man. To Which Is Annex'd by the Publisher, a Discourse of Mr Boyle, about the Possibility of the Resurrection* (London, 1675), pp. 19, 24.

[19] Boyle, 'Some Physico-Theological Considerations', p. 206.

bigness that there may be at several times between the portions of matter whereto the human soul is united'.[20]

The notion that the bones were somehow more important to bodily resurrection than the flesh was reproduced in numerous 'essentials' resurrection arguments. In 1694, for instance, Humphrey Hody disagreed with the extent to which Boyle believed that much of the risen body could be composed of unrelated matter. However, he too viewed only certain parts of the body as 'necessary':

> [T]hough the same Body that died is to rise again, yet it is not necessary that all the Particles of it should be rais'd up. 'Tis enough that such Particles are rais'd up as made up the integrant and necessary Parts of the Body. By necessary Parts, I mean those which remain after the utmost degree of Maceration [wasting], without which the Body would not be Integral, but Imperfect. And these are chiefly the Bones, the Skin, the Nerves, the Tendons, the Ligaments, and the Substance of the several Vessels. As long as these, and all that are necessary to Life, remain, the body is truly Whole, though never so much macerated. All the Flesh that is added makes nothing at all to the Wholeness or Integrality of the Body, tho' it conduce to Strength and Ornament.[21]

Hody seems to regard 'necessity' as related to the survival of certain parts after bodily wasting; he implies that one can imagine an emaciated living body which is skin and bones, but not one *without* skin and bones. Like Boyle, he too suggests that any deficit in the flesh of the risen body can be made up with matter from elsewhere, just as long as the essential parts are the same as those which were buried. Shortly afterward, Thomas Beconsall made a similar point, attesting that the risen body might be considered the same provided that 'a fit Construction and Organization of certain Particles of Matter, whereby one common Principle of Life is begun, [is] continued, and the Integral Parts of the Man are perfected and maintained'.[22] The rest of the matter necessary to make up a human being could, as Hody had argued, be made from the lived body's surplus matter (fingernails, hair, and so on), or from 'common' matter. In effect this once again meant that bones, blood vessels, nerves, and perhaps skin and muscles were numerically the same in the risen body, but other parts need

---

[20] Ibid.

[21] Humphrey Hody, *The Resurrection of the (Same) Body Asserted: From the Traditions of the Heathens, the Ancient Jews, and the Primitive Church. With an Answer to the Objections Brought Against It* (London: printed for Awnsham and John Churchill, 1694), pp. 187–8.

[22] Thomas Beconsall, *The Doctrine of a General Resurrection: Wherein the Identity of the Rising Body Is Asserted, against the Socinians and Scepticks* (Oxford: printed by Leon. Lichfield, for George West, 1697), p. 19.

not be. Beconsall ventured that the 'Integral' constituents might be viewed as the most 'serviceable' to life, or perhaps to 'the received idea of the Animal Part'.[23]

In many respects, the resurrection of 'essential' parts of the body seemed an intuitive solution. It seemed reasonable, for example, to insist that one's heart was more important to continuing selfhood than one's toenails. However, problems attended this view of resurrection, particularly when considered in relation to the altered body. Scholars such as Boyle and Hody evidently believed that the same numerical bones would be raised from the grave because these were what gave the body its framework – as Donne put it, its 'rafters'. Thus, for Boyle in particular, this resurrected body depended on the bones being a 'durable' aspect of the body, relatively impervious to decay and destruction. Boyle claimed to have proved this with chemical experiments, but not everyone agreed with his findings. There were other problems too. For Locke, Boyle did not go far enough in disavowing bodily sameness as a criterion for continuing identity.[24] Conversely, Hody admitted that while he adhered to this theory, it wasn't precisely resurrection of the *same* body.[25]

Where did this intellectual tussle leave people with altered bodies? On one matter, the different voices in the debate, across chronological and doctrinal divides, agreed. The risen body would be a perfected body, and that meant that sick and impaired people would be 'fixed'. Over and over in early modern texts, churchmen detailed how the resurrected body would be free from disease, vulnerability, and disability. There would be, argued John Bunyan in 1665, 'no lame legs, nor Crump-shoulders, no blare-eyes, nor yet wrinkled faces'.[26] Hody likewise claimed that

> Had our Bodies heretofore many Infirmities? Were they *sickly*, or *maim'd*, or *crooked*, or *old*, or otherwise deformed? These Infirmities and all Imperfections are now done away. The Body is *new-cast*, the *Mold* work'd better, and the *Mettal* refin'd: The whole *Figure* comes out with Vast Improvements; though, the same as to all the *Ideal Rudiments*, yet a much more curious and delicate Piece of Workmanship.[27]

[23] Ibid.
[24] K. Joanna S. Forstrom, *John Locke and Personal Identity: Immortality and Bodily Resurrection in 17th-Century Philosophy* (London: Bloomsbury, 2011), p. 112.
[25] Strickland, 'The Doctrine of "the Resurrection of the Same Body" in Early Modern Thought', 174.
[26] John Bunyan, *The Resurrection of the Dead and Eternall Judgement, or, The Truth of the Resurrection of the Bodies Both of Good and Bad at the Last Day Asserted and Proved by Gods Word: Also, the Manner and Order of Their Coming Forth of Their Graves, as Also, with What Bodies They Do Arise: Together with a Discourse of the Last Judgement, and the Finall Conclusion of the Whole World* (London: Francis Smith, 1665), p. 38.
[27] Hody, *The Resurrection of the (Same) Body Asserted*, p. 201.

Isaac Watts, in 1755, asserted that even bodies 'in some Part defective, or redundant' would be made whole, with the missing parts being made up from the surplus matter of corpulent or dropsical bodies.[28] Thomas Watson (1692) assured readers that the 'deformed' bodies of saints would be made 'amiable and beautiful'.[29]

What the perfected body looked like was unclear. John Dunton, in 1698, suggested that the body would be resurrected as it was at the age of thirty or thirty-three (the latter being Christ's age when he died).[30] Thomas Burnet, meanwhile, attempted to suggest that heavenly bodies would not have bowels or legs:

> The parts below the Belly will be taken away likewise, or be entirely useless ... Then the Leg, Thighs, and Feet, made for walking upon some firm and solid Pavement, as there is no such thing, and Motion will not be after the manner of walking, but as Angels move; these will be taken away as unnecessary and superfluous.[31]

Burnet's idea of a less *corporeal* sort of body suggested a return to a prelapsarian, quasi-angelic state, free from the demands of physical appetites. The dismemberment of the self, like a sort of divine drawing and quartering, marked one's purification for heaven, and mirrored the torments of the damned. As in many surgical narratives, the healer looks and acts remarkably like the torturer.

Whatever its specifics, it was made clear that the risen body would not have any impairments, and this made resurrection a matter of scientific as well as religious interest. Pondering on what kinds of monsters would undergo resurrection (all those with rational souls, but not hybrid

---

[28] Isaac Watts, *Philosophical Essays on Various Subjects, Viz. Space, Substance, Body, Spirit, the Operations of the Soul in Union with the Body, Innate Ideas, Perpetual Consciousness, Place and Motion of Spirits, the Departing Soul, the Resurrection of the Body, the Production and Operations of Plants and Animals: With Some Remarks on Mr Locke's Essay on the Human Understanding. To Which Is Subjoined a Brief Scheme of Ontology, or the Science of Being in General, with Its Affections*, 4th edition (London: printed for T. Longman and J. Buckland, J. Oswald, J. Waugh, and J. Ward, 1755), p. 189.

[29] Thomas Watson quoted in Darren Oldridge, *Strange Histories: the Trial of the Pig, the Walking Dead, and Other Matters of Fact from the Medieval and Renaissance Worlds* (Florence: Taylor and Francis, 2004), p. 34.

[30] John Dunton, *An Essay Proving We Shall Know Our Friends in Heaven* (London: printed and sold by E. Whitlock, 1698), p. 35.

[31] Thomas Burnet, *De Statu Mortuorum & Resurgentium Tractatus. Of the State of the Dead, and of Those That Are to Rise. Translated from the Latin Original of Dr Burnet*, trans. Matthias Earbery, 2nd edition, vol. 1 (of 2) (London: E. Curll, 1728), p. 189.

creatures or abortive births), Levinus Lemnius assured readers of his *Secrets of Nature*:

> by rising again they [monsters] shall lay aside all deformities of their bodies that were ill favoured to behold, and be well formed like as men are, and all lame crooked imperfect limbs shall be made perfect. And though in some the force of reason shines lesse, because of the unaptnesse of the organ, as in children, old men, drunkards, mad-men, in whom the force of the Soul is hindred, or oppressed. Yet every one of them hath a reasonable soul; and what is defective shall be made up at the resurrection.[32]

Accounts such as this one must have been reassuring to readers suffering from diseases and impairments for which effective cures were often unavailable, and who faced economic and social hardship as a result of their anomalous bodies. At the same time, however, they presented an obvious problem. How could a body which was thus altered be said to be meaningfully identical?

Irina Metzler has considered this question in relation to medieval accounts of disability. In Thomas Aquinas' influential work on this subject, she finds, continuity between body and self was emphasised, such that 'the soul takes on a similar position to what psychologists would now term the location of identity'.[33] In this formulation,

> The soul does not just accidentally possess a body with a with a specific gender, skin colour, impairment or age, but the soul carries the structure of the self, of the 'ego', and this is what determines the body which will be resurrected, with all its physical characteristics . . . So the 'ego' is neither just the soul nor just the body, that 'ego' is a 'person' with an identity.[34]

Despite this argument, however, Metzler finds that theologians consistently asserted that the risen body would not suffer impairment. Ultimately, she concludes, this apparently 'schizophrenic' stance probably indicates that disability was not an identity category in the same way as, for example, gender:[35]

> Could it be, in the medieval intellectual discourse, at least, that though corporeal identity was recognised, impairment as a form of corporeality was just not considered important? Though sex, age or skin colour may have

---

[32] Levinus Lemnius, *The Secret Miracles of Nature in Four Books: Learnedly and Moderately Treating of Generation, and the Parts Thereof, the Soul, and Its Immortality, of Plants and Living Creatures, of Diseases, Their Symptoms and Cures, and Many Other Rarities* (London: Jo. Streater, 1658), p. 58.

[33] Irina Metzler, *Disability in Medieval Europe: Thinking about Physical Impairment in the High Middle Ages, c. 1100–c. 1400* (Abingdon: Routledge, 2006), p. 59.

[34] Ibid.   [35] Ibid., p. 61.

been important, physical impairment was not? This seems to be the most fruitful approach. ... I therefore propose that though the Thomist notion of body and soul may be reminiscent of a twentieth-century psychology of identity, this is not the case entirely or unreservedly. It needs qualifying to allow for the idea that although certain physical characteristics (such as sex) may matter, others do not. Among the latter, physical impairments must be grouped.[36]

In the intellectual discourse of the early modern period, this may still have been true. As the Introduction to this book has discussed, 'disability' was not a distinct category in the seventeenth and eighteenth centuries in the same sense that it is today. David Turner and Kevin Stagg, for instance, describe disability as having been 'subsumed' into, though not identical with, other categories such as deformity and monstrosity.[37] Notably, the accounts of bodily perfection above place disabilities on a continuum with other instances of human frailty such as ageing and sickness. Despite these caveats, however, it seems clear that impairments *were* an important part of identity, both for the impaired person and for those around them. As we have seen, authors disagreed on the nature of the risen body. Nonetheless, scholars such as Katherine Eisamann Maus and Christopher Tilmouth have shown the importance of social relationships in constituting subject identity during the first half of the seventeenth century, and by extension the importance of recognising and being recognised.[38] How this could occur if the body was entirely transformed was unclear to say the least. As Roy Porter notes, this issue was thrust even more prominently into the public consciousness by Locke's bringing into question the importance of the physical body to the continuous 'self'.[39] Samuel Johnson, for instance, contended in a 1725 sermon that 'the same Marks, Features, and Lineaments are visible in Persons after the Resurrection, by which they were known and

[36] Irina Metzler, 'Disability in the Middle Ages: Impairment at the Intersection of Historical Inquiry and Disability Studies', *History Compass* 9:1 (2011): 61, https://doi.org/10.1111/j.1478-0542.2010.00746.x.

[37] David M. Turner and Kevin Stagg, *Social Histories of Disability and Deformity: Bodies, Images and Experiences* (Abingdon: Routledge, 2006), p. 4; Katherine Schaap Williams, 'Performing Disability and Theorizing Deformity', *English Studies* 94:7 (2013): 757–72, https://doi.org/10.1080/0013838X.2013.840125.

[38] Katharine Eisaman Maus, *Inwardness and Theater in the English Renaissance* (Chicago: University of Chicago Press, 1995); Christopher Tilmouth, 'Passion and Intersubjectivity in Early Modern Literature', in *Passions and Subjectivity in Early Modern Culture*, ed. Freya Sierhuis and Brian Cummings (Farnham: Ashgate, 2013), pp. 13–32.

[39] Roy Porter, *Flesh in the Age of Reason* (London: Allen Lane, 2003).

distinguish'd from one another in their mortal Body'.[40] In this respect, ordinary humans would have something in common with Jesus, who appeared with the marks of crucifixion visible on his risen body. Notably, Johnson maintained this opinion despite also believing that only the 'Stamen', or kernel, of the mortal body was necessary to ensure the risen body's 'Sameness'.[41]

As well as providing recognisability, disability was self-evidently a shaping influence on one's way of being in the world; if not an identity category as such, it was still something that could be defined (albeit loosely) and reproduced (albeit imperfectly). The expanded welfare provisions of early modern England meant that those applying for certain kinds of poor relief would have to identify themselves as dis-abled from working. Some people faked impairments in order to access sympathy and financial aid, and these people's activities were a matter of fascination for many pamphlet readers and theatre audiences.[42] Furthermore, disability was understood to shape one's character, opening up some possibilities and limiting others. In his 1613 *Essays*, Francis Bacon solemnly explained how 'deformed' people were often morally bankrupt, adding that 'it is good to consider of deformity, not as a sign which is more deceivable, but as a cause which seldom faileth of the effect'.[43] In contrast to 'monster' narratives, his repositioning of deformity as a *cause* of sinfulness encompassed acquired, as well as congenital, disabilities. Moreover, Simon Dickie has shown how stereotypes of the jealous or conceited cripple endured despite the supposed 'civilising process' of the seventeenth century. In the eighteenth century, he records, people with anomalous bodies were still routinely mocked according to well-worn caricatures, such that 'one was

---

[40] Samuel Johnson, *The Resurrection of the Same Body, as Asserted and Illustrated by St Paul. A Sermon Preach'd in the Parish-Church of Great Torrington, Devon. on Easter-Day, March 25, 1733*, 2nd edition (London: printed for Lawton Gilliver, Charles Rivington, William Parker, and Samuel Birt, 1741), p. 28.

[41] Ibid., p. 18.

[42] Patricia Fumerton, 'Making Vagrancy (In)Visible: the Economics of Disguise in Early Modern Rogue Pamphlets', *English Literary Renaissance* 33:2 (2003): 211–27, https://doi.org/10.1111/1475-6757.00026; Tobias Hug, *Impostures in Early Modern England: Representations and Perceptions of Fraudulent Identities* (Manchester: Manchester University Press, 2010).

[43] Francis Bacon, 'Of Deformity', in *The Essays, or Councils, Civil and Moral of Sir Francis Bacon … With a Table of the Colours of Good and Evil. And a Discourse of the Wisdom of the Ancients (Done into English by Sir Arthur Gorges). To This Edition Is Added the Character of Queen Elizabeth; Never before Printed in English* (London: published for George Sawbridge, 1696), pp. 117–18, www.bl.uk/collection-items/bacons-essays-on-revenge-envy-and-deformity.

defined by one's body in eighteenth-century culture'.[44] The association was not only negative: William Hay's 1754 *Deformity: An Essay* argued that by dint of such ill-treatment, 'deformed persons' commonly had fewer worldly attachments than their able-bodied counterparts, and were in this respect better Christians.[45] This defence once again had its correlate in the early seventeenth century: Robert Burton's *Anatomy of Melancholy* suggested that disability might aid one's moral development.[46] Furthermore, bodily alteration and anomaly did not necessarily mean disability, as we have seen. It is difficult to believe that the castrato's 'impairment', if one could call it such, was not constitutive of his identity. As shown in Chapter 1, castration was widely believed to confer character traits as well as physical differences, and the whole course of a eunuch's or castrato's life was shaped by his castration. Likewise, cosmetic surgeries, as described in Chapter 3, were understood to fundamentally alter the way in which the altered person interacted with the world around them.

The complexity of this issue is attested to by the fact that debate over the status of disability in Christian soteriology continues within modern theology. Since the rise of disability activism, the image of the 'perfected' unimpaired body has been challenged by scholars who view it as a denial of disabled identity. Amos Yong, for instance, notes that some – though by no means all – people with disabilities object to the notion that they need 'healing'.[47] The modern response to this seems to be analogous with that of early modern writers, in arguing that disability is not an intrinsic part of selfhood. Terrence Ehrman employs what he calls a 'Thomistic hylemorphism' to distinguish between 'proper accidents' of matter, which are determined by an object's form (e.g. flying for birds), and 'contingent accidents', which are not (e.g. a broken wing in a particular bird).[48] This theory seems closest to the early modern conception in which disability merely masked or stunted intrinsic human capacities, such that madmen or 'idiots' may be called those 'in whom the force of the Soul is hindred, or

[44] Simon Dickie, *Cruelty and Laughter: Forgotten Comic Literature and the Unsentimental Eighteenth Century* (Chicago: University of Chicago Press, 2011), p. 103.

[45] William Hay, *Deformity: An Essay* (London: printed for R. and J. Dodsley, and sold by M. Cooper, 1754), p. 42.

[46] Robert Burton, *The Anatomy of Melancholy: what it is. With all the kindes, causes, symptomes, prognosticks, and seuerall cures of it* (Oxford: John Lichfield and James Short, for Henry Cripps, 1621), p. 387.

[47] Amos Yong, *Theology and Down Syndrome: Reimagining Disability in Late Modernity* (Waco: Baylor University Press, 2007).

[48] Terrence Ehrman, 'Disability and Resurrection Identity', *New Blackfriars* 96:1066 (2015): 723–38, https://doi.org/10.1111/nbfr.12126.

oppressed'.[49] Ultimately, however, such an explanation remains at odds with the sort of individuated and personal resurrection which most early modern writers imagined, and which underpinned the notion that resurrected people would know one another in heaven.

The Miracle of the Black Leg

The strong association perceived to exist between a disabled person's impairment and their character highlighted a truth about identity in general: that one's *self*, in some essential way, seemed to be inextricably linked to the body, frailties and all. Donne, Boyle, Hody, and others strove to imagine a way in which the body could rise from the grave precisely because the body was felt to be integral to a person's subjectivity. These debates, however, were not confined to abstract philosophising. Rather, they were creatively played out in medieval and early modern miracle accounts in which limbs were restored to the faithful.

A surprising number and variety of such narratives existed. In their *Wounds in the Middle Ages*, Anne Kirkham and Cordelia Warr describe several miraculous limb restoration accounts from the tenth and eleventh centuries, as well as the better-known twelfth-century story of Peter of Grenoble. Having been struck by lightning after cursing and swearing on a feast day, Peter lost one of his legs, but regained it when the Virgin Mary and Saint Hippolytus appeared to him in a vision:

> At the Virgin's command, Hippolytus took the leg's scattered pieces, which had come together again 'in the likeness of the future resurrection', and proceeded 'to join them to Peter's body, as a slip is joined to a tree'. A year later, the Virgin and Hippolytus returned to perfect the restored leg, which in its first state had been weak and small. These miracles inspired Peter to go into religious seclusion.[50]

This tale has numerous similarities with those I shall describe below, including the intervention of the saint during a dream or vision, and the gradual return to normality of the 'restored' limb. While miraculous healings of this sort were unsurprisingly more prominent in the medieval period, early modern equivalents existed. Douglas Price and Neil J. Twombly identify five limb restoration miracles in fifteen separate

---

[49] Dunton, *An Essay Proving We Shall Know Our Friends in Heaven*, p. 58.
[50] Anne Kirkham and Cordelia Warr, *Wounds in the Middle Ages* (Abingdon: Routledge, 2016), p. 235–6.

accounts dating from the late fifteenth to the eighteenth century.[51] These include the Miracle at Calanda, said to have taken place in Spain in 1640. Michel Pellicero, a young man from Spain, had lost his leg in an accident, and was consigned to a life of begging. The devout young man eventually made his way home to live with his parents. Thus followed the miracle in which he regained his leg:

> Soon after about midnight, his Mother entering into the place where her son lay, espied in his bed a man lying with two legs, imagined him to be another Souldier, not dreaming what had happened to her sonne, frightened and amazed, went and told her husband of the matter, who came along with her to the chamber, being much troubled with fear and admiration untill they knew and discovered that it was their son that was most strangely cured.

> Whereupon, they awaked him not without difficulty, being very fast asleep, to whom his Father spake thus: Son, what is the matter, how came this that we see you with two legs? He replied; saying, he knew not, onely that as he slept he dreamed he was in the holy Chapel of Pilar, annointing himself with the oyl of the lamps there: his Father powring tears of meer joy, desired him to render infinite thanks to our mercifull Lord and Saviour Christ Jesus and his ever blessed Mother . . . because this glorious Virgin as he conceived obtained this cure, whence he was restored to his leg most miraculously.[52]

Despite its Catholic character, the Miracle at Calanda was recounted in numerous English texts including Davenport's 1653 *Enchiridion* and Daniel Turner's 1741 *Art of Surgery*. Though the latter treated the account with scepticism, he included a lengthy account in the *Art* with the justification that it had been the topic of debate among his friends and colleagues at Oxford.[53] The Calanda miracle, like that of Peter of Grenoble, emphasised the devotion of the healed person and the spiritual, as well as physical, effect of their miraculous healing.

Both Michel Pellicero and Peter of Grenoble have their original limbs restored to them, and in both cases, it is clear that this restoration represents more than a simple return to bodily function. In Pellicero's

[51] Douglas B. Price and Neil J. Twombly, *The Phantom Limb Phenomenon: a Medical, Folkloric, and Historical Study. Texts and Translations of 10th to 20th Century Accounts of the Miraculous Restoration of Lost Body Parts* (Washington: Georgetown University Press, 1978).
[52] Christopher Davenport, *An Enchiridion of Faith. Presented in a Dialogue, Declaring the Truth of Christian Religion in Generall* (Douay [Douai, France]: S.N., 1655), pp. 139–40.
[53] Daniel Turner, *The Art of Surgery: In Which Is Laid down Such a General Idea of the Same, as Is . . . Confirmed by Practice, . . . In Two Volumes. The Sixth Edition, Corrected. By Daniel Turner*, 6th edition, vol. 1 (of 2) (London: printed for C. Rivington, and J. Clarke, 1741), p. 216.

case, in particular, the restoration of the limb is a return to wholeness, in a broad sense. The deposition of the Archbishop of Saragossa, which is reproduced in Turner's *Art of Surgery*, specifies that the new leg is known to be Pellicero's own by some distinguishing marks upon it. Moreover, we know that the amputated leg has been treated as a part of the human subject rather than as a piece of meat. Davenport reports that, when Pellicero lost his leg, 'His leg being cut off, some four inches below the knee; was carried to be interred in the place of that holy Church where dead bodies and all such members cut off, are dayly buried.'[54]

Even within the context of a miracle, however, restoration to bodily wholeness is a tricky affair. Restoring the lost limbs in these cases entails reconstituting those limbs from the decayed or obliterated fragments created by burial or by lightning. It is thus shown to be important that the restored limbs are made of the same numerical flesh, whatever may have happened to that flesh in the interim. Yet, what is restored is not the perfect body promised in resurrection discourses. Peter's leg and Michel's are both said to be *im*perfect when they are restored. Where Peter's is stunted and small, Michel's is – in some accounts at least – 'much wrested to one side'.[55] The limbs, we are told, return to normal over time. This detail implies that return to full bodily health is a process which takes place alongside the spiritual work of accepting and proselytising from the healing miracle. Seeing the join in this way raises questions about the status of body parts in relation to bodies whole.

These questions are explored more fully – if peculiarly– in the Miracle of the Black Leg. Also known as the Miracle of Cosmas and Damian, this account had circulated since the medieval period. It appeared in Jacob de Voragine's *Golden Legend* and in William Caxton's 1483 translation of the same, which was widely read throughout the early modern period. Moreover, as I describe below, it remained the subject of artistic representations and re-workings throughout the seventeenth century. The account centres on a pious sacristan, afflicted with cancer of the leg, who falls asleep in the church after praying to Saints Cosmas and Damian:

> as he slept, the holy martyrs Cosmo and Damian, appeared to him their devout servant, bringing with them an instrument and ointment of whom that one said to that other: Where shall we have flesh when we have cut away the rotten flesh to fill the void place? Then that other said to him:

[54] Davenport, *An Enchiridion of Faith*, p. 138.
[55] E.W., *Reason and Religion, or, The Certain Rule of Faith* (Antwerp: Michael Cnobbaert, 1672), p. 330.

There is an Ethiopian that this day is buried in the churchyard of S. Peter ad Vincula, which is yet fresh, let us bear this thither, and take we out of that man's flesh and fill this place withal. And so they fetched the thigh of the sick man and so changed that one for that other. And when the sick man awoke and felt no pain, he put forth his hand and felt his leg without hurt, and then took a candle, and saw well that it was not his thigh, but that it was another.[56]

The Miracle of the Black Leg implies a certain interchangeability of flesh: what is important is not the origin of one's limbs but their usefulness. In this respect it rehearses the preoccupation with prosthetic functionality which I explored in Chapter 4. However, the apparent pragmatism of the surgeon-saints in swapping a healthy for a diseased limb is also deeply problematic. There are obvious questions to be asked here. Given the saints' ability to perform miracles, why do they remove the sacristan's leg rather than healing it? Why do they replace it with that of the recently buried Ethiopian, when presumably they do not require the expediency of a local and recently deceased limb? Moreover, why is that intact but dead limb considered healthier than the sacristan's cankerous but nonetheless living flesh?

As textual and pictorial accounts of the miracle circulated, this strangeness was apparently exacerbated. Sheetal Lodhia traces representations of the black leg miracle from the early to late medieval period. Over this period, she argues, the blackness of the 'donor' is steadily emphasised, with descriptions switching from 'Moor' – a category of religious difference – to the racially determined 'Ethiopian'.[57] In so doing, successive retellers of the story amplify the gulf between the white and the non-white body, and raise the possibility of the sacristan's 'contamination' by racial and/or religious Otherness. Furthermore, early and late versions of the miracle differ in their description of the donor corpse. As Lodhia observes, the diseased white leg is consistently said to have been placed in the tomb with the Moor/Ethiopian, but whether it is grafted on to that body is often unclear.[58] Caxton's rendition is typically indeterminate: when the onlookers realised what had happened, 'they sent hastily to the tomb of the dead man, and found the thigh of him cut off, and *that other thigh in*

---

[56] Jacob de Voragine, *Legenda Aurea*, ed. F. S. Ellis, trans. William Caxton, vol. v (of 7) (Temple Classics, 1900), n.p. Via Fordham University Internet History Sourcebooks Project, https://sourcebooks.fordham.edu, accessed 17 March 2019.

[57] Sheetal Lodhia, 'Material Self-Fashioning and the Renaissance Culture of Improvement', Ph.D. (Queen's University, 2008), pp. 30–88.

[58] Ibid., p. 52.

the tomb instead of his' (emphasis added).[59] If, as this phrase implies, the white leg does not belong to the Moor, can the Moor's leg belong to the sacristan? The burial of the white leg with the donor body implies that this flesh is put aside for some purpose. At the resurrection, will the sacristan have his white leg restored to him, healed by God though not by the saints? Or will he retain the donor leg, which is, after all, the flesh which more properly 'belongs' to him at the time of his death?

The black leg miracle raises these questions but fails – or refuses – to answer them. Both the black and white legs in this story have the potential, though not always realised, to change the fate of their new 'owner'. In this respect, they closely resemble the prostheses I describe in Chapters 3 and 4, which both integrate with and impose upon the body. One might expand that reading, however, to note that the indeterminate status of the black leg raises questions which we have seen recur throughout this book – questions about the status of the body per se as object or subject, mere 'stuff' or inhabited self. Furthermore, there is evidence that audiences hearing or reading about this miracle understood its relevance to matters of bodily alteration. Lodhia describes how in pictorial representations, the apparel and instruments of the operating saints change over time. At first standing with hands off the sacristan's body and replete with aureoles, in later images of the miracle the saints' apparel becomes identical with that of contemporary surgeons, and they are shown manipulating the new leg. An earthy description of the miracle account by a 1623 Protestant text betrays how far the miracle might come to be seen as surgical in character:

> Pope *Felix*, the eighth after S. *Gregory*, built a Church in the honour of S. *Cosmas*, and S. *Damian*, wherein one had his thigh almost rotted off with a canker: but these Saints came with Salves and Ointments, yea tooke very excrements to cure the fellow: but when they sawe they could doe no good, they cut off a legge of an Aethiopian newly buried, and put it to the man, and so cured him.[60]

If the saints are surgeons in this image, it follows that the ideal surgeon – one who could restore as well as take away parts of the body – might be imagined as divine. For their part, Cosmas and Damian were (and are) known in Catholic countries as the patron saints of surgery and physic. (See Figures 5.1 and 5.2.)

[59] De Voragine, *Legenda Aurea*, n.p.
[60] T.G., *The Friers Chronicle: Or, The True Legend of Priests and Monkes Liues* (London: John Budge, 1623), sig. G2v.

Figure 5.1   Detail from 'A Verger's Dream: Saints Cosmas and Damian, 1495'
by Master of Los Balbases.
Credit: Wellcome Collection. CC BY

The medical and metaphysical implications of the Miracle of the Black
Leg may be most strikingly highlighted by the account's parallel with a
modern instance of limb transplantation. In 1998, Clint Hallam received a
hand transplant from a brain-dead donor, having lost his own hand in an
accident fourteen years earlier. The operation was the first of its kind, but
bore odd similarities with the medieval sacristan's leg restoration. Hallam's
new hand and his body were both Caucasian, but the 'join' between the
two remained clearly visible, with the new limb somewhat larger and paler
than his other 'original' hand. In this case, however, the difference between
new and old limbs became construed as something uncanny rather than
evidence of a miracle. Hallam reported that other people avoided shaking
his new hand, and his relationship with his wife deteriorated. He later
stopped taking immunosuppressant drugs in order to force medical staff to
perform an amputation, complaining that his limb felt alien to him: 'As it
began to be rejected, I realised that it wasn't my hand after all.'[61]

---

[61] Donna Dickenson and Guy Widdershoven, 'Ethical Issues in Limb Transplants', *Bioethics* 15:2
(2001): 117.

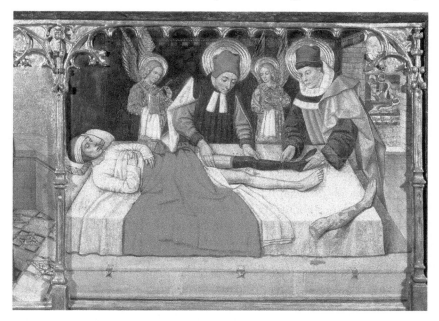

Figure 5.2   Saints Cosmas and Damian, *c.* 1370–5, Master of the Rinuccini Chapel (Matteo di Pacino) (Italian, active 1350–75), tempera and gold leaf on panel. North Carolina Museum of Art, Raleigh, gift of the Samuel H. Kress Foundation

Analysing this episode through a phenomenological lens, Jenny Slatman and Guy Widdershoven conclude: 'Being able to be the body one has, implies for the hand transplant recipient being able to appreciate and accept both the strange body's visual features . . . and its haptic, affective aspects.'[62] In spite of having sensorimotor and proprioceptive abilities in the new hand, Hallam could not accept the visual aspects of the limb or its role in his intersubjective experience of his body. Despite its impressive abilities, the transplanted part thus remained, for Hallam, a foreign object. Though bodily integrity is for Slatman and Widdershoven a psychological rather than spiritual issue, the 'alien' quality of Hallam's mismatched hand strongly evokes the conspicuous difference between the sacristan and his black leg. Furthermore, the surgeons in the Hallam case – just as in that of the sacristan – endeavoured to replace the limb of the donor body. The deceased person was buried with a prosthetic hand in order

[62] Jenny Slatman and Guy Widdershoven, 'Hand Transplants and Bodily Integrity', *Body and Society* 16:3 (2010): 75, https://doi.org/10.1177/1357034X10373406.

'to restore ... dignity'.[63] This gesture belies the clinical nature of the procedure. At some level, those involved still believed that the corpse-object retained some relation to the person-subject, and therefore needed to be buried with all its parts.

Returning to the Grave

As we have seen thus far, early modern people were consistently inconsistent in their beliefs about the resurrection of the body, and in particular of the impaired or altered body. This is not to say that their views on the risen body were not fully developed, or deeply considered. Rather, they kept at the forefront of their thinking questions that seemed to have no clear answer – questions about the relationship between body and soul, object and subject, and lived and risen selves. In light of this complexity, how did early modern citizens treat their disembodied parts and altered corpses? What should have happened to the amputated leg at the beginning of this chapter, which ended up ownerless in a London cellar window?

In the twenty-first century, patients undergoing amputations in the United Kingdom can expect the removed limb to be incinerated as clinical waste, though some patients have established a burial ground for the removed parts.[64] In the early modern period, the picture was less clear. The report of the leg in the window suggests that disembodied parts were treated rather casually, and there is evidence elsewhere for this. We know that, at sea, severed limbs were tossed into the water. This book began with an excerpt from John Moyle's *Abstract of Sea Chirurgery*, which advised young ship's-surgeons on preparing for engagement day. Moyle rather grimly informs the aspiring ship's-surgeon that, before a battle, one should prepare two tubs of water: 'the one to throw amputated Limbs into until there is conveniency to heave them over-board; and the other to dip your dismembring Bladders in'.[65] Such advice suggests that early modern surgeons did not worry much about where the limbs ended up, or the fact that parts of different bodies were mixed in together.

In less pressing circumstances, however, there is evidence that people undergoing amputations thought carefully about what to do with their severed limbs. In 1725, five years after the discovery of the leg in the cellar

---

[63] Dickenson and Widdershoven, 'Ethical Issues in Limb Transplants', 119.

[64] Pamela Parkes, 'Leg-Loss Patients Left in Limbo', *BBC News*, 17 January 2016, www.bbc.co.uk/news/uk-england-somerset-34879100.

[65] John Moyle, *Abstractum Chirurgiae Marinae, or, An Abstract of Sea Chirurgery* (London: printed by J. Richardson for Tho. Passinger, 1686), p. 22.

window documented at the start of this chapter, the *Weekly Journal* reported that

> A Gentleman in the North of England having lost a Leg by Amputation, caused a Monument to be erected over it in the Church-yard where it was buried, with this Inscription:
>
> > Here lies the Leg of Master Conder:
> > But he's alive, and that's a Wonder.
> > It was cut off by Dr Johnson,
> > The famousest Surgeon of the Nation.[66]

This jovial inscription may have been undertaken as a display of the patient's wit and a means of asserting his continuing economic and social agency. Nonetheless, it suggests that Master Conder hoped to be reunited with his leg at death, and was prepared to pay to secure that right. A less pithy example of the same practice can be found in Strata Florida, Wales, where Henry Hughes Cooper buried his amputated limb in a grave complete with tombstone bearing the inscription 'The left leg and part of the thigh of Henry Hughes Cooper, was cut off and interr'd here, June 18, 1756.'[67] Such examples are few and far between, but they bespeak a desire among some amputees to bury their body parts in hallowed ground, and possibly to have their bodies buried with or near the severed part at their eventual death. Sarah Tarlow asserts that numerous examples exist in the early modern period of 'care taken to inter amputated limbs alongside other whole bodies', indicating that the people in question felt that the amputated parts continued to house part of their 'individuated self'.[68] Henry Hughes Cooper and Mr Conder clearly felt that their severed legs retained some connection to the living body and therefore to its subjectivity, rather than being merely decaying objects.

The mixed treatment of amputated limbs in this context reflects the heterogeneity of early modern burial practices in general. Even as theologians asserted God's capacity to reunite scattered parts wherever they might be, early modern people continued to engage in rituals which treated the lived body, the buried corpse, and the risen body as continuous in a very literal sense. Claire Gittings, for instance, describes early modern burials in which the individuals concerned specified that only they were to be allowed space in their plot or tomb, even to the exclusion of their

---

[66] *Weekly Journal or British Gazetteer*, 9 October 1725

[67] Cited in Sarah Tarlow, *Ritual, Belief and the Dead in Early Modern Britain and Ireland* (Cambridge: Cambridge University Press, 2010), p. 66.

[68] Ibid.

children.[69] As Gittings recognises, these requests reflect a fear that at the day of resurrection, parts of different corpses might get mixed up with one another in the melee of bodily reassembly.[70] The shrouding of corpses was likewise deemed to be of material importance. Gittings writes that a tightly wound shroud was sometimes recommended to prevent the ghost of the dead person from walking, but in other instances it was suggested that the shroud should be loose 'lest it impede the wearer on the day of resurrection'.[71] A sense of literal continuity between living, dead, and risen bodies was also apparent in the burying of items with the deceased. Putting pennies in the mouth of a corpse was by the seventeenth century viewed as a popish and superstitious practice, but this did not stop Donne from imagining a similar talismanic power when he proposed carrying a bracelet of his mistress's hair from life into death.[72] Did people similarly take their prostheses with them to the grave? Evidence of prosthesis burial in early modern England is entirely absent, but this does not necessarily mean that no such burials took place. The majority of prostheses, as we have seen, were wooden, and would rot away in the grave. According to virtually all theologians, prostheses would be unnecessary for the risen, perfected body. Nonetheless, there are a handful of examples of medieval Europeans having been buried with their prosthetic limbs: a sixth-century wearer of a foot prosthesis was excavated in Austria in 2013.[73]

The existence of such practices does not imply that theologians believed one thing about bodily resurrection and 'ordinary' people another. It does, however, point to a tension in practice, as in theological argument, about whether the risen body would be composed of all and only the material belonging to the corpse. In her analysis of medieval heart burial and relic worship, Bynum argues that medieval believers' apparent readiness to divide up the body did not preclude a general horror and fear of bodily partition. On the contrary, the pious practice which invested saints' body parts with holy powers also implied that subject identity inhered in all the parts of one's body wherever they might be. It was therefore desirable,

[69] Mass graves, in which the bodies of some plague victims and war dead were interred, must have had a profound effect on beliefs about bodily integrity, but this topic remains relatively unstudied. See Sarah Covington, *Wounds, Flesh, and Metaphor in Seventeenth-Century England* (Basingstoke: Palgrave Macmillan, 2009), p. 91.
[70] Clare Gittings, 'Eccentric or Enlightened? Unusual Burial and Commemoration in England, 1689–1823', *Mortality* 12:4 (2007): 332, https://doi.org/10.1080/13576270701609667.
[71] Ibid., 112.   [72] Ibid., 111.
[73] M. Binder et al., 'Prosthetics in Antiquity: an Early Medieval Wearer of a Foot Prosthesis (6th Century AD) from Hemmaberg/Austria', *International Journal of Paleopathology* 12 (2016): 29–40, https://doi.org/10.1016/j.ijpp.2015.11.003.

though not theologically necessary, for the whole body to be buried in one grave.[74] The Church of England may have rejected reliquary culture, but it retained, both theoretically and ritually, the notion that subject identity inhered in the body. It therefore just *felt* better to have the body buried in certain ways in certain places. In his work on Reformation-era burials, Peter Marshall notes how people writing their wills couched the desire to be interred among their ancestors as an expression of belief that did not detract from their faith in God's ability to resurrect their bodies from any place, in any state:

> In North Yorkshire a woman stipulated that her body was to be buried 'in Askrigg church yeard amongst my ancestors, trusting that I shall receve the same againe, not a corruptible, mortall and vile body, but an immortall, uncorruptible and a glorious body'. In his will of 1585, Thomas Andrew of Bury St Edmunds requested burial 'in the churche yarde nighe unto the southe syde of St James Churche wheare myne Auncestors lye buried, not for that I thinke any place better then other but to declare my hope and beleve that they and I shall ryse together in the last day throughe Jesus Christ our onely saviour and Redemer to lyfe everlasting'.[75]

Though some modes and rites of burial changed over the seventeenth century, this theme endured through all kinds of burial practices which sought to keep the body intact. In the eighteenth century, embalming of corpses became commonplace. The best embalmers were those who could keep the body from putrefaction for the longest time. This was not merely for funerary purposes: skilled embalmers used multiple coffins of various materials to preserve the body in the grave.[76] Yet the embalmers, like the will-makers above, insisted that they were not keeping bodies intact in order for them to rise intact. In fact, as the author of one 1705 text pointed out, even burial was not really *necessary*:

> Neither is our Faith in his [Jesus'] assured Promise so frail, as to think ravenous Beasts or Birds of Prey can any ways make the Body want any part at the *Resurrection*; but on the contrary, we are well satisfied that in a Moment there shall be given such a new Restitution, not only out of the Earth, but out of the most minute Particles of all the other Elements, wherein any Bodies can possibly be included, that not a hair of our Heads shall be missing.[77]

[74] Bynum, 'Material Continuity, Personal Survival, and the Resurrection of the Body', 78–9.
[75] Peter Marshall, *Beliefs and the Dead in Reformation England* (Oxford: Oxford University Press, 2002), p. 210.
[76] Jolene Zigarovich, 'Preserved Remains: Embalming Practices in Eighteenth-Century England', *Eighteenth-Century Life* 33:3 (2009): 65–104.
[77] Thomas Greenhill, *Nekrokedeia: Or, the Art of Embalming* (London, 1705), p. 19.

The writer of this text, Thomas Greenhill, drew explicitly on the Bible, where it was promised that each hair on the heads of the faithful was under God's superintendence (Luke 12:7, 21:18). In talking of extracting human matter from the minutest particles, he was also clearly influenced by thinkers such as Donne, Boyle, and Hody, for whom belief in resurrection was bound up with their understanding of atomism. The desire to embalm the body was, as Zigarovich has acknowledged, linked to the incorrupt-ibility (and implied virtue) of saints' bodies. Yet, as Greenhill admitted, the desire to take any care of the body after death – including preserving it or gathering up its amputated parts – might be viewed as incompatible with earnest belief in bodily resurrection. In theory, the body would rise perfected regardless of what happened to it on earth. In practice, missing a body part was clearly a cause for concern.

Conclusion

At many points in the foregoing chapters I have argued that early modern people exercised a remarkable mental flexibility in their discourses about the body. This is nowhere more evident than in approaches to bodily resurrection, and the paradoxes of resurrection become particularly evident when one considers the fate of the altered body. As we have seen, most learned debate on the risen body accepted that God might gather up one's scattered parts wherever they might be. As Donne evocatively put it, He could pluck an amputated arm from one continent and a leg from another as easily as reaching for coins strewn across a table. As Donne's own work reveals, however, this solution failed to quell people's anxieties about whether and in what form their body would rise at the Last Day. If maintaining the *same* body – at least in essentials – was so important, then how was sameness to be measured? The surgical alteration of the body demonstrably affected every aspect of a person's life, so that it was sometimes difficult to conceive of a 'perfected' body which maintained an identity with the lived, impaired individual.

While theologians tried to square this circle, in pious practice, people lived with and even embraced the contradictions. In creative expressions of belief such as Donne's poems, in the miracle stories people favoured, and the ways they buried their dead, one sees the body treated as object and subject, 'me' and 'mine', exterior carcase and lived identity. As so often, anxiety about this matter was most pointedly illustrated through satire. In a 1782 cartoon (Figure 5.3), Thomas Rowlandson depicted William Hunter's famous anatomy museum at the day of the resurrection.

Figure 5.3   'The Resurrection or an Internal View of the Museum [of William Hunter] in Windmill Street, on the Last Day', attributed to Thomas Rowlandson, 1782.
Credit: Wellcome Collection. CC BY

The unfortunate 'owners' of Hunter's collections of disembodied limbs scramble to retrieve their missing parts, which have been lost, stolen, or misappropriated in the confusion. Despite the promises of churchmen, even of the Bible, they are neither recompacted nor miraculously restored. God has forgotten about these altered bodies.

CHAPTER 6

Phantom Limbs and the Hard Problem

In the previous chapters, I have shown how different aspects of bodily alteration may illuminate for us different early modern anxieties and fantasies about the possible uses of the body as a commodity, a relational object, a sign, and a sign-maker. This final chapter will look at a strange phenomenon which affected many surgically altered bodies and posed questions about bodily experience in general. Phantom limb pain (PLP) was an affective phenomenon that was parsed in terms of science, medicine, and philosophy. It provoked those who looked upon it (in person or through the medium of text) to consider what distinguished their own 'real' pains from these 'unreal' bodily sensations. Phantoms provided the most influential natural philosophers of the early modern period with a puzzle in which the role of the body as both subject and object was uppermost.

As Drew Daniel observes of the early modern melancholic, the phantom pain sufferer 'always seems to both require and exceed explanation, at once to need no introduction and to never be able to stop introducing himself'.[1] In my analysis of the topic, I trace the under- and over-determination of phantom limbs through medical and philosophical works. I will, however, consciously avoid the use of phantom limbs as analogy for that which is missing from literary texts. Phantoms, like prostheses, make useful tools for thought. The 'presence of an absence', as Vivian Sobchack terms this phenomenon, is a provocative way of thinking about how a text's omissions might make meaning.[2] Yet, I wish to attend to the historical specificities of phantom limb pain, and in particular to the literature that was generated by thinking about phantom limbs. The 'hard problem' of

---

[1] Drew Daniel, *The Melancholy Assemblage: Affect and Epistemology in the English Renaissance* (New York: Fordham University Press, 2013), p. 6.
[2] Vivian Sobchack, 'Living a "Phantom Limb": On the Phenomenology of Bodily Integrity', *Body and Society* 16:3 (2010): 51–67, https://doi.org/10.1177/1357034X10373407.

this chapter's title is a modern phrase, but one of relevance to the quandary felt by seventeenth- and eighteenth-century natural philosophers in regard to the body. Popularised as a term by David Chalmers in the 1990s, the hard problem describes the puzzle of how consciousness can arise from matter. As Chalmers describes:

> It is undeniable that some organisms are subjects of experience. But the questions of how it is that these systems are subjects of experience is perplexing. Why is it that when our cognitive systems engage in visual and auditory information-processing, we have visual or auditory experience: the quality of deep blue, the sensation of middle C? How can we explain why there is something it's like to entertain a mental image, or to experience an emotion? It is widely agreed that experience arises from a physical basis, but we have no good explanation of why and how it so arises. Why should physical processing give rise to a rich inner life at all?[3]

In modern neuroscience, one can look at a brain scan and see a 'lighting up' which represents what occurs in the brain when we listen to music, or see the colour red. Nonetheless, it remains unclear how exactly the electrical impulses which flow between synapses generate the subjective, abstract experience of melodic sound, or of 'red'. In early modern investigations of the same question, I will argue, concrete representation of thought – the 'lighting up' of the brain – was provided by bodily phenomena. Anomalous bodies or body parts could provide the most illuminating examples, and phantom limbs were arguably the most anomalous body parts of all. The picture was complicated, moreover, by a fundamental difference between early modern and modern philosophies of mind. Whereas today's neuroscientists commonly seek to find a material process to explain the seemingly immaterial phenomenon of thought, seventeenth- and eighteenth-century physicians and philosophers worked against a backdrop of Christian faith which commonly, though not always, assumed the existence of an immaterial and immortal soul as a starting point.

Thinking with Phantoms: Early Modern Theories of Sensation

The first extant observation of what we now call phantom limb pain appears in Ambroise Paré's 1564 *Ten Books of Surgery*.[4] Paré was a skilled

[3] David Chalmers, 'The Hard Problem of Consciousness', in *The Blackwell Companion to Consciousness*, ed. Max Velmans and Susan Schneider (Oxford: Blackwell, 2007), p. 226, https://doi.org/10.1002/9780470751466.ch18.
[4] I am speaking here of the European medical tradition only. Even within this, it is entirely possible that other works on phantom limb pain exist and have not been studied, or once existed and are no

and renowned military surgeon, and he drew on his experiences to suggest remedies for common combat injuries such as burns, fractures, and contusions. In the seventh book, on 'gangrene and mortification', he advises surgeons not to be fooled by patients who report feeling pain in limbs which appear gangrenous. Such sensations, he argues, are merely referred, in the same way that tugging on a garment produces a touch on the skin. Further proof of the tricks pain can play on the brain is evident in the complaints of patients after limb amputation:

> Of this false feeling you will have manifest argument after the amputation of the mortified parts. For the patients, long after the amputation is made, say they still feel pain in the dead and amputated parts. Of this they complain strongly, a thing worthy of wonder, and almost incredible to people who have not experienced this.[5]

What drove this mysterious pain? Another passage in the same book offers this explanation:

> Now, it is so that a long time after the amputation, the patients think they still have in its entirety the member which has been amputated from them (as I have said). This happens to them, as it seems to me, because the nerves withdraw toward their origin and in withdrawing make great pain, almost similar to the retractions which are made in spasms. To remedy this, it is necessary to rub the nape of the neck and the whole affected part with the liniment which follows.[6]

These passages are notable for several reasons. The *Ten Books* were not published in English, but may nonetheless have been read by many English surgeons, who often received training on the continent, and who were substantially influenced by Paré's work. Interestingly, however, the passages were reformulated in the English translation of Paré's *Oeuvres* (first published as the *Workes* in 1634). In this translation, the more

---

longer extant. Certainly, Paré's treatment of the subject implies that he thought other surgeons would be familiar with the phenomenon he describes.

[5] Ambroise Paré, *Ten Books of Surgery with the Magazine of the Instruments Necessary for It*, trans. Robert White Linker and Nathan Womack (Athens: University of Georgia Press, 2010), p. 134. This translation was first published in 1969. Prior to this, the work (published in French in 1564) had not been translated into English, though it is likely to have been read by some English surgeons in the original language, or in the Latin version. Linker and Womack speculate that the reason it was not translated in the early modern period is because most of the material therein was included in some form in Paré's *Oeuvres* and thus in the (widely available) *Workes*.

[6] Ibid., p. 142. The liniment Paré mentions is a concoction of sage, marjoram, rosemary, mint, rue, lavender, camomile, dill, hypericum, laurel, juniper, pellitory, mastic, laserwort, Venice turpentine, 'sweet gum', oil of earthworms, oil of puppies, oil of turpentine, human fat, crocus, white wine, and wax.

detailed aspects of this explanation for phantom limbs were omitted, and emphasis was instead placed on the mystery which surrounded this strange phenomenon. Again, the passage was positioned as a warning to surgeons about patients who reported sensation in gangrenous limbs:

> Here I must admonish the young Chirurgeon, that he be not deceived concerning the loss, or privation, of the sense of the part. For I know very many deceived as thus; the Patients pricked on that [gangrenous] part would say, they felt much pain there. But that feeling is oft deceitful, as that which proceeds rather from the strong apprehension of great pain which formerly raigned in the part, than from any faculty of feeling as yet remaining. A most clear and manifest argument of this false and deceitful sense appears after the amputation of the member; for a long while after they will complain of the part which is cut away.
>
> Verily it is a thing wondrous strange and prodigious, and which will scarse be credited, unless by such as have seen with their eyes, and heard with their ears the Patients, who have many months after the cutting away of the Leg, grevously complained that they yet felt exceeding great pain of that Leg so cut off.[7]

This passage clearly takes much from the first example cited from *Ten Bookes*. However, it substantially adds to that passage, and the choice of language by both author and translator here is worth unpacking.[8] Multiple parties are in danger of 'deception': the patient, the surgeon, and the reader/viewer. Yet Paré's description itself reinforces the 'existence' of the phantom limb. The various onlookers in this case must 'see with their eyes' and 'hear with their ears' to know the case reliably. However, the phantom pain sufferer, by Paré's own admission, feels 'with her limb', inasmuch as they complain 'of the Leg' as distinct from the stump. To 'apprehend' in this period means 'to lay hold of' in many different senses: to restrain with the hands, to grasp with the intellect, to perceive sensorially, to feel emotionally, and to learn of.[9] The translator's choice of this term thus

---

[7] Ambroise Paré, *The Workes of That Famous Chirurgion Ambrose Parey Translated out of Latine and Compared with the French. by Th: Johnson* (London: printed by Th. Cotes and R. Young, 1634), p. 457.

[8] The influence of the translator on this text may need further study – a brief but informative article from the James Lind Library suggests that 'It is unfortunate that this, the only fairly complete English edition of Paré's works, was derived from the less than perfect Latin editions; though the title claims "compared with the French" it seems that Johnson's French was not equal to the task. In spite of this, the Jacobean English of the translation suits Paré's often racy style very well and the book is in many ways delightful, if not always very accurate.' 'Paré A (1575)', *James Lind Library*, 26 May 2010, accessed 7 November 2019, www.jameslindlibrary.org/pare-a-1575/.

[9] 'Apprehension, N.', in *OED Online* (Oxford University Press), accessed 4 August 2017, www.oed.com/view/Entry/9808.

reflects the multivalency of the phantom, which is at once absent and present, unable to be apprehended by the eye and unable to *stop* being apprehended by nociception. Likewise, this phenomenon is at once 'prodigious' (that is, both 'causing wonder' and 'portentous', with connotations of the supernatural), and a natural response to be expected by the diligent surgeon.[10]

In the *Workes*, Paré's description of the phantom limb was pragmatic, but clearly fascinated by the 'wondrous strange[ness]' of the phenomenon. However, his earlier analysis of 'spasms' as the cause of PLP was ignored, and only resurfaced more than fifty years later in the composite text *Somatographia Anthropine*. Published in 1634, this text took a far more confident stance on phantom pain:

> it is ordinary for the Patient, long after the member is cut off to imagine he yet hath it, and that he feeles paine in it. Now you must know that this is not altogether without cause. For the nerve or sinew which is cut in sunder, contracts it selfe towards his originall, and that contraction induces a paine much like a convulsion. For as Galen writeth in his booke, *De motu musculorum*, the proper action of a nerve and a muscle is contraction. Their tension is not so much an action as a motion. Wherefore you may ease that convulsive paine, by annointing the ridge of the backe, and the whole member also, with this following Liniment.[11]

The language in which these authors proffer a cure suggests that they too are not immune to the hypnotic effects of the phantom limb, talking of anointing the 'whole member' despite the fact that it is the 'unwholeness' of the member which generates the ailment in the first place. Gone, however, is the *Workes'* emphasis on the parallel apprehensions of the viewer/reader and the patient, along with its admission of PLP's strangeness. Where Paré's account is awestruck, that of *Somatographia Anthropine*

---

[10] 'Prodigious, Adj. (and Int.) and Adv.', in *OED Online* (Oxford University Press), accessed 13 December 2019, www.oed.com/view/Entry/151951.

[11] Alexander Read, *Somatographia Anthropine, or, a Description of the Body of Man. With the Practise of Chirurgery, and the Use of Three and Fifty Instruments*, 2nd edition (London: printed by Thomas Cotes, and sold by Michael Sparke, 1634), p. 114. First published in 1616, this text was designed as an octavo-sized companion volume to Helkiah Crooke's anatomical treatise *Mikrokosmographia: a Description of the Body of Man* (a text commissioned by the printer William Jaggard in 1615). *Somatographia* contains illustrations from *Mikrokosmographia*, some of which are altered. It has a preface by Alexander Read, and is usually listed as authored by Read, sometimes by Jaggard or Crooke. The most comprehensive explanation of this relationship I have found is Jillian Faith Linster, 'Books, Bodies, and the "Great Labor" of Helkiah Crooke's *Mikrokosmographia*,' Ph.D. (University of Iowa, 2017), pp. 43–73. See also Lauren Kassell, 'Medical Understandings of the Body', in *The Routledge History of Sex and the Body*, ed. Kate Fisher and Sarah Toulalan (Abingdon: Routledge, 2013), pp. 57–74.

is remarkable for its coolness, accepting as entirely natural and 'ordinary' a bodily event without any perceptible cause.[12] Moreover, the sufferer of phantom pain is no longer united with the surgeon in perplexity at this 'deceitful' sensation. It is the patient who 'imagine[s]' that he 'yet hath' his amputated limb, and that it causes him pain. By contrast, for the medical professional, the phantom limb is both entirely explicable and eminently curable.

What changed between the *Workes*' account of 'wondrous strange' phantom pains and *Somatographia Anthropine*'s description of the same phenomenon as 'ordinary'? Why was the nerve spasm theory advanced in *Ten Bookes* omitted from English translations of Paré, and then picked up several decades later? Part of the shift clearly involves the distancing of the medical practitioner from their patient, as part of a teleology of professionalisation among surgeons. In addition, however, the explanation offered by *Ten Bookes*, and later by *Somatographia Anthropine*, was engaged with theories about pain which became popular in England during the first half of the seventeenth century. Early seventeenth-century philosophers and physicians became increasingly focussed on sensation as an area for investigation.[13] Bolstered by Pierre Gassendi's revival of atomism in France, many came to regard those sensations as produced and relayed, in some hydraulic fashion, by the nerves and spinal cord.[14] As Darren Wagner describes

> Among the contending theories, that of a nervous fluid coursing through a minuscule tubal structure of nerves gained the most credence. Publications by individuals such as René Descartes (1596–1650), William Harvey (1578–1657), Renier de Graaf (1641–1673), Thomas Bartholin (1616–1680), Walter Charleton (1619–1707) and especially Thomas Willis (1621–1675) advanced theories and principles about that nervous fluid, the animal spirits ... Animal spirits were see as a protean and fluid substance, extremely subtle, easily agitated, highly rarefied, fine and thin, lying just beyond the scope of visual observation. Produced in the brain and

---

[12] In this respect it is odd that more surgical texts do not mention phantom limb pain, particularly as modern research estimates that up to 80 per cent of amputees will experience the sensation, usually soon after surgery (Laxmaiah Manchikanti, Vijay Singh, and Mark V. Boswell, 'Phantom Pain Syndromes', in *Pain Management*, ed. Steven D. Waldman (Philadelphia: W. B. Saunders, 2007), pp. 304–15, https://doi.org/10.1016/B978-0-7216-0334-6.50032-7). However, at least some of this reticence may be explained by the fact that most surgeons were not involved in long-term aftercare for their patients, and that a much smaller proportion of amputees survived their operation to be able to report such sensations.

[13] Sydney Ochs, *A History of Nerve Functions: From Animal Spirits to Molecular Mechanisms* (Cambridge: Cambridge University Press, 2004), pp. 63–107.

[14] Ibid., p. 63.

circulated via nerves, they seemed to move 'quicker than the twinkling of an Eye'. In function, they conveyed sensation, desire and motion. This ethereal fluid bridged the gap between the physical and the metaphysical, the body and the soul.[15]

While 'animal spirits' had long been a part of the lexicon for describing sensation, they were increasingly situated within theories of nerve vibration and tension. Matthew Cobb notes that 'Through a precise mechanical analogy, the original vague vitalism was transformed into a modern mechanistic conception.'[16] Scholars of various stripes were growing used to the notion that feeling had some material basis, though that basis might be mysterious and ill-understood. In so doing, they became increasingly interested in what phantom limbs could reveal about the nature of pain.

Descartes and Phantom Pain

Appropriately, the most famous figure in the project to understand sensation was also the man who had most to say about the phantom limb phenomenon. In a handful of passages from across his philosophical works, René Descartes established a way of thinking about phantom limb pain that lasted for well over a century. For its part, PLP furnished Descartes with a test case that shaped his ideas about perception and sensation, and exposed vulnerabilities in the dualist model. His interest in this topic began relatively early in his philosophical career. In a 1637 letter addressed to 'Plempius', but intended for the Belgian theologian Libert Froidmont, Descartes expresses his fascination with phantom limbs and the philosophical usefulness he finds in this phenomenon:

> He [Froidmont] expresses surprise that on page 30 I recognize no sensation save that which takes place in the brain. On this point I hope that all doctors and surgeons will help me to persuade him; for they know that those whose limbs have recently been amputated often think they still feel pain in the parts they no longer possess. I once knew a girl who had a serious wound in her hands and had her whole arm amputated because of a creeping gangrene. Whenever the surgeon approached her they blindfolded her eyes so that she would be more tractable, and the place where her arm

[15] Darren N. Wagner, 'Body, Mind and Spirits: the Physiology of Sexuality in the Culture of Sensibility', *Journal for Eighteenth-Century Studies* 39:3 (2016): 337, https://doi.org/10.1111/1754-0208.12336.
[16] Matthew Cobb, 'Exorcizing the Animal Spirits: Jan Swammerdam on Nerve Function', *National Review of Neuroscience* 3:5 (2002): 397, https://doi.org/10.1038/nrn806. On animal spirits and mechanistic models, see also Julian Jaynes, 'The Problem of Animate Motion in the Seventeenth Century', *Journal of the History of Ideas* 31:2 (1970): 219–34, https://doi.org/10.2307/2708546.

had been was so covered with bandages that for some weeks she did not know she had lost it. Meanwhile she complained of feeling various pains in her fingers, wrist, and forearm; and this was obviously due to the condition of the nerves in her arm which formerly led from her brain to those parts of her body. This would certainly not have happened if the feeling or, as he says, sensation of pain occurred outside the brain.[17]

The explanation Descartes gives for phantom pain here concurs broadly with that given in *Somatographia Anthropine*: pain arises from the irritation of the severed nerves which previously led to the amputated part. Importantly, the fact that Descartes uses PLP as evidence to bolster the claims of his own natural philosophical writings shows how interwoven the philosopher's concept of pain was with his concept of vision. Both, as I will demonstrate, rested on the fundamental belief that one could not take the veracity of the object world for granted – could not, in fact, assume certain knowledge of anything beyond *cogito ergo sum*. The text to which Descartes refers above is presumably his *Discourse on Method*, published in the same year. In the sixth discourse of that text, 'Of Vision', Descartes explains that while the eye is the instrument of vision, it is not the eye that *perceives* objects:

> Now although this picture [of the physical world] in being so transmitted into our head, always retains some resemblance to the objects from which it proceeds, nevertheless, as I have already shown, we must not hold that it is by means of this resemblance that the picture causes us to perceive the objects as if there were yet other eyes in our brain with which we could apprehend it; but rather, that it is the movements of which the picture is composed which, acting immediately on our mind inasmuch as it is united to our body, are so established by nature as to make it have such perceptions.[18]

Much as in the case of pain sensations, Descartes believed that stimulation of the nerves on the retina provoked a movement of animal spirits, which would then pass into a ventricle of the brain and on to the pineal gland, which caused the perception of a sighted object. As Ochs explains,

> The soul, the rational cognitive thinking soul ... expresses its actions through the pineal gland. Sensory inputs passing by means of animal spirits

---

[17] Extract from a letter to Plempius for Fromondus [Libert Froidmont, Belgian theologian and scientist], 3 October 1637, in René Descartes, *The Philosophical Writing of Descartes, Volume III: The Correspondence*, trans. John Cottingham et al. (Cambridge: Cambridge University Press, 1991), p. 64.

[18] René Descartes, *Discourse on Method, Optics, Geometry, and Meteorology* (1637), trans. Paul J. Olscamp (Indianapolis: Hackett, 2001), p. 101.

in nerve tubules project them onto the pineal gland. There, sensations are perceived and animal spirits are directed by the soul into the proper nerve tubules to effect muscle movements.[19]

Descartes' thoughts on vision were not only a matter for physiologists. As the hot topic of seventeenth-century natural philosophy, 'the problematics of vision' were, in Stuart Clark's words, '[t]he agenda for all really serious thought'.[20] Central to Cartesian wisdom on the issue was the principle of 'non-resemblance' between objects and visual perceptions. Though material things possessed the properties of extension (i.e. taking up space in the world) and geometry (shape, size, and motion), other qualities, such as colour, existed in the eye of the beholder. A group of onlookers might agree, for instance, that an object was red, but the perception of 'redness' was generated individually in each person's mind, rather than inhering in the viewed object. Clark explains:

> Sensing is occurring [in the eye], but not perception – not 'seeing' – the functioning of a machine (which, by definition, is without judgement), not the understanding of a thinking mind: '[I]t is the soul which sees', declared Descartes famously, 'and not the eye; and it does not see directly, but only by means of the brain.'[21]

The preceding chapters have shown that early modern people conceived of embodiment in varied and often fluctuating ways: the body could be imagined as entirely entwined with one's mental subjectivity, or as utterly divorced from it. Feelings of every kind were felt to be generated in a complex relationship between the passions, intellect, and soul, such that raw affect and mediated emotion were in practice virtually impossible to separate.[22] Descartes' theory of non-resemblance appeared to offer clarity in these murky waters. Non-resemblance meant that there was no innate correspondence between outside stimuli and cognitive experience. Impulses provoked in the nerves by exogenous stimuli had no affective meaning in themselves, and to experience pain 'in' one's finger was as illusory as experiencing dread 'in' the pit of one's stomach.

---

[19] Ochs, *A History of Nerve Functions*, p. 64.
[20] Stuart Clark, *Vanities of the Eye: Vision in Early Modern European Culture* (Oxford: Oxford University Press, 2007), p. 332.
[21] Ibid., p. 342.
[22] 'Affect' is used here in the way suggested by Jan Plamper, to signify 'nonconscious, nonsignified, inchoate states'. 'Jan Plamper On the History of Emotions | The History of Emotions Blog', accessed 5 September 2017, https://emotionsblog.history.qmul.ac.uk/2017/09/jan-plamper-on-the-history-of-emotions/.

Because they generated a false picture of the body, phantom limbs seemed to exemplify non-resemblance, and so Descartes returned to this phenomenon throughout his philosophical career. In 1644, for instance, his *Principles* mentioned again the case of the girl with the phantom hand:

> She had various pains, sometimes in one of the fingers of the hand which was cut off, and sometimes in another. This could clearly only happen because the nerves which previously had been carried all the way from the brain to the hand, and afterwards terminated in the arm near the elbow, were there affected in the same way as it was their function to be stimulated for the purpose of impressing on the mind residing in the brain the sensation of pain in this and that finger.[23]

In this case, phantom limb pain was presented as proving the non-resemblance of pain sensations specifically. Descartes explained: 'the soul feels those things that affect the body not in so far as it is in each member of the body, but only in so far as it is in the brain'.[24] Thus it was possible that in rare cases, '[w]e sometimes feel pain as though it were in certain of our members, and yet its cause is not in those members where it is felt, but in others through which the nerves pass that extend to the brain from the parts where the pain is felt'.[25] Phantom limb pain was thus explained by, and simultaneously taken as evidence for, the 'bell-cord' theory of pain which Descartes famously outlined in his *On Man* (written 1630–3 but published posthumously in 1662). Aided by the illustration shown in Figure 6.1, Descartes argued:

> if the fire A is close to the foot B, the small particles of fire, which as you know move very swiftly, are able to move as well the part of the skin which they touch on the foot. In this way, by pulling at the little thread cc, which you see attached there, they at the same instant open e, which is the entry for the pore d, which is where this small thread terminates; just as, by pulling one end of a cord, you ring a bell which hangs at the other end . . . Now when the entry of the pore, or the little tube, de, has thus been opened, the animal spirits flow into it from the cavity F, and through it they are carried partly into the muscles which serve to pull the foot back from the fire, partly into those which serve to turn the eyes and the head to look at it, and partly into those which serve to move the hands forward and to turn the whole body for its defense.[26]

---

[23] René Descartes, 'Principles of Philosophy', in *The Philosophical Works of Descartes*, trans. Elizabeth S. Haldane and G. R. T. Ross, vol. 1 (of 2) (Cambridge: Cambridge University Press, 1912), pp. 293–4.
[24] Ibid., p. 293.   [25] Ibid., pp. 294.
[26] René Descartes, *Treatise of Man* (1662), trans. Thomas Steele Hall (Amherst: Prometheus Books, 2003), pp. 33–4.

Figure 6.1   Descartes, 'The Path of Burning Pain. Comme elle est incitee par les objets
exterieurs a se mouvoir en plusiers manieres'.
Credit: Wellcome Collection. CC BY

The bell-cord theory proved immensely appealing to generations
of physicians.[27] In particular, its presentation of pain as reliant on
the transmission of some substance through the nerves seemed to
anticipate the biochemical model of nociception which emerged some

---

[27] Joanna Bourke discusses the long and varied afterlife of Descartes' model in her *The Story of Pain:
From Prayer to Painkillers* (Oxford: Oxford University Press, 2014), especially pp. 12–13.

250 years later.[28] Furthermore, the wide reach of Descartes' work ensured that both the principle of non-resemblance and the phantom pain phenomenon used to illustrate that model influenced writers on a surprisingly broad range of topics. These writers included Antoine de Courtin, the author of *A Treatise of Jealousie* (1684). De Courtin speculated that jealousy might have a physiological basis – something which he argued was possible because of the capacity of the senses to deceive the understanding. This capacity relied in turn on a neurocentric model of sensation, in which de Courtin clearly drew from Descartes' works:

> Now as it is this Organ [the brain] that receives the Impressions or the Species that are sent thither by the External Organs or Senses, it must by Consequence be in this Place, and in the Brain that Sensation or the Perception which we have of things is perform'd, and not at all in the External Senses themselves, or any other part of the Body. For although the outward Senses are as the Instruments, that the Imagination makes use of, for the Reception of the Species of Sensible Objects; although they are as the ports of the Soul, by which the Species do enter; yet the Objects are Imprinted, and as it were Limned in these Organs (for we find by Experience that we see by the Eyes, hear with the Ears, and that the Hand or Foot gives us the Sense of Pain) nevertheless without all doubt, we can have no Sensation, no Perception or discerning, if the Species or Impressions have not passage to the Principal Seat of the Imagination or Common Sense. We have experience thereof in this, that if we [are] very attentive to any thing, we perceive not the Pain of any hurt received, nor do we see the things that are before our Eyes; as it happens to these that are Apoplectick, they perceive not at all when they are pricked, no nor when they are Wounded, which must proceed from hence, that the Organ of the Imagination ceasing its Action, it receives no Impression, and consequently it produces no Sensation; And what is more, these that have, for Example, their hand Amputated, do complain of great Pains in that very Hand, that was cut off.[29]

De Courtin's use of phantom limbs as an example in a text entirely unrelated to that subject shows that, following Descartes, this

---

[28] S. Scott Graham, *The Politics of Pain Medicine: a Rhetorical-Ontological Inquiry* (Chicago: University of Chicago Press, 2015), pp. 49–50.

[29] Antoine de Courtin, *A Treatise of Jealousie, or, Means to Preserve Peace in Marriage Wherein Is Treated of I. The Nature and Effects of Jealousie, Which for the Most Part Is the Fatal Cause of Discontents between Man and Wife, II. And Because Jealousy Is a Passion, It's Therefore Occasionally Discoursed of Passions in General, Giving and Exact Idea of the Production of Passions, and of the Oeconomie of the Body so Far as It Relates Thereunto. III. The Reciprocal Duties of Man and Wife, with Infallible Means to Preserve Peace in the Family, by Avoiding Dissentions That May Arise from Jealousie, or Any Other Cause Whatever* (London: printed for W. Freeman, 1684), pp. 14–15.

phenomenon acquired scholastic interest as a set-piece, a physical anomaly meant to prove the rule that inward perceptions did not always match up with outward realities. De Courtin's language here bespeaks his interest in the subject of perception in general; the encroachment of 'species' on the nervous system was an Aristotelian idea, rooted in the notion that objects in the world consisted of both matter and form ('species'). Though the neurocentric model de Courtin embraces jettisoned the idea of 'species', this term clearly remained in the minds of omnivorous readers. At the same time, however, de Courtin's reading of the bell-cord theory, understood through the prism of phantom limb pain, downplayed the role of the body and the sense organs in perception by casting them as mere 'instruments' for the use of a subjective self which was apparently located elsewhere. In de Courtin's interpretation, both affect and emotions – including jealousy – are reoriented from visceral to purely cognitive, a departure from the humoral schema in which melancholy, anger and so forth were conditions of both body and soul. 'Sensation', argued de Courtin, 'is perform'd in the imagination, and not in the External Organs, or parts of the Body, whereon the first Impression is made, so likewise the Passions are not form'd in the Heart; as some believe, but in the same Imagination also.'[30] Notably, in this formulation, 'External Organs' include not only those organs, such as the skin, which interface with outside stimuli, but *any* organ which is not the mind.

De Courtin's passage was clearly meant to be an endorsement of Descartes' non-resemblance theory, and it is notable that he saw phantom limbs as among the most pertinent proofs of that theory. At the same time, however, some of the examples which de Courtin cited as evidence of sensory unreliability were clearly problematic. Apoplexies and other mental disorders were believed to be caused by disordered passions or animal spirits, but it was by no means clear how the material substance of those spirits acted on the immaterial mind to cause symptoms such as insensibility. Descartes' explanation for phantom limb pain was that since the mind was connected to the body at a single point (the brain, specifically the pineal gland), it was possible that motions of the pineal gland might be effected from time to time by stimuli which did not accord with what was typical (nerve impulses that did not 'really' come from a limb, for instance). This provoked both neurophysiological and epistemological questions. Physiologically, phantom limb pain was described as seeming to come from one point in a nervous pathway when in fact it derived from

[30] Ibid., p. 17.

another. However, as Tommy Lott has noted, it was unclear how Descartes supposed that nerve impulses conveyed information about the location of a pain signal at all.[31] He seems to have believed that location was somehow intrinsic in the response that stimulation of the neural pathways produced in the brain, though exactly how this occurred was ambiguous.

More troubling for Descartes, and for many of his critics, was the epistemological issue of human reason versus sensory unreliability. The fact of non-resemblance meant that the body could deceive the person 'inside', and, as Descartes noted, this worrying potential was epitomised by phantom limb pain:

> I have learned from some persons whose arms or legs have been cut off, that they sometimes seemed to feel pain in the part which had been amputated, which made me think that I could not be quite certain that it was a certain member which pained me, even although I felt pain in it.[32]

It was thus necessary to doubt not only the existence of outside objects, but even the nature of pain in one's own body. Despite this observation, Descartes argued that God had paired sensations with effects on the pineal gland in the way that worked in the majority of cases, and could not have done otherwise given the nature of the connection between mind and body.[33] 'It is quite clear,' he argued, 'that, notwithstanding the supreme goodness of God, the nature of man, inasmuch as it is composed of mind and body, cannot be otherwise than sometimes a source of deception.'[34] However, in the rare case where a nerve 'message' was deceptive – as in phantom pain – a human being's God-given rationality was capable of sorting out the confusion, since one would look at one's stump, remember the amputation, and be corrected. This accorded with a central tenet of Descartes' world-view – the notion that a benevolent God would not allow humans to be deceived, and that one could therefore (with the help of reason) trust in the reality of the perceived world. Wilson notes that

> In considering God's benevolence in the Fourth Meditation Descartes maintained that such a benign creator could not have given him a faculty

[31] Tommy L. Lott, 'Descartes on Phantom Limbs', *Mind and Language* 1:3 (1986): 248–9, https://doi.org/10.1111/j.1468-0017.1986.tb00103.x.

[32] René Descartes, 'Meditation VI', in *The Philosophical Works of Descartes*, vol. 1 (of 2), trans. Elizabeth S. Haldane and G. R. T. Ross (Cambridge: Cambridge University Press, 1912), p. 189.

[33] Sarah Patterson, 'Descartes on the Errors of the Senses', *Royal Institute of Philosophy Supplement* 78 (2016): 73–108.

[34] Descartes, 'Meditation VI', p. 198.

that would lead him into error if he used it rightly. The partial vindication of the senses, however, is made to rest on a different principle: that God would not allow me to fall into any error which He did not give me the power to correct. This principle is needed to affirm the existence of material objects, since Descartes apparently wants to hold back from saying their existence is clearly and distinctly perceived.[35]

While this approach seemed to reconcile bodily deception and divine design, it fell short as an explanation for phantom limb pain, in which 'the power to correct' sensory anomaly was conspicuously absent. Looking at Descartes' example in the context of contemporary medical texts, we can see how the 'faulty senses corrected by reason' explanation elides the particular 'strangeness' of phantom limbs which had long been identified by Paré and Read. These authors recognised that knowing intellectually that a phantom limb is not real *does not* stop the 'limb' from hurting; rather, it is the cognitive dissonance between what is seen and what is felt that makes phantom limb pain so distressing.

Whether Descartes recognised that phantom limbs were immune to reason in this way is debatable. As was the case for many of this book's sources, he seemingly regarded people with disabilities – in this case, phantom limb pain sufferers – as people to think with, rather than to talk to. Nonetheless, it is clear that the experience and the theory of pain were hard to reconcile, even for avowed adherents of dualism. This was demonstrably the case for the eighteenth-century scientist William Porterfield (*c.* 1696–1771). Porterfield was an eminent Scottish physician, who shared with Descartes, Thomas Willis, Hobbes, and others a particular interest in the mechanics of vision.[36] He was also the first person to publish an autobiographical account of phantom limb pain, as a part of his *Treatise on the Eye* (1759). Just as Descartes had done more than a century earlier, he marshalled the phantom limb in service of his understanding of sensory perception, and his account is worth citing at length:

> It is ... evident, that, did the Mind perceive Pictures in the *Retina*, it behoved to be there present: And for the same Reason, did it perceive in the other Organs of Sense, it behoved to be there present: And for the same Reason, did it perceive in the other Organs of Sense, it behoved also to be present to all the parts of the Body; because the Sense of Feeling is diffused thro' all the Body: Nay in some Cases it behoved to be extended beyond the

[35] Margaret Dauler Wilson, *Descartes* (Abingdon: Routledge and K. Paul, 1978), p. 202.
[36] Nicholas J. Wade, 'The Vision of William Porterfield', in *Brain, Mind and Medicine: Essays in Eighteenth-Century Neuroscience*, ed. Harry Whitaker, C. U. M. Smith, and Stanley Finger (Leiden: Springer, 2007), pp. 163–77.

Body itself, as in the Case of Amputations, where the Person, after the Loss of his Limb, has the same Perception of Pain, Itching, &c. as before, and feels them as if they were in some Part of his Limb, tho' it had long ago been amputated, and removed from that Place where the Mind places the Sensation. Having had this Misfortune myself, I can the better vouch the Truth of this Fact from my own Experience; for I sometimes still feel Pains and Itching, as if in my Toes, Heel or Ancle, &c. tho' it be several Years since my Leg was taken off. Nay, these Itchings have sometimes been so strong and lively, that, in spite of all my Reason and Philosophy, I could scarce forbear attempting to scratch the Part, tho' I well knew there was nothing there in the Place where I felt the Itching. And however strange this may appear to some, it is nevertheless no way miraculous or extraordinary, but very agreeable to the usual Course and Tenor of Nature; for, tho' all our Sensations are Passions or Perceptions produced in the Mind itself, yet the Mind never considers them as such, but, by an irresistible Law of our Nature, it is always made to refer them to something external, and at a Distance from the Mind; for it always considers them as belonging either to the Object, the Organs, or both, but never as belonging to the Mind itself, in which they truly are; and therefore, when the nervous Fibres in the Stump are affected in the same manner as they used to be by Objects acting on their Extremities in the Toes, Heel or Ancle, the same Notice or Information must be carried to the Mind, and the Mind must have the same Sensation, and form the same Judgment concerning it, *viz.* that it is at a Distance from it, as if in the Toes, Heel or Ancle, tho' these have long ago been taken off and removed from that Place where the Mind places the Sensation.

If this should prove hard to be conceived, It may be illustrated by what happens in the Sensation of Colours; for tho' the Colours we perceive are present with the Mind, and in the *Sensorium*, yet we judge them at a Distance from us, and in the Objects we look at; and it is not more difficult to conceive how Pain may be felt at a Distance from us, than how Colours are seen at a Distance from us.[37]

As Nicholas Wade recognises, Porterfield 'displayed considerable sophistication in the analysis of his phantom limb, by associating the projective features of the experience with other aspects of perception'.[38] Porterfield's treatment of his own pain as merely a useful example for illustrating his theory of vision reflects both the intellectual idealism of the Enlightenment and the subordination of the physical to the mental which is implied in the Cartesian world-view. Porterfield developed Descartes'

---

[37] William Porterfield, *A Treatise on the Eye, the Manner and Phænomena of Vision*, vol. 1 (of 2) (Edinburgh: printed for A. Miller at London, and for G. Hamilton and J. Balfour at Edinburgh, 1759), pp. 363–5.
[38] Wade, 'The Vision of William Porterfield', p. 174.

theory of optics by developing a much more detailed understanding of the anatomy of the eye, and by dwelling at greater length on the fact that objects perceived in the mind were nonetheless sensorially positioned as 'out' in the world. His reference to colour here also demonstrates his indebtedness to Newtonian colour theory, which posited that the experience of colour was subjective, rather than intrinsic in rays of light.[39] Of particular interest to Porterfield was the spatiality of perception: the fact of sensations seeming to be produced 'at a distance' from the mind, which was as much a product of his work on physiology as of his philosophy.[40] Throughout Porterfield's investigations into perceptual theory, his ideological debt to Cartesianism is evident:

> Now, as Objects seen by Reflection or Refraction appear and are seen, not in their true Place, but in some other Place from which they are absent, and that because the Rays fall upon the Eyes, and make a Picture on their Bottom, in the very same Manner as if they had come from the Object really placed there, without the Interposition of the Glass; so, when the Impression made upon the nervous Fibres of the Stump is the same as if it had come from an Object acting on their Extremities, the Sensation must also be the same, and the Mind, by forming the same Judgment concerning it, must feel it as in the Toes, Heel, or Ancle, &c. in which those nervous Fibres terminated before the Leg was taken off.[41]

Here Porterfield seems to be referring specifically to Descartes' example of the stick placed in water, which appears bent but is, by reason, understood merely to seem that way because of the effect of refraction.[42] He does so in service of a theory of perception which identifies both phantom limb pain and optical illusions as evidence for sensory non-resemblance. The use of phantom limbs to support the notion that sensation and perception were localised in the brain rather than the body was, as Wade notes, also taken up in the late eighteenth century by Charles Bell and Johannes Müller.[43] Indeed, in her work on pain, Roselyne Rey argues that a dualist

---

[39] Ibid., p. 174.

[40] Porterfield was the first to describe the 'accommodation' of the eye, whereby structures such as the lens and pupil alter in response to focussing on a near or distant object. 'William Porterfield | Portraits of European Neuroscientists', accessed 7 August 2017, http://neuroportraits.eu/portrait/william-porterfield.

[41] Porterfield, *A Treatise on the Eye*, vol. 1, pp. 366–7.

[42] Bruce Stansfield Eastwood, 'Descartes on Refraction: Scientific versus Rhetorical Method', *Isis* 75:3 (1984): 481–502, https://doi.org/10.1086/353568.

[43] Of note, phantom penises were also reported by several late eighteenth-century physicians, including John Hunter. Nicholas J. Wade and Stanley Finger, 'Phantom Penis: Historical Dimensions', *Journal of the History of the Neurosciences* 19:4 (2010): 299–312, https://doi.org/10.1080/09647040903363006).

explanation of phantom limb syndrome was conceptually necessary to mechanistic investigations of the body and brain:

> It was necessary to explain mental phenomena such as the hallucinations of madness or the pains of amputees, which were lumped together since in neither case could one blame an external cause that would have been liable to affect the nerves. In so doing, the 'mechanist' physicians conceded that 'one cause, whatever it might be, would produce the same change in the brain as would have happened had there been a nerve fibre ... so disposed that its dissolution could have been a consequence.'[44]

The most interesting part of Porterfield's account, however, may be less his rationalisation of his pains than his admission that 'I could scarce forbear attempting to scratch the Part, tho' I well knew there was nothing there'. In Porterfield's frustration with his own response to the painful 'part', one sees another irony of phantom limb pain. As Descartes recognised, pain was a profoundly intimate phenomenon, seemingly more immediate than any other. Notwithstanding this fact, pain was also, as phenomenologists and historians of emotion have shown, socially and culturally mediated.[45] While one might not be able to feel another's pain directly (though as Chapter 3 has shown, the limits of sympathy were up for debate), one can at least liken it to similar feelings from one's own experience, or can look at a person's injury and surmise its painfulness. In the case of phantom limb pain, this possibility is diminished. The phantom limb's lack of objective existence also shuts down the intersubjective networks within which bodily experience is partly lived out.[46] For Porterfield, the nature of his pain seems to have been particularly galling because of his status as a man of science, who could not resist scratching his missing leg *'in spite* of all my Reason and Philosophy'; this man dedicated to mapping the human body found that his own proprioceptive

---

[44] Roselyne Rey, *The History of Pain*, trans. Louise Elliot Wallace, J. A. Cadden, and S. W. Cadden (Cambridge: Harvard University Press, 1995), pp. 103–4.

[45] The topic of pain has been prominent in recent scholarship of the early modern period, with all analyses recognising the cultural specificity and sociality of pain: see Louise Hide, Joanna Bourke, and Carmen Mangion, 'Perspectives on Pain: Introduction', *19: Interdisciplinary Studies in the Long Nineteenth Century*, 15 (2012), https://doi.org/10.16995/ntn.663; Bourke, *The Story of Pain*; Jonathan Sawday, '"I Feel Your Pain": Some Reflections on the (Literary) Perception of Pain', in *The Hurt(Ful) Body: Performing and Beholding Pain, 1600–1800*, ed. Tomas Macsotay, Cornelis Van der Haven, and Karl Vanhaesebrouck (Manchester: Manchester University Press, 2017) pp. 97–114; Jan Frans van Dijkhuizen and Karl Enenkel, *The Sense of Suffering: Constructions of Physical Pain in Early Modern Culture* (Leiden: Brill, 2009); Michael C. Schoenfeldt, 'Shakespearean Pain', in *Shakespearean Sensations: Experiencing Literature in Early Modern England*, ed. Katharine A. Craik and Tanya Pollard (Cambridge: Cambridge University Press, 2013), pp. 191–207.

[46] See Tilmouth, 'Passion and Intersubjectivity in Early Modern Literature', pp. 24–31.

powers had failed him. Indeed, his use of this experience to explicate his scientific theory of vision may have been in part an attempt to exercise control over his uncontrollable phantom by bringing it into line with his vision of himself as a rational creature. Phantom limbs thus exemplified the resistance of the body to sociability and to intellectualism, its resistance to being understood 'from the outside'. As Betty Bayer eloquently suggests,

> quickened by historical struggles and negotiations around doubt, contro-versy, and skepticism troubling the subject of Enlightenment science, phantoms open science onto the terrain of subjectivism, fears, and desires (secret and known). To inquire into the transversals of spirits animating relations between humans and nonhumans, bodies and machines in the production of scientific knowledge is to raise the specter of divine truth, to query those ways in which the imaginary and the rational coextend and dwell in one another.[47]

The Hard Problem

Offering up bodily feeling unbounded by the body itself, phantom limbs proffered a disconcerting excess of subjectivity, whereby the perceived limits of the body failed to contain the feeling 'self'. This de-segregation of 'the imaginary and the rational', or of self-subject and body-object, also presented Cartesian dualism with its most serious stumbling block. In his wider discussion of sensation, Porterfield found it necessary to refute the notion of the soul as extended throughout the body (a notion explored in Chapter 5 of this book). Such an idea, he insisted, implied that the soul had different capabilities in the different areas in which it existed – that of seeing in the eyes, hearing in the ears, and so on. Though Porterfield scoffed at this notion, however, it exposed a weakness in the dualist model which troubled even its most devoted proponents: the question of *how*, exactly, the body and soul could interact. This dilemma – the so-called 'hard problem' – had been raised with Descartes many times. Most notably, it was a central theme of his extensive correspondence with Princess Elisabeth of Bohemia (1618–80), the grand-daughter of James I. As Lisa Shapiro has observed, in the pair's correspondence Elisabeth repeatedly presses Descartes on the issue of how the immaterial and the

---

[47] Betty M. Bayer, 'Between Apparatuses and Apparitions: Phantoms of the Laboratory', in *Reconstructing the Psychological Subject: Bodies, Practices, and Technologies*, ed. John Shotter and Betty M. Bayer (London: Sage, 1998), p. 188.

material (the mind and the animal spirits) can influence one another, and in particular, why it should be the case that a physical indisposition can affect the mind. In June 1643, for example, she writes:

> I admit *that it would be easier for me to concede matter and extension to the* *soul than to concede the capacity to move a body and to be moved by it to an* *immaterial thing.* For, if the first is achieved through information, it would be necessary that the spirits, which cause the movements, were intelligent, a capacity you accord to nothing corporeal. And even though . . . you show the possibility of the second, it is altogether very difficult to understand that a soul, as you have described it, after having had the faculty and the custom of reasoning well, can lose all of this by some vapors, *and that, being able to* *subsist without the body, and having nothing in common with it, the soul is still* *so governed by it.*[48]

Elisabeth's attention was drawn to this issue once again after she wrote to the philosopher complaining of a cough. He, considering the ailment to be caused by stress, advised her to meditate upon her soul and her own strength as a means to wellness. His response provoked another question from Elisabeth. If mind and body were truly separate, she wondered, how could mental attitude affect physical wellbeing?

> I do not yet know how to rid myself of the doubt that one can arrive at the true happiness of which you speak without the assistance of that which does not depend absolutely on the will. For there are diseases that destroy altogether the power of reasoning and by consequence that of enjoying a satisfaction of reason. There are others that diminish the force of reason and prevent one from following the maxims that good sense would have forged and that make the most moderate man subject to being carried away by his passion.[49]

Judging by her correspondence, Elisabeth was never truly satisfied with Descartes' responses to her questions, though she politely framed them as the products of her own 'stupidity'.[50] As Shapiro argues, Descartes

---

[48] Elisabeth of Bohemia, 'Elisabeth to Descartes [The Hague] 10 June 1643 (AT 3:683)', in Princess Elisabeth of Bohemia and René Descartes, *The Correspondence between Princess Elisabeth of Bohemia and René Descartes*, ed. Lisa Shapiro (Chicago: University of Chicago Press, 2007), pp. 67–9 (emphases added).

[49] Elisabeth of Bohemia, 'Elisabeth to Descartes [The Hague] 16 August 1645 (AT 2:268)', in *The Correspondence between Princess Elisabeth of Bohemia and René Descartes*, pp. 128–30.

[50] In fact, Elisabeth was a highly educated woman with extensive intellectual connections. In 1660 she became abbess of the Lutheran convent at Herford, Germany, where she remained until her death in 1680. Lisa Shapiro, 'Elisabeth, Princess of Bohemia', in *The Stanford Encyclopedia of Philosophy*, ed. Edward N. Zalta, Winter 2014 (Metaphysics Research Lab, Stanford University, 2014), https://plato.stanford.edu/archives/win2014/entries/elisabeth-bohemia/.

repeatedly seems to fudge the issue of body–mind interactionism in his replies to the princess, and Elisabeth appears eventually to have navigated her own way through this maze, finding a path that avoided 'the kind of substance dualism that Descartes appears to espouse'.[51]

These issues were also struggles for Descartes himself, whom Wilson characterises as having oscillated between two visions of the mind–body interaction. In the *Meditations*, Descartes proposed that pain 'in' a certain part of the body was felt as such only by God's ordinance. It so happened that the stimulation of the nerves in a particular area created a sensation in the mind as if it occurred in (for example) the foot. Wilson explains:

> The mind must be said to perceive 'in the brain,' since if it perceived 'in the limbs,' for example, we should be able directly to distinguish cases of peripheral stimulation from cases of intermediate nervous disorder, and this we cannot do ... The prevailing tendency *to ascribe pains* to our feet and hands is said to be deluded for the reason that pains are after all *sensations*, and feet and hands are nothing but bits of *res extensa*, and assigning sensations to some bits of *res extensa* is just as intelligent as assigning them to any other bits – say to the chalk or the blackboard.[52]

This reading of sensation as a phenomenon of *res cogita* was that which proved influential on decades of writing about phantom limb pain. Yet, Descartes at points appeared to espouse a quite different idea of mind–body interaction. The theory of 'co-extension', as Wilson terms it, saw mind and body as 'in union' or 'intermixed'. In a famous passage from 'Meditation VI', Descartes cast the mind–body relationship as more than intellectual:

> Nature also teaches me, by these sensations of pain, hunger, thirst and so on, that I am not merely present in my body as a sailor is present in a ship, but that I am very closely joined and, as it were, intermingled with it, so that I and the body form one thing. If this were not so, I, who am nothing but a thinking thing, would not feel pain when the body was hurt, but would perceive the damage by the pure intellect, just as a sailor perceives by sight if anything in his ship is broken. Similarly, when the body needs food or drink, I should have an explicit understanding of the fact, instead of having confused sensations of hunger and thirst. For these sensations of hunger,

[51] Lisa Shapiro, 'Princess Elizabeth and Descartes: the Union of Soul and Body and the Practice of Philosophy', *British Journal for the History of Philosophy* 7:3 (1999): 515, https://doi.org/10.1080/09608789908571042.
[52] Wilson, *Descartes*, p. 209.

thirst, pain and so on are nothing but confused modes of thinking which arise from the union, and as it were, intermingling of the mind with the body.[53]

Viewed in relation to phantom limb pain, this passage seems to recognise the problem identified above, that the mind does not rationalise all bodily experience. Hunger and thirst are experienced as 'confused sensations' rather than items of information. Phantom limbs resist rationalisation despite the fact that the sufferer knows them to be illusory.

Philosophers have pored over Descartes' writings on this topic, looking for an answer to the 'hard problem' which does not seem to be forthcoming. In light of the altered body, however, and in particular of phantom limb pain, the question takes on an interesting significance. Reading Descartes' varied interpretations of *res extensa* versus *res cogita*, Wilson comments that the latter seems to have no *necessary* relationship to the former, but only interacts with it as it is ordained by God that impulse X in the body should produce sensation Y in the mind. Therefore, she argues, 'It is, at best, hard to see how our unjustified tendency to ascribe experiences to parts of what we call our body could justify us in calling this thing *our body*.'[54] That is, if the relationship between impulse X and sensation Y is only incidental, God might as easily locate the pain which we experience 'in' our bodies 'in' other bodies – even animal or inanimate bodies. Seemingly this thought also occurred to Descartes, as he makes an effort in his writings to Elisabeth and elsewhere to explain how he believes the soul can be extended through the body in a non-corporeal sense (Elisabeth, like many of Descartes' readers, found the idea of non-corporeal extension illogical). In a series of letters to the Jesuit Denis Mesland in 1644–5, Descartes explained that he conceived of selfhood as inhering in the combination of body and mind. Thus, the body could be called a divisible *object*, but the identity of the body of a particular person was an indivisible *subject*. The soul was the form of the body, and one could therefore claim to have the same body throughout one's life regardless of whether it was fat or thin, infant or elderly, or even whether it had all its original parts. In explanation, he returned to the altered body:

> In that sense [a human body] ... can even be called indivisible, because if an arm or a leg of a man is amputated, we think that it is only in the first [object] sense of 'body' that this body is divided – we do not think that a man who has lost an arm or a leg is less a man than any other.[55]

---

[53] Descartes, 'Meditation VI', p. 192.   [54] Wilson, *Descartes*, p. 218 (emphasis added).
[55] René Descartes, 'Letter to Mesland, 9 February 1645', cited in Deborah Brown, 'The Sixth Meditation: Descartes and the Embodied Self', in *The Cambridge Companion to Descartes' Meditations*, edited by David Cunning (Cambridge: Cambridge University Press, 2014), p. 253.

Descartes' definition of identity here is notably similar to Locke's definition of 'man'. In Locke's estimation, to be the man X involves having the
body and mind of X. The *principium individuationis* which makes a tree a
tree or a man a man, rather than (or as well as) a mere collection of
particles, consists in its 'organisation of a common life'. Thus Locke, like
Descartes, believed one could claim to look at the same man (or tree) as
one had ten years previously, even if that entity contained none of the
same material as it had at first view.[56]

Of course, Locke diverged radically from Descartes in that he distinguished between 'man', thus defined, and 'person'. Personhood, for Locke,
implied a continued consciousness, such that one might legitimately claim
that an amputated limb was a whole person, *if* personality and memories
could be shown still to inhere in that organ. Conversely, what made a body
one's own was the experience of sensation and perception related to that
body.[57] Locke writes, in his 1690 *Essay Concerning Human Understanding*:

> That this is so, we have some kind of evidence in our very bodies, all whose
> particles, whilst vitally united to this same thinking conscious self, so that
> we *feel* when they are touched, and are affected by, and are conscious of
> good or harm that happens to them, are a part of our *selves* i.e. of our
> thinking conscious *self*. Thus the limbs of his body are to everyone a part of
> himself; he sympathizes and is concerned for them. Cut off an hand, and
> thereby separate it from that consciousness he had of its heat, cold, and
> other affections; and it is then no longer a part of that which is *himself*, any
> more than the remotest part of matter.[58]

Locke, despite having read and critiqued Descartes, did not make the
connection between his own conception of selfhood and the phantom
limb phenomenon which was both exemplar and problem for
Descartes' theory. We, however, can do just that. Locke's formulation
of bodily identity, as Quassim Cassam states, specifies that 'To
experience a limb as part of oneself is necessary and sufficient for it to

---

[56] K. Joanna S. Forstrom, *John Locke and Personal Identity: Immortality and Bodily Resurrection in 17th-Century Philosophy* (London: Bloomsbury, 2011), p. 20.

[57] Interestingly, William Bynum notes that Locke advised the Earl of Shaftesbury to try 'powder of sympathy' on three occasions. The implications of this for Locke's philosophy are unclear since the workings of sympathy were themselves up for debate, but it may imply that in practice Locke believed in some form of identity inhering in atoms, or simply that he had tried and approved the remedy himself. See William F. Bynum, 'The Weapon Salve in Seventeenth Century English Drama', *Journal of the History of Medicine and Allied Sciences* 21:1 (1966): 10, https://doi.org/10.1093/jhmas/XXI.1.8.

[58] John Locke, *An Essay Concerning Human Understanding*, ed. Roger Woolhouse, revised edition (London: Penguin Classics, 1998), p. 303.

be a part of one.'[59] Taken to its logical conclusion, then, it implies that phantom limbs – *experienced* as having feeling, being moved by volition, and so forth in spite of their physical absence – are truly a part of one's body. To a lesser extent, the same could be said of 'incorporated' prostheses, those which, as explored in Chapter 4, become experienced not as an addition to, but rather as a part of the body.

Including phantom limbs in the bodily schema may seem a sticking point for Locke's theory. Viewed from a different perspective, however, Locke's theory of embodiment actually accords neatly with some modern descriptions of phantom limb syndrome. Influenced by Merleau-Ponty and by Leder's theory of the absent body, amputee Vivian Sobchack describes her phantom limb as both objectively absent and subjectively present. That is, while physically absent, her painful and perplexing 'phantom' leg dys-appears to her consciousness, 'figuring itself in odd ways against the ground of where it once had lived its ordinary form of disappearance, its transparent and enabling absence in presence'.[60] The phantom limb ironically makes its presence felt, not least by animating Sobchack's prosthesis.[61] By contrast, the healthy, objectively present leg recedes from consciousness:

> whereas I subjectively experienced the objective 'no-thing' *there* of my absent left leg as 'some thing' *here* [i.e. in her consciousness], I subjectively experienced the objective 'some thing' *there* of my 'real' leg as almost 'no-thing' *here* at all ... Despite, and because of, their reversed inflection, there is, then, a mirrored form of *structural homology* – of recognition and, indeed, of possible reconciliation – that exists between my two legs: the so-called 'phantom' and the so-called 'real' one.[62]

Though it seems counterintuitive, Sobchack's description of 'the presence of an absence' speaks powerfully to Porterfield's account of the phantom limb's 'strong and lively' illusions. Douglas Robinson poetically

---

[59] Quassim Cassam, 'Introspection and Bodily Self-Ascription', in *The Body and the Self*, ed. Jose Luis Bermudez, Anthony Marcel, and Naomi Eilan (Cambridge: MIT Press, 1995), p. 320.

[60] Sobchack, 'Living a "Phantom Limb"', 57.

[61] This relation between phantom and prosthesis is now used to design artificial limbs with proprioceptive feedback. This involves designing the limb such that it utilises remaining movement through the nearest natural joint, an idea known as *extended physiological proprioception* (EPP). On this and other anomalies of limb perception such as the rubber hand illusion (in which one's hands seem to be moved by somebody else), see Jose Luis Bermudez, 'Ownership and the Space of the Body', in *The Subject's Matter: Self-Consciousness and the Body*, ed. Frédérique de Vignemont and Adrian J. T. Alsmith (Cambridge: MIT Press, 2017), p. 125.

[62] Sobchack, 'Living a "Phantom Limb"', 59.

refers to PLP as a creative transgression of the proprioceptive system which usually helps one to differentiate one's body from the 'outside' world:

> The phantom limb phenomenon might even be thought of as proprioception's 'literary' creativity: making the amputee care as deeply about a limb that exists 'only in the imagination' as about one that can be seen and poked and prodded, and indeed infusing the mechanical/scientific artificiality of the prosthetic device with the estranging/enlivening power of the 'only imagined' phantom limb.[63]

Moreover, as Cassandra Crawford has shown, phantoms have the power now, no less than in Descartes' lifetime, to challenge our notions of embodiment. These 'embodied ghosts', she argues, remind us of the limits of rigid theoretical models.[64] Despite scientific advances, phantom pains remain inchoate subject-objects, which persist in somatic, relational, and social terms, acting on and with the person from whom they are 'absent'.

Conclusion

Debates about phantom limbs were very different in tone to those about resurrection. Where discussions of the latter were necessarily spiritual, and often poetic, discourses around phantoms strove – with varying degrees of success – for rationalist, mechanistic explanations of this mysterious phenomenon. This emphasis was both a product of and cause for the fascination of Enlightenment thinkers with phantom limb syndrome; to explain this phenomenon would be to delineate and tame the irrational and unruly body. This project has continued intermittently ever since. In the eighteenth century, John Hunter reported two cases of phantom sensations in a missing penis. He interpreted these in a broadly similar way to Descartes, speculating that stimulation of a nerve would produce the same sensation regardless of where along the nerve that stimulation was received.[65] In the 1800s, Silas Weir Mitchell coined the phrase

---

[63] Douglas Robinson, *Estrangement and the Somatics of Literature: Tolstoy, Shklovsky, Brecht* (Baltimore: Johns Hopkins University Press, 2008), pp. 103–4.

[64] Cassandra S. Crawford, 'Body Image, Prostheses, Phantom Limbs', *Body and Society* 21:2 (2015): 221–44, https://doi.org/10.1177/1357034X14522102; Cassandra S. Crawford, '"You Don't Need a Body to Feel a Body": Phantom Limb Syndrome and Corporeal Transgression', *Sociology of Health and Illness* 35:3 (2013): 434–48, https://doi.org/10.1111/j.1467-9566.2012.01498.x.

[65] Nicholas J. Wade, 'The Legacy of Phantom Limbs', *Perception* 32:5 (2003): 521, https://doi.org/10.1068/p3205ed.

'phantom limb'.[66] Neurological research in this area continues, most notably in V. S Ramachandran's use of mirrors to induce synaesthesia of the phantom limb with its 'real' counterpart.[67] At length, however, many of the questions raised by these experiments are similar to those posed by Descartes and his early modern counterparts: how can our feelings be 'all in the mind'? What makes my body mine? These queries stretch the limits of the imagination, and blur the boundaries between medicine, philosophy, and faith.

---

[66] Ibid., 511. On the history of phantom limb syndrome, see Douglas B. Price and Neil J. Twombly, *The Phantom Limb Phenomenon: a Medical, Folkloric, and Historical Study. Texts and Translations of 10th to 20th Century Accounts of the Miraculous Restoration of Lost Body Parts* (Washington: Georgetown University Press, 1978); Nicholas J. Wade and Stanley Finger, 'William Porterfield (ca. 1696–1771) and his Phantom Limb: an Overlooked First Self-Report by a Man of Medicine', *Neurosurgery* 52:5 (2003): 1196–9, https://doi.org/10.1227/01.NEU.0000057837.74142.68;.

[67] V. S. Ramachandran and D. Rogers-Ramachandran, 'Synaesthesia in Phantom Limbs Induced with Mirrors', *Proceedings: Biological Sciences* 263:1369 (1996): 377–86.

Conclusion

The stories in this book are by turns moving, humorous, shocking, and bizarre. Above all, they have shown that experiences of bodily alteration were almost infinitely varied. Bodily difference could signify in vastly different ways, from the destitute cripple to the desirable castrato. The nobleman amputee with a sophisticated articulate prosthetic lived his body in a way profoundly different from the discharged soldier with an unhealed stump. The female mastectomy survivor found that her bodily difference went unmentioned, whereas the woman with facial difference might be used to being commented on and stared at. The questions of categorisation raised in the Introduction to this book therefore remain live concerns. This is not only because we lack terms appropriate to the early modern period, but because even in that period, the lines between bodily wholeness and partition, impairment and disability, and health and illness were constantly shifting.

It is also clear, however, that the body remains a fruitful object of study despite (perhaps because of) its slipperiness. The repetition of similar questions about identity and subjectivity across various kinds of narrative about various kinds of bodily change shows that there was a conceptual thread which linked 'altered people' together. By making visible the continuities and fissures between flesh and identity, surgically changed bodies crystallised a metaphysical question surrounding all bodies: *how* did one 'have a body'? Embodiment was, on the one hand, an inseparable facet of being, yet, on the other hand, the body often seemed a quasi-alien thing, available for manipulation and liable to exert demands upon the person 'inside'. The flesh was both thinking, feeling subject, and lumpen object. Early modern people were alive to these contradictions, and not only in philosophical terms. Concern with the relationship between mind and body permeated the moral panic over castrati and the satirical jibes levelled at those who underwent cosmetic surgery. It helped to determine what people prioritised when they commissioned artificial limbs, and where and how they buried their loved ones. Thinking about embodiment was therefore not a discrete subject for the learned, but a problematic woven through culture, from medicine, to trade, the arts, formal worship, and informal devotion.

These discussions did not take place exclusively in the terms we now tend to imagine them, with substance dualists on one side and others advocating for embodied cognition through the humours. In reality, even the most formal philosophy struggled to assert that the body was entirely irrelevant to one's way of being in the world. Equally, when they spoke of the body as deeply and complexly related to the mind or soul, or of the soul as being embodied, early modern people did not necessarily think in humoral terms. Rather, they spoke directly of the social and cultural functionality of the body, treating the body itself as a relational object-subject without recourse to a narrative of animating passions. Even developments or processes which appear to us to promote a mechanistic idea of the body – the advent of articulated prostheses, for instance – could be read as exemplifying the interconnectedness of somatic and emotional experience. In this landscape, the possibilities for bodily alteration were both broad and deep. Increasingly, it seemed that there was almost no part of the body which might not be changed in some way.

While this story is characterised by variance and individuality, we can nonetheless trace some broad influences at work. The shift from Galenic to iatrochemical medical models over the early modern period has been much discussed. The stories in this book confirm that this shift was incomplete and far from linear; humoral ideas were incorporated into new medical philosophies rather than supplanted by them.[1] Nonetheless, the notion of bodily processes as governed by discrete chemical entities – informed in turn by belief in atomism – was a necessary precondition to the theories of sympathy which allowed writers to imagine a piece of transplanted flesh communicating across distances with its original owner.[2] Anxieties about transplanting flesh from one person to another had been around for a long time by the seventeenth century, but scientific credibility, or at least the appearance thereof, gave those fears extra bite. More generally, Paracelsian and Helmontian medical models were associated with a democratic

---

[1] See, for instance, Silva de Renzi, 'Old and New Models of the Body', in *The Healing Arts: Health, Disease and Society in Europe, 1500–1800*, ed. Peter Elmer (Manchester: Manchester University Press, 2004), pp. 166–9; Mary Lindemann, *Medicine and Society in Early Modern Europe*, 2nd edition (Cambridge: Cambridge University Press, 2010), especially p. 8.

[2] See Ann E. Moyer, 'Sympathy in the Renaissance', in *Sympathy: a History*, ed. Eric Schliesser (Oxford: Oxford University Press, 2015), pp. 71–102.

medical marketplace, in which cures no longer needed to be tailored to the individual. This shift away from individualised medicine accompanied a rise in tonics and cure-alls which did not require prescription. It also fostered the idea that the human body was eminently comprehensible, and therefore fixable, thus paving the way for the narratives of restoration we have seen in facial and limb prostheses.

Such changes were enmeshed with shifts in economic behaviour. The popularity of castrati, the rise of 'cosmetic' surgery, and the development of articulated prostheses all depended for their existence on a burgeoning consumer culture.[3] This does not necessarily imply that eighteenth-century consumers cared more or less about physical appearances than their Elizabethan forebears, but they had more avenues at their disposal to alter their bodies and faces. We might also view self-improvement technologies as an arms race: the more it was possible to smooth over one's physical differences, the greater the social requirement to do so. In 1729, Joshua Gee inveighed against 'Creatures that go about the Streets to shew their maim'd Limbs, nauseous Sores, stump Hands or Feet, or any other Deformity'.[4] His suggestion that all such people could be housed in one large hospital was typical of the eighteenth- and nineteenth-century tendency to categorise and institutionalise people with disabilities. However, his concern that the sight of such beggars might cause infants to be 'deformed' in the womb relied on beliefs about maternal imagination which were almost two hundred years old.[5] Perceived ties between physical attributes and moral worth were thus renegotiated rather than loosened over this period. The indexing of social privilege to an innately 'noble' body may have declined in the latter half of the seventeenth century. However, new forms of reading the body, such as physiognomy, readily emerged to supplant that model, confirming that people still wanted and needed a way of connecting physical and moral virtues and deficiencies. Rather than sickening and dying, questions about bodily integrity and

[3] On the economic evidence about this period, see Darron Dean et al., *Production and Consumption in English Households, 1600–1750* (Florence: Routledge, 2004). On consumerism and luxury, see Helen Berry, 'Polite Consumption: Shopping in Eighteenth-Century England', *Transactions of the Royal Historical Society* 12 (2002): 375–94; Maxine Berg, *Luxury and Pleasure in Eighteenth-Century Britain* (Oxford: Oxford University Press, 2007); Maxine Berg and Elizabeth Eger, 'The Rise and Fall of the Luxury Debates', in *Luxury in the Eighteenth Century: Debates, Desires and Delectable Goods* (Basingstoke: Palgrave Macmillan, 2016), pp. 7–28; for an overview of historiography of this period, see Sara Pennell, 'Consumption and Consumerism in Early Modern England', *Historical Journal* 42:2 (1999): 549–64.
[4] Joshua Gee, *The Trade and Navigation of Great-Britain Considered* (London: printed by Sam Buckley, 1729), p. 42.
[5] Ibid.

moral worth mutated and adapted, in concert with new forms of expression. This book has briefly considered how the burgeoning form of print advertising encouraged readers to view bodies – both their own and those of other people – as commodities. However, the link between advertising, perceptions of the body, and the emergence of the novel is an intriguing area for further study.

Considering questions of bodily identity as unevenly influenced by socio-economic and intellectual factors is both more painstaking and more productive than ascribing change to the Enlightenment, as if this were a blunt force sweeping the nation. Kinds of bodily alteration are micro-histories in which we can see how early modern people accrued new languages with which to describe their hopes and fears. At the same time, they may supply a broader perspective with which to consider modern innovations in the remaking of the body. In the course of writing this book, it has become apparent that experiences of and questions about embodiment raised in the seventeenth and eighteenth centuries remain powerfully relevant. In its extraordinary capacity to restore the body, modern medicine appears in places to be reaching towards what Drew Leder terms 'the Cartesian dream of remaking the body at will'.[6] Certainly the ableist ideal hinted at in early modern discourses about artificial arms and legs is prominent in modern narratives of prosthesis. Prosthetic limbs and other devices are more sophisticated than ever before. Largely funded by military agencies (notably the United States' Defense Advanced Research Projects Agency [DARPA]), technologists have created artificial limbs capable of connectivity with the body's nervous system, such that they can be said to be brain-controlled. Often, these limbs are capable of feats of strength or speed unavailable to 'natural' bodies. Publicity material for a prosthetic arm unveiled in 2016, for instance, proudly notes that the arm can lift a 45lb dumbbell and never gets tired.[7] Like the mechanical prostheses of the early modern period, these technologies aim to erase disability by erasing the economic and social disadvantages associated with impairment. Where early modern surgeons imagined prosthesis users walking and riding confidently, modern technologists have created a

---

[6] Drew Leder, 'Whose Body? What Body? The Metaphysics of Organ Transplantation', in *Persons and their Bodies: Rights, Responsibilities, Relationships*, Philosophy and Medicine (Dordrecht: Springer, 1999), p. 239, https://doi.org/10.1007/0-306-46866-2_10.

[7] Darren Weaver, Corey Protin, and Paul Szoldra, 'The Military Just Built the Most Advanced Prosthetic Arm We've Ever Seen', *Business Insider*, accessed 28 May 2018, http://uk.businessinsider.com/advanced-darpa-prosthetic-arm-2016-5; DARPA, 'Revolutionizing Prosthetics', accessed 28 May 2018, www.darpa.mil/program/revolutionizing-prosthetics.

vision of re-ablement in which the prosthesis user is less restored than
augmented. This 'supercrip', it is imagined, may possess an assembly of
parts which is superior to the natural body, such that some transhumanist
thinkers imagine a future in which people elect to 'upgrade' themselves
with prosthetics.[8]
Moreover, the surgical alteration of the body may be moving into new
territories. Among other projects disclosed by DARPA is the development of 'Iron Man' style exoskeletons, aimed as much at protecting and
augmenting able-bodied soldiers as at allowing those with spinal injuries
to walk again.[9] The most radical transhumanists seek to alter the body
from the inside out using so-called insideables, neural and physiological
implants designed to enhance human performance and confer new
abilities.[10] These range from cochlear and retinal implants designed to
restore lost senses, to so-called memory implants, silicon chips capable of
mimicking the signal processing which occurs naturally in the brain.[11]
Of particular interest to both military-focussed and academic transhumanists is the possibility of 'tech-lepathy'. An implanted device would
convert the nerve impulses on their way to the vocal cords into sounds,
which might then be radio-transmitted and reverse-translated into neural
signals for another implant-wearer, thus erasing the need for vocal
communication altogether.[12] In pursuit of morphological freedom,
transhumanists thus happily seek to jettison the human body as it
currently exists. In Max More's words, 'Transhumanists regard human

[8] Dave Lee, 'When Your Body Becomes Eligible for an Upgrade', *BBC News*, 15 July 2017, www.bbc
     .co.uk/news/technology-40616561.
[9] Roberto Manzocco, *Transhumanism: Engineering the Human Condition: History, Philosophy and
     Current Status* (Leiden: Springer, 2019), p. 173.
[10] I am indebted here to Professor Tracy Harwood and Dr Camille Baker, who kindly spoke about art,
     bodily technologies, and transhumanism at a public engagement event connected to this book
     project in April 2018. Their discussion of future directions in bodily alteration informed the book
     in unexpected ways.
[11] Jon Cohen, 'Brain Implants Could Restore the Ability to Form Memories', *MIT Technology Review*,
     accessed 29 May 2018, www.technologyreview.com/s/513681/memory-implants/.
[12] Manzocco, *Transhumanism: Engineering the Human Condition*, pp. 179–80. On these topics, and
     other forms of transhumanism, see Mark O'Connell, *To Be a Machine: Adventures among Cyborgs,
     Utopians, Hackers, and the Futurists Solving the Modest Problem of Death* (London: Granta Books,
     2017); Tim Adams, 'When Man Meets Metal: Rise of the Transhumans', *The Observer*, 29 October
     2017,   www.theguardian.com/technology/2017/oct/29/transhuman-bodyhacking-transspecies-
     cyborg; Steven John Kraftchick, 'Bodies, Selves, and Human Identity: a Conversation between
     Transhumanism and the Apostle Paul', *Theology Today* 72:1 (2015): 47–69, https://doi.org/10
     .1177/0040573614563530; Max More and Natasha Vita-More, eds, *Transhumanist Reader:
     Classical and Contemporary Essays on the Science, Technology, and Philosophy of the Human Future*
     (Somerset: Wiley, 2013).

nature not as an end in itself, not as perfect, and not as having any claim on our allegiance.'¹³

In these circumstances, it may appear that the 'Cartesian dream' is complete – that the body itself has come to be regarded as a prosthesis which is firmly, but not inalienably, attached to the 'real self' of *res cogita*. Transhumanists are often at pains to point out that they are not dualists, since they believe that cognition requires a physical instantiation. They do, however, believe that the nature of the substrate for thought is relatively unimportant, and may become non-biological.¹⁴ Yet cases such as that of Clint Hallam, the hand transplant recipient who rejected his new hand on psychological grounds, demonstrate that outside the rarefied world of transhumanist innovation, bodies still matter. The body may no longer uniformly be considered as eternally linked to an immortal soul, but it retains a link to one's personhood which is hard to ignore. Discussing the ethics of transplantation, Leder contends that 'the self is an integrated whole whose subjectivity is embodied, and whose body is "mentalized" through and through'.¹⁵ Body-altering sex reassignment, along with some kinds of cosmetic surgery, demonstrates that people may view a sense of estrangement from their bodies not as an inevitable effect of dualist embodiment but rather as a problem which is in need of redress. In these cases, medical intervention implies that the 'normal' mode of embodiment is one in which subjectivity is experienced through and in the body.¹⁶ Moreover, a greater attention to the subjectivity of the body might potentially offer a counter to the tendency of modern physic to treat the body rather than the person. It has been suggested that in order to improve health outcomes, a greater emphasis on preventive care is needed, which might be fostered in part by emphasising one's *being* rather than *having* a body.¹⁷

One way in which these discourses have been brought together is in the idea of '4E' cognition.¹⁸ Investigations into this area are the province of

¹³ Max More, "The Philosophy of Transhumanism," in *Transhumanist Reader*, ed. Vita-More and More, p. 4.
¹⁴ Ibid., p. 7.   ¹⁵ Leder, 'Whose Body?', p. 254.
¹⁶ As part of public engagement work connected to this project, in 2017 I held an event discussing voice and gender identity. Among the attendees were transgender men and women seeking advice on how to train their voice to reflect this gender identity. For these people, changing the body was a case not of exceeding natural limits, but of 'passing' in day-to-day life – reflecting the way in which discourses of bodily alteration extend beyond those of disability studies and transhumanism.
¹⁷ Drew Leder, 'Medicine and Paradigms of Embodiment', *Journal of Medicine and Philosophy: a Forum for Bioethics and Philosophy of Medicine* 9:1 (1984): 29–44, https://doi.org/10.1093/jmp/9.1.29.
¹⁸ For a full explanation of the differences between the four 'Es' of extended, embodied, embedded, and enacted cognition, see Mark Rowlands, *The New Science of the Mind: From Extended Mind to Embodied Phenomenology* (Cambridge: MIT Press, 2010).

neuroscientists, philosophers, phenomenologists, and psychologists. The 'Es' most relevant to altered bodies are *embodied* and *extended* cognition, as summarised by Mark Rowlands:

> The idea that mental processes are *embodied*, is very roughly, the idea that they are partly constituted by, partly made up of, wider (i.e. extraneural) bodily structures and processes ... The idea that mental processes are *extended* is the idea that they are not located exclusively inside an organism's head but extend out, in various ways, into the organism's environment.[19]

Work on embodied cognition has lately sought to prove that which early modern people instinctively assumed – that thinking takes place through the flesh as well as in the brain. In his *How the Body Shapes the Mind*, Shaun Gallagher summarises numerous examples in which the attitudes and motions of the body are shown to affect perception and thought. For example:

> Body posture can affect attention and certain kinds of judgement. If subjects turn head and eyes to one side just prior to making a judgement, the direction of turning influences cognitive performance. When subjects listen to a sentence with head and eyes turned right, their performance in cued recall is better than when they listened with head and trunk turned toward the left.[20]

Unsurprisingly, the hands have a particularly potent role in cognitive processes. In brain-damaged subjects, the hands may be capable of manipulating an object in the appropriate way even when the person is unable to identify that object, implying a degree of what Gallagher terms 'manual thinking'.[21] It has also been observed that 'Objects located near one's hands receive enhanced visual attention ... the hands facilitate the evaluation of objects for potential manipulation.'[22] If one can think through movement, then gesture takes on a new significance as not only expressive of thought, but integral to the formation of ideas. Andy Clark describes how gesture has been shown to help in tasks such as remembering a list or solving maths problems. Gesturing, he argues,

> is not simply a motor act expressive of some fully neurally realized process of thought. Instead, the physical act of gesturing is part and parcel of a coupled neural-bodily unfolding that is itself usefully seen as an

---

[19] Ibid., p. 3
[20] Shaun Gallagher, *How the Body Shapes the Mind* (Oxford: Oxford University Press, 2005), p. 9.
[21] Shaun Gallagher, 'The Enactive Hand' in *The Hand, an Organ of the Mind: What the Manual Tells the Mental*, ed. Zdravko Radman (Cambridge: MIT Press, 2013), p. 213.
[22] Ibid., p. 214.

organismically extended process of thought. In gesture, we plausibly con-
front a cognitive process whose implementation involved machinery that
loops out beyond the purely neural realm.[23]

Clark's contention may seem radical, but as he recognises, it reiterates the
contention of phenomenologists that all language is body language. As
Elena Cuffari asserts, 'Speech is already gesture: the use of words is an
instance of body movement and expression. Gesture is the happening, or
enactment, of thought.'[24]

Such work expresses in a renewed form that which is imaginatively
conveyed in *Titus Andronicus* or the Miracle of the Black Leg: losing a
body part is a psychic as well as physical change. It also overlaps with
extended cognition by positioning the use of prostheses in a new light, as a
kind of environmental scaffolding which facilitates thought.[25] I have argued
that Lavinia's use of prostheses allows her to express an 'inward' self which is
ignored by those around her. Extended cognition might go further, arguing
that the prostheses allow her to think as well as act differently. Moreover,
the extended mind hypothesis touches most closely on early modern
themes when it goes beyond the individual, positing intersubjectivity as a
constitutive part of the cognitive process.[26] Joel Krueger takes the bold step
of arguing for interpersonal interactions as cognitive in nature, such that
encounters between people may constitute thinking-in-action:

> I argue that social cognition is a kind of extended cognition. Specifically,
> I argue that social cognition is fundamentally an interactive form of space
> management – the negotiation and management of 'we-space' – and that
> some of the expressive actions involved in the negotiation and management
> of we-space (gesture, touch, facial and whole-body expressions, etc.) drive
> basic processes of interpersonal understanding ... Some social-cognitive
> processes are therefore partially driven by and composed of non-neural
> scaffolding; and social cognition is in this way not reducible to individual,
> intracranial mechanisms but instead emerges from within the dynamics of
> the interactive process itself. Put otherwise, social *interaction* is a form of
> social *cognition*.[27]

[23] Andy Clark, 'Gesture as Thought?', in *The Hand, an Organ of the Mind*, ed. Radman, p. 257.
[24] Elena Cuffari, 'Gestural Sense-Making: Hand Gestures as Intersubjective Linguistic Enactments', *Phenomenology and the Cognitive Sciences* 11:4 (2012): 615, https://doi.org/10.1007/s11097-011-9244-9.
[25] Joel Krueger, 'Extended Cognition and the Space of Social Interaction', *Consciousness and Cognition* 20:3 (2011): 643–57, https://doi.org/10.1016/j.concog.2010.09.022.
[26] Richard Menary, 'The Encultured Hand', in *The Hand, an Organ of the Mind*, ed. Radman, pp. 349–67.
[27] Krueger, 'Extended Cognition and the Space of Social Interaction', 643.

While Krueger's formulation of 'body-centric action space' is abstract, it receives some support from research into mirror neurons, through which social interactions may be concretely played out in the brain:

> The recent discovery of 'mirror neurons' in the premotor cortex, neurons that are activated by the subject's own motor behavior *or* by the subject's visual observation of someone else's motor behavior, shows a direct and active link between the motor and sensory systems and has important implications for explaining how we understand other people.[28]

The potential links between research of this kind and early modern considerations of embodiment are striking. Jonathan Sawday has noted that mirror neurons may provide a modern correlate for the early modern understanding of pain as 'historically and socially contingent'.[29] The neuroscientific idea of pain sensations as stimulated by the sight of another's distress concretises the 'imaginative participation' which made gazing on images of Christ or watching *King Lear* almost unbearably painful.[30] More generally, new research into the role of the body and intersubjectivity in phenomenological experience is often redolent of early modern writing on the passions as jointly somatic and cerebral. This book has shown that flesh and thought were often deeply imbricated with one another, to the extent that even after death, personal identity might be argued to inhere in the body. Numerous scholars have recently explored the implications of embodied and extended cognition for the study of early modern culture in general and Shakespeare in particular, as part of a growing field of cognitive humanities.[31] In this process, we should be careful not to equate modern and early modern ideas too closely. It is important to remember that early modern belief in an immortal soul

---

[28] Gallagher, *How the Body Shapes the Mind*, p. 9.

[29] Jonathan Sawday, '"I Feel Your Pain": Some Reflections on the (Literary) Perception of Pain', in *The Hurt(Ful) Body: Performing and Beholding Pain, 1600–1800*, ed. Tomas Macsotay, Cornelis Van der Haven, and Karl Vanhaesebrouck (Manchester: Manchester University Press, 2017), p. 110.

[30] Ibid.

[31] There is much emerging work on this topic, and a brief summary can be found in the "Introduction", in Raphael Lyne and Timothy Chesters, eds., *Movement in Renaissance Literature: Exploring Kinesic Intelligence* (Basingstoke: Palgrave, 2017), pp. 1–12. Other works of note include Mary Thomas Crane, *Shakespeare's Brain: Reading with Cognitive Theory* (Princeton: Princeton University Press, 2010); Laurie Johnson, John Sutton, and Evelyn Tribble, *Embodied Cognition and Shakespeare's Theatre: the Early Modern Body-Mind* (Abingdon: Routledge, 2014); Evelyn Tribble, *Cognition in the Globe: Attention and Memory in Shakespeare's Theatre* (New York: Palgrave Macmillan, 2011); Steve Mentz, 'Half-Fish, Half-Flesh: Dolphins, the Ocean, and Early Modern Humans', in *The Indistinct Human in Renaissance Literature*, ed. Jean E. Feerick and Vin Nardizzi (New York: Palgrave Macmillan, 2012), pp. 27–46; John Sutton, 'Spongy Brains and Material Memories', in *Environment and Embodiment in Early Modern England*, ed. Mary Floyd-Wilson and Garrett A. Sullivan, Jr. (Basingstoke: Palgrave Macmillan, 2007), pp. 14–34.

provided an animating principle for all action, such that the matter of the brain itself could be viewed as *res extensa*. Nonetheless, discourses from this period provide a valuable context for transhumanist and neuroscientific debates which are often presented as ahistorical, and which raise troubling ethical questions. When it came to altered bodies, early modern people showed nuance and humility in their beliefs. They had rich epistemological languages in which to imagine their own embodiment, and they used those languages fluidly. Though their spiritual convictions were deeply held, they were capable of embracing heteroglossic, even contradictory modes of thought about the body. In order to examine bodily alterations both modern and historic, we need to be like the early moderns: flexible, curious, ready to change our minds.

Bibliography

Primary Sources

Addison, Joseph. 'Non Cuicunque Datum Est Habere Nasum'. *Tatler.* 1710.

Alarum for London, or The Siedge of Antwerpe VVith the Ventrous Actes and Valorous Deeds of the Lame Soldier. London: William Ferbrand, 1602.

Allen, Charles. *Curious Observations on the Teeth* (1687). Edited by L. Lindsay. London: John Bale, Sons and Danielsson, 1924.

Ancillon, Charles. *Italian Love: Or, Eunuchism Displayed. Describing All the Different Kinds of Eunuchs; Shewing the Esteem They Have Met with in the World, and How They Came to Be Made so, Wherein Principally Is Examined, Whether They Are Capable of Marriage, and if They Ought to Be Suffered to Enter into That Holy State ... Occasioned by a Young Lady's Falling in Love with One, Who Sung in the Opera at the Hay-Market, and to Whom She Had like to Have Been Married. Written by a Person of Honour.* 2nd edition. London: printed for E. Curll, 1740.

Bacon, Francis. 'Of Deformity'. In *The Essays, or Councils, Civil and Moral of Sir Francis Bacon ... With a Table of the Colours of Good and Evil. And a Discourse of the Wisdom of the Ancients (Done into English by Sir Arthur Gorges). To This Edition Is Added the Character of Queen Elizabeth; Never before Printed in English*, 117–18. London: published for George Sawbridge, 1696. Accessed 3 October 2017, www.bl.uk/collection-items/bacons-essays-on-revenge-envy-and-deformity.

Barrough, Philip. *The Method of Physick.* London, 1583.

Beckett, William. *New Discoveries Relating to the Cure of Cancers, Wherein a Method of Dissolving the Cancerous Substance Is Recommended, with Various Instances of the Author's Success in Such Practice, on Persons Reputed Incurable, in a Letter to a Friend. To Which Is Added, a Solution of Some Curious Problems, Concerning the Same Disease.* London, 1711.

Beconsall, Thomas. *The Doctrine of a General Resurrection: Wherein the Identity of the Rising Body Is Asserted, against the Socinians and Scepticks.* Oxford: printed by Leon. Lichfield, for George West, 1697.

Bon, Ottaviano. *A Description of the Grand Signour's Seraglio or Turkish Emperours Court.* Translated by John Greaves. London: Jo. Ridley, 1653.

Boyle, Robert. 'Some Physico-Theological Considerations about the Possibility of the Resurrection (1675)'. In *Selected Philosophical Papers of Robert Boyle*, edited by M. A. Stewart, 192–208. Manchester: Manchester University Press, 1979.

With T.E. *Some considerations about the reconcileableness of reason and religion. By T.E. a lay-man. To which is annex'd by the publisher, a discourse of Mr. Boyle, about the possibility of the resurrection.* London, 1675.

'Tryals Proposed by Mr Boyle to Dr Lower, to Be Made by Him, for the Improvement of Transfusing Blood out of One Live Animal into Another'. *Philosophical Transactions*. 11 February 1666. Folger Shakespeare Library.

Budgell, Eustace, ed. 'Notice of a Sale of Beauties, at Temple-Oge'. *Bee, or Universal Weekly Pamphlet Revived, May 1733–June 1733* 2, no. 17 (16 June 1733): 738–40.

Bulwer, John. *Anthropometamorphosis: = Man Transform'd: Or, the Artificiall Changling.* London: printed by William Hunt, 1653.

Chirologia, or, The Naturall Language of the Hand Composed of the Speaking Motions, and Discoursing Gestures Thereof: Whereunto Is Added Chironomia, or, The Art of Manuall Rhetoricke, Consisting of the Naturall Expressions, Digested by Art in the Hand, as the Chiefest Instrument of Eloquence, by Historicall Manifesto's Exemplified out of the Authentique Registers of Common Life and Civill Conversation: With Types, or Chyrograms, a Long-Wish'd for Illustration of This Argument. London: Tho[mas] Harper, sold by R. Whitaker, 1644.

Philocophus, or, The Deafe and Dumbe Mans Friend Exhibiting the Philosophicall Verity of That Subtile Art, Which May Inable One with an Observant Eie, to Heare What Any Man Speaks by the Moving of His Lips: Upon the Same Ground . . . That a Man Borne Deafe and Dumbe, May Be Taught to Heare the Sound of Words with His Eie, & Thence Learne to Speake with His Tongue. London: printed for Humphrey Moseley, 1648.

Bunyan, John. *The Resurrection of the Dead and Eternall Judgement, or, The Truth of the Resurrection of the Bodies Both of Good and Bad at the Last Day Asserted and Proved by Gods Word: Also, the Manner and Order of Their Coming Forth of Their Graves, as Also, with What Bodies They Do Arise: Together with a Discourse of the Last Judgement, and the Finall Conclusion of the Whole World.* London: Francis Smith, 1665.

Burnet, Thomas. *De Statu Mortuorum & Resurgentium Tractatus. Of the State of the Dead, and of Those That Are to Rise. Translated from the Latin Original of Dr Burnet.* Translated by Matthias Earbery. 2nd edition. Vol. 1 (of 2). London: E. Curll, 1728.

Burney, Frances. 'Letter from Frances Burney to Her Sister Esther about Her Mastectomy without Anaesthetic, 1812'. Paris, 1812. Berg Coll. MSS Arblay. British Library.

Burton, Robert. *The Anatomy of Melancholy: what it is. With all the kindes, causes, symptomes, prognosticks, and seuerall cures of it.* Oxford: John Lichfield and James Short, for Henry Cripps, 1621.

Butler, Samuel. *Hudibras*. London: John Murray, 1835.

Case, Thomas. *Mount Pisgah, or, A Prospect of Heaven Being an Exposition on the Fourth Chapter of the First Epistle of St Paul to the Thessalonians, from the 13th Verse, to the End of the Chapter, Divided into Three Parts*. London: Thomas Milbourn, for Dorman Newman, 1670.

Chambers, Ephraim. *Cyclopædia, or, An Universal Dictionary of Arts and Sciences*. London, 1728. Accessed 3 August 2015, https://uwdc.library.wisc.edu/collections/HistSciTech/.

Cooke, James. *Mellificium Chirurgiæ, or the Marrow of Many Good Authors Enlarged: Wherein Is Briefly, Fully, and Faithfully Handled the Art of Chirurgery in Its Four Parts, with All the Several Diseases unto Them Belonging: Their Definitions, Causes, Signes, Prognosticks, and Cures, Both General and Particular*. London: printed by T.R. for John Sherley, 1662.

Cowper, Sarah. 'Diary, Volume 1, 1700–1702'. Defining Gender, 1450–1910, n. d. Accessed 7 May 2013. www.gender.amdigital.co.uk.

Davenport, Christopher. *An Enchiridion of Faith. Presented in a Dialogue, Declaring the Truth of Christian Religion in Generall*. Douay [Douai, France]: S.N., 1655.

Day, Martin. *Doomes-Day, or, a Treatise of the Resurrection of the Body*. London: 1636.

Deeds against Nature, and Monsters by Kinde Tryed at the Goale Deliuerie of Newgate, at the Sessions in the Old Bayly, the 18. and 19. of Iuly Last, 1614. the One of a London Cripple Named Iohn Arthur, That to Hide His Shame and Lust, Strangled His Betrothed Wife. The Other of a Lasciuious Young Damsell Named Martha Scambler, Which Made Away the Fru[i]t of Her Own Womb, That the World Might Not See the Seed of Her Owne Shame: Which Two Persons with Diuers Others were Executed at Tyburne the 21. o[f] Iuly Folowing. With Two Sorrowfull Ditties of These Two Aforesaid Persons, Made by Themselues in Newgate, the Night before Their Execution. London: printed [by G. Eld] for Edward Wright, 1614.

de Courtin, Antoine. *A Treatise of Jealousie, or, Means to Preserve Peace in Marriage Wherein Is Treated of I. The Nature and Effects of Jealousie, Which for the Most Part Is the Fatal Cause of Discontents between Man and Wife, II. And Because Jealousy Is a Passion, It's Therefore Occasionally Discoursed of Passions in General, Giving and Exact Idea of the Production of Passions, and of the Oeconomie of the Body so Far as It Relates Thereunto. III. The Reciprocal Duties of Man and Wife, with Infallable Means to Preserve Peace in the Family, by Avoiding Dissentions That May Arise from Jealousie, or Any Other Cause Whatever*. London: printed for W. Freeman, 1684.

de la Charriére, Joseph. *A Treatise of the Operations of Surgery. Wherein Are Mechanically Explain'd the Causes of the Diseases in Which They Are Needful, ... To Which Is Added, a Treatise of Wounds, ... Translated from the Third Edition of the French, Enlarg'd, Corrected and Revis'd by the Author, Joseph de La Charriere*. London: printed by R. Brugis, for D. Brown, and W. Mears; and T. Ballard, 1712.

de la Vauguion, M. *A Compleat Body of Chirurgical Operations, Containing the Whole Practice of Surgery. With Observations and Remarks on Each Case. Amongst Which Are Inserted, the Several Ways of Delivering Women in Natural and Unnatural Labours. The Whole Illustrated with Copper Plates, Explaining the Several Bandages, Sutures, and Divers Useful Instruments. By M. de La Vauguion. M.D. and Intendant of the Royal Hospitals about Paris. Faithfully Done into English*. London: printed for Henry Bonwick Yard, T. Goodwin, M. Wotton, B. Took, and S. Manship, 1699.

de Voragine, Jacob. *Legenda Aurea*. Edited by F. S. Ellis. Translated by William Caxton. Vol. v. Temple Classics, 1900. Via Fordham University Internet History Sourcebooks Project. accessed 17 March 2019, https://sourcebooks .fordham.edu.

Descartes, René. *Discourse on Method, Optics, Geometry, and Meteorology* (1637). Translated by Paul J. Olscamp. Indianapolis: Hackett, 2001.

'Letter to Mesland, 9 February 1645', cited in Deborah Brown, 'The Sixth Meditation: Descartes and the Embodied Self', in *The Cambridge Companion to Descartes' Meditations*, edited by David Cunning, pp. 240–57 (cited p. 253). Cambridge: Cambridge University Press, 2014.

'Letter to Plempius for Fromondus, 3 October 1637'. In *The Philosophical Writing of Descartes, Volume III: The Correspondence*, translated by John Cottingham, Robert Stoothoff, Dugald Murdoch, and Anthony Kenny, 64. Cambridge: Cambridge University Press, 1991.

'Meditation VI'. In *The Philosophical Works of Descartes*, translated by Elizabeth S. Haldane and G. R. T. Ross. Vol. 1 (of 2), 185–99. Cambridge: Cambridge University Press, 1912.

'Principles of Philosophy'. In *The Philosophical Works of Descartes*, translated by Elizabeth S. Haldane and G. R. T. Ross. Vol. 1 (of 2), 201–302. Cambridge: Cambridge University Press, 1912.

Treatise of Man (1662). Translated by Thomas Steele Hall. New York: Prometheus Books, 2003.

Digby, Kenelm. *A Late Discourse, Made in a Solmne Assembly of Nobles and Learned Men at Montepellier in France: By Sr Kenelme Digby, Knight, &c. Touching the Cure of Wounds by the Powder of Sympathy; With Instructions How to Make the Said Powders; Whereby Many Other Secrets of Nature Are Unfolded*. Translated by R. White. London: printed for R. Lownes and T. Davies, 1658.

Dionis, Pierre. *A Course of Chirurgical Operations, Demonstrated in the Royal Garden at Paris. By Monsieur Dionis, Chief Chirurgeon to the Late Dauphiness, and to the Present Dutchess of Burgundy. Translated from the Paris Edition*. London, 1710.

Donne, John. 'From a Sermon Preached on Easter Day, 1626'. In *John Donne: the Major Works*, edited by John Carey, 369. Oxford: Oxford University Press, 2000.

'Obsequies to the Lord Harrington, Brother to the Countess of Bedford'. In *John Donne: the Major Works*, edited by John Carey, 252. Oxford: Oxford University Press, 2000.

'Preached at Lincolns Inne'. In *The Sermons of John Donne*, edited by Evelyn Simpson and George Potter, 1–24. Vol. III (of 10), no. 3. Berkeley: University of California Press, 1957.

'A Sermon Preached At the Earl of Bridge-Waters House in London at the Marriage of His Daughter, the Lady Mary, to the Eldest Son of the Lord Herbert of Castle-Iland, November 19 1627'. In *The Sermons of John Donne*, edited by Evelyn Simpson and George Potter, 1–16. Vol. VIII (of 10), no. 7. Berkeley: University of California Press, 1956.

'A Valediction: Of My Name in the Window'. In *John Donne: the Major Works*, edited by John Carey, 102. Oxford: Oxford University Press, 2000.

Dunton, John. *An Essay Proving We Shall Know Our Friends in Heaven*. London: printed and sold by E. Whitlock, 1698.

Elisabeth of Bohemia. 'Elisabeth to Descartes [The Hague] 10 June 1643 (AT 3:683)'. In *The Correspondence between Princess Elisabeth of Bohemia and René Descartes*, edited by Lisa Shapiro, 67–9. Chicago: University of Chicago Press, 2007.

'Elisabeth to Descartes [The Hague] 16 August 1645 (AT 2:268)'. In *The Correspondence between Princess Elisabeth of Bohemia and René Descartes*, edited by Lisa Shapiro, 128–30. Chicago: University of Chicago Press, 2007.

E.W. *Reason and Religion, or, The Certain Rule of Faith*. Antwerp: Michael Cnobbaert, 1672.

Fauchard, Pierre. *The Surgeon Dentist, or, Treatise on the Teeth*. Translated by Lillian Lindsay. 2nd edition. Pound Ridge, NY: Milford House, 1969.

Fletcher, John, and Philip Massinger. 'The Sea Voyage'. In *Three Renaissance Travel Plays*, edited by Anthony Parr, 135–216. Manchester: Manchester University Press, 1995.

Fludd, Robert. *Doctor Fludds Answer Vnto M⸱ Foster or, The Squeesing of Parson Fosters Sponge, Ordained by Him for the Wiping Away of the Weapon-Salve Wherein the Sponge-Bearers Immodest Carriage and Behauiour towards His Bretheren Is Detected; the Bitter Flames of His Slanderous Reports, Are by the Sharpe Vineger of Truth Corrected and Quite Extinguished: And Lastly, the Verrtuous Validity of His Sponge, in Wiping Away of the Weapon-Salve, Is Crushed out and Cleane Abolished*. London: printed for Nathaneal Butter, 1631.

Gauden, John. *A Discourse of Auxiliary Beauty. Or Artificiall Hansomnesse. In Point of Conscience between Two Ladies*. London: printed for R. Royston, 1656.

Gee, Joshua. *The Trade and Navigation of Great-Britain Considered*. London: printed by Sam Buckley, 1729.

Greenhill, Thomas. *Nekrokedeia: Or, the Art of Embalming*. London, 1705.

Guillemeau, Jacques. *Childbirth, or, the Happy Delivery of Women*. London, 1612.

Hay, William. *Deformity: an Essay*. London: printed for R. and J. Dodsley, and sold by M. Cooper, 1754.

Helmont, Johan [Jean] Baptiste van. *A Ternary of Paradoxes. The Magnetick Cure of Wounds*. Translated by Walter Charleston. 2nd edition. London, 1650.

Herrick, Robert. 'Upon Glasco. Epig'. In *Robert Herrick*, edited by Stephen Romer, n.p. London: Faber and Faber, 2010.

Heywood, Thomas. *Gynaikeion: Or, Nine Bookes of Various History. Concerninge Women Inscribed by Ye Names of Ye Nine Muses*. London, 1624.

Hody, Humphrey. *The Resurrection of the (Same) Body Asserted: From the Traditions of the Heathens, the Ancient Jews, and the Primitive Church. With an Answer to the Objections Brought Against It*. London: printed for Awnsham and John Churchill, 1694.

Horne, Johannes van. *Micro-Techne; or, a Methodical Introduction to the Art of Chirurgery*. London: printed by J. Darby, for T. Varnam and J. Osborne, and J. and B. Sprint, 1717.

James, Robert. 'Amputatio''. In *A Medicinal Dictionary*, vol. 1 (of 3), sig. 5GV. London, 1743.

Johnson, Samuel. *The Resurrection of the Same Body, as Asserted and Illustrated by St Paul. A Sermon Preach'd in the Parish-Church of Great Torrington, Devon, on Easter-Day, March 25, 1733*. 2nd edition. London: printed for Lawton Gilliver, Charles Rivington, William Parker, and Samuel Birt, 1741.

La Calprenède, Gaultier de Coste. *Hymen's Præludia, or Loves Master-Peice Being That so Much Admired Romance, Intituled Cleopatra: In Twelve Parts*. London: W.R. and J.R., 1674.

Lemnius, Levinus. *The Secret Miracles of Nature in Four Books: Learnedly and Moderately Treating of Generation, and the Parts Thereof, the Soul, and Its Immortality, of Plants and Living Creatures, of Diseases, Their Symptoms and Cures, and Many Other Rarities*. London: Jo. Streater, 1658.

Locke, John. *An Essay Concerning Human Understanding*. Edited by Roger Woolhouse. Revised edition. London: Penguin Classics, 1998.

Mandeville, Sir John. *The Voyages and Trauailes of Sir John Maundeuile Knight Wherein Is Treated of the Way towards Hierusalem, and of the Meruailes of Inde, with Other Lands and Countries*. London: printed by Thomas Este, 1582.

Mayne, Jasper. *The Amorous Warre*. London: S.N., 1648.

Moyle, John. *Abstractum Chirurgiae Marinae, or, An Abstract of Sea Chirurgery*. London: printed by J. Richardson for Tho. Passinger, 1686.

Mullman, Teresia Constantia. *An Apology for the Conduct of Mrs Teresia Constantia Phillips*. Vol. ii (of 3). London: printed for the booksellers of London and Westminster, 1748.

The Happy Courtezan: Or, the Prude Demolish'd. An Epistle from the Celebrated Mrs C- P-, to the Angelick Signior Far–n–Li. London: printed for J. Roberts, 1735.

The New Atlas, or, Travels and Voyages in Europe, Asia, Africa, and America. London: J. Cleave and A. Roper, 1698.

Paré, Ambroise. *The Apologie and Treatise of Ambroise Paré, Containing the Voyages Made into Divers Places, with Many of His Writings upon Surgery*. Edited by Geoffrey Keynes. London: Falcon Educational Books, 1951.

Ten Books of Surgery with the Magazine of the Instruments Necessary for It. Translated by Robert White Linker and Nathan Womack. Athens: University of Georgia Press, 2010.

The Workes of That Famous Chirurgion Ambrose Parey Translated out of Latine and Compared with the French. by Th: Johnson. London: printed by Th. Cotes and R. Young, 1634.

Pepys, Samuel. *The Diary of Samuel Pepys* (1660–9). Accessed 6 April 2018, www.pepysdiary.com/diary.

Plutarch. *Plutarch's Lives.* London: Jacob Tonson, 1683.

Porterfield, William. *A Treatise on the Eye, the Manner and Phænomena of Vision.* Vol. 1 (of 2). Edinburgh: printed for A. Miller at London, and for G. Hamilton and J. Balfour at Edinburgh, 1759.

The Priest Gelded: Or Popery at the Last Gasp. Shewing . . . the Absolute Necessity of Passing a Law for the Castration of Popish Ecclesiastics. London: A. M'Culloh, 1747.

Pulter, Hester. *Poems, Emblems, and The Unfortunate Florinda.* Edited by Alice Eardley. Toronto: Iter Incorporated, 2014.

'To Sir W.D. upon the Unspeakable Loss of the Most Conspicuous and Chief Ornament of His Frontispiece'. In *Women's Works: 1625–1650*, edited by Donald W. Foster and Tobian Banton. 1st edition, 160–1. New York: Wicked Good Books, 2013.

Rabelais, François. *Gargantua and Pantagruel.* Translated by M. A. Screech. London: Penguin, 2006.

Raleigh, Walter. *Discovery of the Large, Rich, and Beautiful Empire of Guiana, by Sir W. Ralegh: With a Relation of the Great and Golden City of Manoa (Which the Spaniards Call El Dorado), Etc. (1596).* London: Hakluyt Society, 1848.

Read, Alexander. *Chirurgorum Comes; or, The Whole Practice of Chirurgery.* London: Edw. Jones, for Christopher Wilkinson, 1687.

Somatographia Anthropine, or, a Description of the Body of Man. With the Practise of Chirurgery, and the Use of Three and Fifty Instrument. London: printed by Thomas Cotes, and sold by Michael Sparke, 1634.

Ryder, Hugh. *New Practical Observations in Surgery.* London: printed for James Partridge, 1685.

Salmon, William. *Ars Chirurgica.* London, 1698.

Scultetus, Johannes. *The Chyrurgeons Store-House.* Translated by E.B. London: printed for John Starkey, 1674.

Sewers, John. 'Advertisement'. Printed by John Cluer in Twelve-Bell-Court in Bow Church-Yard, Cheapside, 1710. EPH 528:3. Wellcome Library.

Shakespeare, William. *The Oxford Shakespeare: Complete Works*, edited by John Jowett, William Montgomery, Gary Taylor, and Stanley Wells. 2nd edition. Oxford: Clarendon Press, 2005.

The Signior in Fashion: Or the Fair Maid's Conveniency. A Poem on Nicolini's Musick-Meeting. Dublin, 1711.

Sinibaldi, Giovanni Benedetto. *Rare Verities.* London: P. Briggs, 1658.

Smollet, Tobias. *The Adventures of Roderick Random, in Two Volumes.* Vol. 1 (of 2). London: John Osborn, 1748.

Swift, Jonathan. *The Complete Poems*. Edited by Pat Rogers. London: Penguin, 1983.

Tagliacozzi, Gaspare. *De Curtorum Chirurgia per Institionem*. Edited by Robert M. Goldwyn. Translated by Joan H. Thomas. New York: Gryphon Edition, 1996.

'Letter to Hieronymus Mercurialis'. In *The Life and Times of Gaspare Tagliacozzi, Surgeon of Bologna 1545–1599. With a Documented Study of the Scientific and Cultural Life of Bologna in the Sixteenth Century*, by Martha Teach Gnudi and Jerome Pierce Webster, 136–9. New York: H. Reichner, 1950.

T.D. *The Present State of Chyrurgery, with Some Short Remarks on the Abuses Committed under a Pretence to the Practice. And Reasons Offer'd for Regulating the Same*. London, 1703.

T.E. and Robert Boyle. *Some Considerations about the Reconcileableness of Reason and Religion. By T.E. a Lay-Man. To Which Is Annex'd by the Publisher, a Discourse of Mr Boyle, about the Possibility of the Resurrection*. London, 1675.

T.G. *The Friers Chronicle: Or, The True Legend of Priests and Monkes Liues*. London: John Budge, 1623.

The Tryal and Condemnation of Arundel Coke Alias Cooke Esq; and of John Woodburne Labourer, for Felony, in Slitting the Nose of Edward Crispe. London: printed for John Darby and Daniel Midwinter, 1722.

A Trip through the Town. Containing Observations on the Customs and Manners of the Age. 4th edition. London: printed for J. Roberts; and sold by the booksellers of London and Westminster, 1735.

Turner, Daniel. *The Art of Surgery: In Which Is Laid down Such a General Idea of the Same, as Is Confirmed by Practice*. 6th edition. 2 vols. London: printed for C. Rivington and J. Clarke, 1741.

Venette, Nicholas. *The Mysteries of Conjugal Love Reveal'd Written in French by Nicholas de Venette, . . . The 8th Edition. Done into English by a Gentleman*. 2nd edition. London, 1707.

Vicary, Thomas. *The Surgion's Directorie, for Young Practitioners, in Anatomie, Wounds, and Cures, &c. Shewing, the Excellencie of Divers Secrets Belonging to That Noble Art and Mysterie. Very Usefull in These Times upon Any Sodaine Accidents. And May Well Serve, as a Noble Exercise for Gentlewomen and Others; Who Desire Science in Medicine and Surgery, for a Generall Good*. London: printed by T. Fawcett, 1651.

Ward, Edward. *The Second Part of the London Clubs; Containing, the No-Nose Club, the Beaus Club, the Farting Club, the Sodomites, or Mollies Club, The Quacks Club*. London: printed by J. Dutton, 1709.

Ward, John. 'Notebook of John Ward, Vol. 1', n.d. (*c.* 1650–70). Folger Shakespeare Library. V.a. 284–99.

Watts, Isaac. *Philosophical Essays on Various Subjects, Viz. Space, Substance, Body, Spirit, the Operations of the Soul in Union with the Body, Innate Ideas, Perpetual Consciousness, Place and Motion of Spirits, the Departing Soul, the Resurrection of the Body, the Production and Operations of Plants and Animals:*

*With Some Remarks on Mr Locke's Essay on the Human Understanding. To
Which Is Subjoined a Brief Scheme of Ontology, or the Science of Being in
General, with Its Affections.* 4th edition. London: printed for T. Longman, J.
Buckland, J. Oswald, J. Waugh, and J. Ward, 1755.

Weston, John. *The Amazon Queen, or, The Amours of Thalestris to Alexander the
Great.* London: printed for Hen[ry] Harrington, 1667.

Wiseman, Richard. *Several Chirurgical Treatises.* London, 1686.

Woodall, John. 'A Treatise of Gangraena'. In *The Surgeons Mate, or, Military &
Domestique Surgery: Discouering Faithfully & Plainly [the] Method and Order
of [the] Surgeons Chest, [the] Vses of the Instruments, the Vertues and Operations
of [the] Medicines, With [the] Exact Cures of Wounds Made by Gun-Shott; and
Otherwise . . .: With a Treatise of [the] Cure of [the] Plague: Published for the
Service of His Matie. and of the Com. Wealth.* London: printed by Rob.
Young, for Nicholas Bourne, 1639.

Newspapers/Periodicals

The following newspapers and periodicals can be accessed in the Burney
Newspaper Collection, www.galegroup.com.

Daily Courant
Daily Gazetteer
Daily Journal
Daily Post
Flying Post or The Post Master
General Evening Post
London Evening Post
London Journal
Observator
Penny London Post or The Morning Advertiser
Prompter
Tatler
Weekly Journal or British Gazetteer

Secondary Sources

Adams, Tim. 'When Man Meets Metal: Rise of the Transhumans'. *The Observer*,
29 October 2017. www.theguardian.com/technology/2017/oct/29/transhu
man-bodyhacking-transspecies-cyborg.

André, Naomi Adele. *Voicing Gender: Castrati, Travesti, and the Second Woman in
Early-Nineteenth-Century Italian Opera.* Indianapolis: Indiana University
Press, 2006.

Anglin, Sallie J. 'Generative Space: Embodiment and Identity at the Margins on
the Early Modern Stage'. Ph.D. University of Mississippi, 2013.

Appleby, David J. 'Unnecessary Persons? Maimed Soldiers and War Widows in Essex, 1642–1662'. *Essex Archaeology and History*, no. 32 (2001), 209–21.

Arni, Eric Gruber von. *Justice to the Maimed Soldier: Nursing, Medical Care and Welfare for Sick and Wounded Soldiers and their Families during the English Civil Wars and Interregnum.* Aldershot: Ashgate, 2001.

Astbury, Raymond. 'The Renewal of the Licensing Act in 1693 and its Lapse in 1695'. *The Library* 5th series, 33, no. 4 (1978), 296–322. https://doi.org/10.1093/library/s5-XXXIII.4.296.

Bakhtin, Mikhail. *Rabelais and his World.* Translated by Helene Iswolsky. Bloomington: Indiana University Press, 1984.

Bates, Catherine. *Masculinity, Gender and Identity in the English Renaissance Lyric.* Cambridge: Cambridge University Press, 2007.

Bayer, Betty M. 'Between Apparatuses and Apparitions: Phantoms of the Laboratory'. In *Reconstructing the Psychological Subject: Bodies, Practices, and Technologies,* edited by John Shotter and Betty M. Bayer, 187–214. London: Sage, 1998.

Bearden, Elizabeth B. 'Before Normal, There Was Natural: John Bulwer, Disability, and Natural Signing in Early Modern England and Beyond'. *PMLA* 132, no. 1 (2017), 33–50. https://doi.org/10.1632/pmla.2017.132.1.33.

Monstrous Kinds: Body, Space, and Narrative in Renaissance Representations of Disability (Ann Arbor: University of Michigan Press, 2019).

Benhamou, Reed. 'The Artifical Limb in Preindustrial France'. *Technology and Culture* 35, no. 4 (1994), 835–45.

Berek, Peter. '"Looking Jewish" on the Early Modern Stage'. In *Religion and Drama in Early Modern England: the Performance of Religion on the Renaissance Stage,* edited by Jane Hwang Degenhardt and Elizabeth Williamson, 55–70. Farnham: Ashgate, 2011.

Berg, Maxine. *Luxury and Pleasure in Eighteenth-Century Britain.* Oxford: Oxford University Press, 2007.

Berg, Maxine, and Elizabeth Eger. 'The Rise and Fall of the Luxury Debates'. In *Luxury in the Eighteenth Century: Debates, Desires and Delectable Goods,* edited by Maxine Berg and Elizabeth Eger, 7–28. Basingstoke: Palgrave Macmillan, 2016.

Bermudez, Jose Luis. 'Ownership and the Space of the Body'. In *The Subject's Matter: Self-Consciousness and the Body,* edited by Frédérique de Vignemont and Adrian J. T. Alsmith, 117–44. Cambridge: MIT Press, 2017.

Berry, Helen. *The Castrato and his Wife.* Oxford: Oxford University Press, 2012.

'Polite Consumption: Shopping in Eighteenth-Century England'. *Transactions of the Royal Historical Society* 12 (2002), 375–94

Binder, M., J. Eitler, J. Deutschmann, S. Ladstätter, F. Glaser, and D. Fiedler. 'Prosthetics in Antiquity: an Early Medieval Wearer of a Foot Prosthesis (6th Century AD) from Hemmaberg/Austria'. *International Journal of Paleopathology* 12 (March 2016), 29–40. https://doi.org/10.1016/j.ijpp.2015.11.003.

Blackwell, Mark. '"Extraneous Bodies": the Contagion of Live-Tooth Transplantation in Late-Eighteenth-Century England'. *Eighteenth-Century Life* 28, no. 1 (2004), 21–68.

Bourke, Joanna. *The Story of Pain: From Prayer to Painkillers*. Oxford: Oxford University Press, 2014.

Breitenberg, Mark. *Anxious Masculinity in Early Modern England*. Cambridge: Cambridge University Press, 1996.

Burnim, Kalman A. 'Aaron Hill's "The Prompter": an Eighteenth-Century Theatrical Paper'. *Educational Theatre Journal* 13, no. 2 (1961), 73–81. https://doi.org/10.2307/3204685.

Burwood, Stephen. 'The Apparent Truth of Dualism and the Uncanny Body'. *Phenomenology and the Cognitive Sciences* 7, no. 2 (2008), 263–78. https://doi.org/10.1007/s11097-007-9073-z.

Busse, Ashley Denham. '"Quod Me Nutrit Me Destruit": Discovering the Abject on the Early Modern Stage', *Journal of Medieval and Early Modern Studies* 43, no. 1 (2013), 71–98. https://doi.org/10.1215/10829636-1902549.

Bynum, Caroline Walker. 'Material Continuity, Personal Survival, and the Resurrection of the Body: a Scholastic Discussion in its Medieval and Modern Contexts'. *History of Religions* 30, no. 1 (1990), 51–85.

Bynum, William F. 'The Weapon Salve in Seventeenth Century English Drama'. *Journal of the History of Medicine and Allied Sciences* 21, no. 1 (1966), 8–23. https://doi.org/10.1093/jhmas/XXI.1.8.

Cahill, Patricia A. *Unto the Breach: Martial Formations, Historical Trauma, and the Early Modern Stage*. Oxford: Oxford University Press, 2008.

Callaghan, Dympna. *Shakespeare without Women: Representing Gender and Race on the Renaissance Stage*. Accents on Shakespeare. London: Routledge, 2000.

Carlton, Charles. *This Seat of Mars: War and the British Isles, 1485–1746*. New Haven: Yale University Press, 2011.

Cassam, Quassim. 'Introspection and Bodily Self-Ascription'. In *The Body and the Self*, edited by José Luis Bermudez, Anthony Marcel, and Naomi Eilan, 311–37. Cambridge: MIT Press, 1995.

Chalmers, David. 'The Hard Problem of Consciousness'. In *The Blackwell Companion to Consciousness*, edited by Max Velmans and Susan Schneider, 223–35. Oxford: Blackwell, 2007. https://doi.org/10.1002/9780470751466.ch18.

Clark, Andy. 'Gesture as Thought?'. In *The Hand, an Organ of the Mind: What the Manual Tells the Mental*, edited by Zdravko Radman, 255–68. Cambridge: MIT Press, 2013.

Clark, Stuart. *Vanities of the Eye: Vision in Early Modern European Culture*. Oxford: Oxford University Press, 2007.

Cobb, Matthew. 'Exorcizing the Animal Spirits: Jan Swammerdam on Nerve Function'. *National Review of Neuroscience* 3, no. 5 (2002), 395–400. https://doi.org/10.1038/nrn806

Generation: the Seventeenth-Century Scientists Who Unraveled the Secrets of Sex, Life, and Growth. New York: Bloomsbury Publishing USA, 2008.

Cock, Emily. '"Lead[Ing] 'em by the Nose into Publick Shame and Derision":
Gaspare Tagliacozzi, Alexander Read and the Lost History of Plastic Surgery,
1600–1800'. *Social History of Medicine* 28, no. 1 (2015), 1–21. https://doi
.org/10.1093/shm/hku070.
  Rhinoplasty and the Nose in Early Modern British Medicine and Culture.
Manchester: Manchester University Press, 2019.
Cohen, Jon. 'Brain Implants Could Restore the Ability to Form Memories'. *MIT
Technology Review.* Accessed 29 May 2018. www.technologyreview.com/s/
513681/memory-implants/.
Coker-Durso, Lauren G. 'Metatheatricality and Disability Drag: Performing
Bodily Difference on the Early Modern English Stage'. Ph.D. Saint Louis
University, 2014.
Cole, Andrew. 'The Call of Things: a Critique of Object-Oriented Ontologies'.
Minnesota Review no. 80 (2013), 106–18.
Coral, Jordi. '"Maiden Walls That War Hath Never Entered": Rape and Post-
Chivalric Military Culture in Shakespeare's *Henry V*. *College Literature* 44,
no. 3 (2017), 404–35. https://doi.org/10.1353/lit.2017.0021.
Covington, Sarah. *Wounds, Flesh, and Metaphor in Seventeenth-Century England.*
Basingstoke: Palgrave Macmillan, 2009.
Craik, Katherine, and Tanya Pollard, eds. *Shakespearean Sensations: Experiencing
Literature in Early Modern England.* Cambridge: Cambridge University
Press, 2013.
Crane, Mary Thomas. *Shakespeare's Brain: Reading with Cognitive Theory.*
Princeton: Princeton University Press, 2010.
Crawford, Cassandra S. 'Body Image, Prostheses, Phantom Limbs'. *Body and
Society* 21, no. 2 (2015), 221–44. https://doi.org/10.1177/
1357034X14522102.
  '"You Don't Need a Body to Feel a Body": Phantom Limb Syndrome and
Corporeal Transgression'. *Sociology of Health and Illness* 35, no. 3 (2013),
434–48. https://doi.org/10.1111/j.1467-9566.2012.01498.x.
Crawford, Katherine. 'Desiring Castrates, or How to Create Disabled Social
Subjects'. *Journal for Early Modern Cultural Studies* 16, no. 2 (2016),
59–90. https://doi.org/10.1353/jem.2016.0011.
Crawford, Patricia. 'Attitudes to Menstruation in Seventeenth-Century England'.
Past and Present 91 (1981), 46–73.
Cuffari, Elena. 'Gestural Sense-Making: Hand Gestures as Intersubjective
Linguistic Enactments'. *Phenomenology and the Cognitive Sciences* 11, no. 4
(2012), 599–622. https://doi.org/10.1007/s11097-011-9244-9
Cunning, David. *The Cambridge Companion to Descartes' Meditations.*
Cambridge: Cambridge University Press, 2014.
Daniel, Drew. *The Melancholy Assemblage: Affect and Epistemology in the English
Renaissance.* New York: Fordham University Press, 2013.
DARPA (Defense Advanced Research Projects Agency). 'Revolutionizing
Prosthetics'. Accessed 28 May 2018. www.darpa.mil/program/revolutioniz
ing-prosthetics.

Davis, Lennard J. 'Dr Johnson, Amelia, and the Discourse of Disability in the Eighteenth Century'. In *Defects: Engendering the Modern Body*, edited by Helen Deutsch and Felicity Nussbaum, 54–74. Ann Arbor: University of Michigan Press, 2000.

Dawson, Mark S. 'First Impressions: Newspaper Advertisements and Early Modern English Body Imaging, 1651–1750', *Journal of British Studies* 50, no. 2 (2011), 277–306.

de Renzi, Silva. 'Old and New Models of the Body'. In *The Healing Arts: Health, Disease and Society in Europe, 1500–1800*, edited by Peter Elmer, 166–9. Manchester: Manchester University Press, 2004.

Dean, Darron, Andrew Hann, Mark Overton, and Jane Whittle. *Production and Consumption in English Households, 1600–1750*. Florence: Routledge, 2004.

Deutsch, Helen, and Felicity Nussbaum, 'Introduction'. In *Defects: Engendering the Modern Body*, edited by Helen Deutsch and Felicity Nussbaum, 1–30. Ann Arbor: University of Michigan Press, 2000.

Dickenson, Donna, and Guy Widdershoven. 'Ethical Issues in Limb Transplants'. *Bioethics* 15, no. 2 (2001), 110–24.

Dickie, Simon. *Cruelty and Laughter: Forgotten Comic Literature and the Unsentimental Eighteenth Century*. Chicago: University of Chicago Press, 2011.

Doherty, Francis Cecil. *A Study in Eighteenth-Century Advertising Methods: the Anodyne Necklace*. Lewiston: Edwin Mellen Press, 1992.

Dohmen, Josh. 'Disability as Abject: Kristeva, Disability, and Resistance'. *Hypatia* 31, no. 4 (2016), 762–78. https://doi.org/10.1111/hypa.12266.

Donagan, Barbara. 'Law, War and Women in Seventeenth-Century England'. In *Sexual Violence in Conflict Zones: From the Ancient World to the Era of Human Rights*, edited by Elizabeth D. Heineman, 189–201. Philadelphia: University of Pennsylvania Press, 2011.

Dugan, Holly. *The Ephemeral History of Perfume: Scent and Sense in Early Modern England*. Baltimore: Johns Hopkins University Press, 2011.

Duncan, Cheryll. 'Castrati and Impresarios in London: Two Mid-Eighteenth-Century Lawsuits'. *Cambridge Opera Journal* 24, no. 1 (2012), 43–65.

Dupond, Pascal. *Le vocabulaire de Merleau-Ponty*. Paris: Ellipses Marketing, 2001.

Eastwood, Bruce Stansfield. 'Descartes on Refraction: Scientific versus Rhetorical Method'. *Isis* 75, no. 3 (1984), 481–502. https://doi.org/10.1086/353568.

Eccles, Audrey. *Vagrancy in Law and Practice under the Old Poor Law*. Farnham: Ashgate, 2012.

Edmond, Mary. *Rare Sir William Davenant: Poet Laureate, Playwright, Civil War General, Restoration Theatre Manager*. Manchester: Manchester University Press, 1987.

Ehrman, Terrence. 'Disability and Resurrection Identity'. *New Blackfriars* 96, no. 1066 (2015), 723–38. https://doi.org/10.1111/nbfr.12126.

Fawcett, Mary Laughlin. 'Arms/Words/Tears: Language and the Body in *Titus Andronicus*'. *ELH* 50, no. 2 (1983), 261–77. https://doi.org/10.2307/2872816.

Feather, Jennifer. 'Contagious Pity: Cultural Difference and the Language of Contagion in *Titus Andronicus*'. In *Contagion and the Shakespearean Stage*, edited by Darryl Chalk and Mary Floyd-Wilson, 169–87. Basingstoke: Palgrave Macmillan, 2019.

Feldman, Martha. *The Castrato: Reflections on Natures and Kinds*. Oakland: University of California Press, 2015.

Festa, Lynn M. 'Personal Effects: Wigs and Possessive Individualism in the Long Eighteenth Century'. *Eighteenth-Century Life* 29, no. 2 (2005), 47–90.

Finucci, Valeria. *The Manly Masquerade: Masculinity, Paternity, and Castration in the Italian Renaissance*. Durham: Duke University Press, 2003.

Fisher, Will. *Materializing Gender in Early Modern English Literature and Culture*. Cambridge: Cambridge University Press, 2006.

Fissell, Mary Elizabeth. *Vernacular Bodies: the Politics of Reproduction in Early Modern England*. Oxford: Oxford University Press, 2004.

Floyd-Wilson, Mary, Matthew Greenfield, Gail Kern Paster, Tanya Pollard, Katherine Rowe, and Julian Yates. 'Shakespeare and Embodiment: an E-Conversation'. *Literature Compass* 2, no. 1 (2005). https://doi.org/10.1111/j.1741-4113.2005.00180.x.

Forstrom, K. Joanna S. *John Locke and Personal Identity: Immortality and Bodily Resurrection in 17th-Century Philosophy*. London: Bloomsbury, 2011.

Frandsen, Mary E. '"Eunuchi Conjugium": the Marriage of a Castrato in Early Modern Germany'. *Early Music History* 24 (2005), 53–124.

Fraser, Mat. 'Cripping It Up'. *Journal of Visual Art Practice* 12, no. 3 (2013), 245–48. https://doi.org/10.1386/jvap.12.3.245_1.

Freitas, Roger. 'The Eroticism of Emasculation: Confronting the Baroque Body of the Castrato'. *Journal of Musicology* 20, no. 2 (2003), 196–249.

Portrait of a Castrato: Politics, Patronage, and Music in the Life of Atto Melani. Cambridge: Cambridge University Press, 2009.

Fumerton, Patricia. 'Making Vagrancy (In)Visible: the Economics of Disguise in Early Modern Rogue Pamphlets'. *English Literary Renaissance* 33, no. 2 (2003), 211–27. https://doi.org/10.1111/1475-6757.00026.

Gallagher, Shaun. 'The Enactive Hand'. In *The Hand, an Organ of the Mind: What the Manual Tells the Mental*, edited by Zdravko Radman, 209–26. Cambridge: MIT Press, 2013.

How the Body Shapes the Mind. Oxford: Oxford University Press, 2005.

Gittings, Clare. 'Eccentric or Enlightened? Unusual Burial and Commemoration in England, 1689–1823'. *Mortality* 12, no. 4 (2007), 321–49. https://doi.org/10.1080/13576270701609667.

Glaisyer, Natasha. '"The Most Universal Intelligencers"', *Media History* 23, no. 2 (2017), 256–80. https://doi.org/10.1080/13688804.2017.1309971.

Gnudi, Martha Teach, and Jerome Pierce Webster. *The Life and Times of Gaspare Tagliacozzi, Surgeon of Bologna, 1545–1599. With a Documented Study of the Scientific and Cultural Life of Bologna in the Sixteenth Century*. New York: H. Reichner, 1950.

Gowland, Angus. 'Melancholy, Passions and Identity in the Renaissance'. In *Passions and Subjectivity in Early Modern Culture*, edited by Freya Sierhuis and Brian Cummings, 75–94. Farnham: Ashgate, 2013.

Graham, S. Scott. *The Politics of Pain Medicine: a Rhetorical-Ontological Inquiry.* Chicago: University of Chicago Press, 2015.

Grazia, Margreta de, Maureen Quilligan, and Peter Stallybrass, eds. *Subject and Object in Renaissance Culture.* Cambridge: Cambridge University Press, 1996.

Guerrini, Anita. 'The Ethics of Animal Experimentation in Seventeenth-Century England'. *Journal of the History of Ideas* 50, no. 3 (1989), 391–407. https://doi.org/10.2307/2709568.

Hamilton, David. *A History of Organ Transplantation: Ancient Legends to Modern Practice.* Pittsburgh: University of Pittsburgh Press, 2012.

Hargreaves, A. S. *White as Whales Bone: Dental Services in Early Modern England.* Leeds: Northern Universities Press, 1998.

Harris, Michael. 'Timely Notices: the Uses of Advertising and its Relationship to News during the Late Seventeenth Century'. In *News, Newspapers and Society in Early Modern Britain*, edited by Joad Raymond, 141–56. Abingdon: Routledge, 2013.

Hide, Louise, Joanna Bourke, and Carmen Mangion. 'Perspectives on Pain: Introduction'. *19: Interdisciplinary Studies in the Long Nineteenth Century* no. 15 (2012). https://doi.org/10.16995/ntn.663.

Hirsch, David A. Hedrich. 'Donne's Atomies and Anatomies: Deconstructed Bodies and the Resurrection of Atomic Theory'. *Studies in English Literature, 1500–1900* 31, no. 1 (1991), 69–94. https://doi.org/10.2307/450444.

Hobgood, Allison, and David Houston Wood. 'Early Modern Literature and Disability Studies'. In *The Cambridge Companion to Literature and Disability*, edited by Clare Barker and Stuart Murray, 32–46. Cambridge: Cambridge University Press, 2017.

Hollis, Gavin. *The Absence of America: the London Stage, 1576–1642.* Oxford: Oxford University Press, 2015.

Hudson, Geoffrey L. 'Disabled Veterans and the State in Early Modern England'. In *Disabled Veterans in History*, edited by David A. Gerber, 117–44. Ann Arbor: University of Michigan Press, 2012.

Huffman, Shawn. 'Amputation, Phantom Limbs, and Spectral Agency in Shakespeare's *Titus Andronicus* and Normand Chaurette's *Les Reines*'. *Modern Drama* 47, no. 1 (2004), 66–81. https://doi.org/10.1353/mdr.2004.0012.

Hug, Tobias. *Impostures in Early Modern England: Representations and Perceptions of Fraudulent Identities.* Manchester: Manchester University Press, 2010.

Hughes, Bill. 'Wounded/Monstrous/Abject: a Critique of the Disabled Body in the Sociological Imaginary', *Disability and Society* 24, no. 4 (2009), 399–410. https://doi.org/10.1080/09687590902876144.

Hyman, Wendy Beth. 'Introduction'. In *The Automaton in English Renaissance Literature*, edited by Wendy Beth Hyman, 1–18. Farnham: Ashgate, 2011.

Imbracsio, Nicola M. 'Stage Hands: Shakespeare's *Titus Andronicus* and the Agency of the Disabled Body in Text and Performance'. *Journal of Literary and Cultural Disability Studies* 6, no. 3 (2012), 291–306.

'Jan Plamper On the History of Emotions | The History of Emotions Blog'. Accessed 5 September 2017. https://emotionsblog.history.qmul.ac.uk/2017/09/jan-plamper-on-the-history-of-emotions/.

Jarman, Freya. 'Pitch Fever: the Castrato, the Tenor and the Question of Masculinity in Nineteenth-Century Opera'. In *Masculinity in Opera*, edited by Philip Purvis, 51–65. London: Routledge, 2013.

Jaynes, Julian. 'The Problem of Animate Motion in the Seventeenth Century', *Journal of the History of Ideas* 31, no. 2 (1970), 219–34. https://doi.org/10.2307/2708546.

Johnson, Laurie, John Sutton, and Evelyn Tribble. *Embodied Cognition and Shakespeare's Theatre: the Early Modern Body-Mind*. Abingdon: Routledge, 2014.

Kahl, Rebecca A. 'Dog-Faced Deflores: Disability in Early Modern Literature'. MA. Northern Michigan University, 2013.

Kaplan, David M. *Ricoeur's Critical Theory*. New York: State University of New York Press, 2003.

Karim-Cooper, Farah. *Cosmetics in Shakespearean and Renaissance Drama*. Edinburgh: Edinburgh University Press, 2006.

The Hand on the Shakespearean Stage: Gesture, Touch and the Spectacle of Dismemberment. London: Bloomsbury, 2016.

Kassell, Lauren. 'Medical Understandings of the Body'. In *The Routledge History of Sex and the Body*, edited by Kate Fisher and Sarah Toulalan, 57–74. Abingdon: Routledge, 2013.

King, Emily. 'The Female Muselmann: Desire, Violence and Spectatorship in *Titus Andronicus*'. In *Titus out of Joint: Reading the Fragmented Titus Andronicus*, edited by Liberty Stanavage and Paxton Hehmeyer, 125–40. Cambridge: Cambridge Scholars Publishing, 2012.

King, Thomas A. 'The Castrato's Castration'. *SEL Studies in English Literature 1500–1900* 46, no. 3 (2006), 563–83.

Kirkham, Anne, and Cordelia Warr. *Wounds in the Middle Ages*. London: Routledge, 2016.

Kraftchick, Steven John. 'Bodies, Selves, and Human Identity: a Conversation between Transhumanism and the Apostle Paul'. *Theology Today* 72, no. 1 (2015), 47–69.

Kristeva, Julia. *Powers of Horror: an Essay on Abjection*, translated by Leon S. Roudiez. New York: Columbia University Press, 1982; first published in French 1980.

Krueger, Joel. 'Extended Cognition and the Space of Social Interaction'. *Consciousness and Cognition* 20, no. 3 (2011), 643–57. https://doi.org/10.1016/j.concog.2010.09.022

Kuzner, James. *Open Subjects: English Renaissance Republicans, Modern Selfhoods, and the Virtue of Vulnerability*. Edinburgh: Edinburgh University Press, 2011.

Lamb, Caroline. 'Physical Trauma and (Adapt)Ability in *Titus Andronicus*'. *Critical Survey* 22, no. 1 (2010), 41–57.

Leder, Drew. *The Absent Body*. Chicago: University of Chicago Press, 1990.

'Medicine and Paradigms of Embodiment'. *Journal of Medicine and Philosophy: a Forum for Bioethics and Philosophy of Medicine* 9, no. 1 (1984), 29–44. https://doi.org/10.1093/jmp/9.1.29.

'Whose Body? What Body? The Metaphysics of Organ Transplantation'. In *Persons and Their Bodies: Rights, Responsibilities, Relationships*, 233–64. Dordrecht: Springer, 1999. https://doi.org/10.1007/0-306-46866-2_10.

Lee, Dave. 'When your Body Becomes Eligible for an Upgrade'. *BBC News*, 15 July 2017. www.bbc.co.uk/news/technology-40616561.

Lindemann, Mary. *Medicine and Society in Early Modern Europe*. 2nd edition. Cambridge: Cambridge University Press, 2010.

Linster, Jillian Faith. 'Books, Bodies, and the "Great Labor" of Helkiah Crooke's Mikrokosmographia'. Ph.D. University of Iowa, 2017.

Lobis, Seth. *The Virtue of Sympathy: Magic, Philosophy, and Literature in Seventeenth-Century England*. Yale Studies in English. New Haven: Yale University Press, 2015.

Lodhia, Sheetal. 'Material Self-Fashioning and the Renaissance Culture of Improvement'. Ph.D. Queen's University, 2008.

Lott, Tommy L. 'Descartes on Phantom Limbs'. *Mind and Language* 1, no. 3 (1986), 243–71. https://doi.org/10.1111/j.1468-0017.1986.tb00103.x.

Lyne, Raphael, and Timothy Chesters, eds. *Movement in Renaissance Literature: Exploring Kinesic Intelligence*. Basingstoke: Palgrave, 2017.

Manchikanti, Laxmaiah, Vijay Singh, and Mark V. Boswell. 'Phantom Pain Syndromes'. In *Pain Management*, edited by Steven D. Waldman, 304–15. Philadelphia: W. B. Saunders, 2007. https://doi.org/10.1016/B978-0-7216-0334-6.50032-7.

Manzocco, Roberto. *Transhumanism: Engineering the Human Condition: History, Philosophy and Current Status*. Leiden: Springer, 2019.

Marshall, Peter. *Beliefs and the Dead in Reformation England*. Oxford: Oxford University Press, 2002.

'Maunsell [Married Name Kingsman], Dorothea (b. 1749x51), Figure of Scandal', in *Oxford Dictionary of National Biography*, accessed 4 December 2019. https://doi.org/10.1093/ref:odnb/104868.

Maus, Katharine Eisaman. *Inwardness and Theater in the English Renaissance*. Chicago: University of Chicago Press, 1995.

Meer, Theo van der. 'Sodomy and the Pursuit of a Third Sex in the Early Modern Period'. In *Third Sex, Third Gender: Beyond Sexual Dimorphism in Culture and History*, edited by Gilbert Herdt, 137–212. New York: Zone Books, 1994.

Menary, Richard. 'The Enculturated Hand'. In *The Hand, an Organ of the Mind: What the Manual Tells the Mental*, edited by Zdravko Radman, 349–67. Cambridge: MIT Press, 2013.

Mentz, Steve. 'Half-Fish, Half-Flesh: Dolphins, the Ocean, and Early Modern Humans'. In *The Indistinct Human in Renaissance Literature*, edited by Jean E. Feerick and Vin Nardizzi, 27–46. New York: Palgrave Macmillan, 2012.

Metzler, Irina. *Disability in Medieval Europe: Thinking about Physical Impairment in the High Middle Ages, c. 1100–c. 1400* (Abingdon: Routledge, 2006).

'Disability in the Middle Ages: Impairment at the Intersection of Historical Inquiry and Disability Studies'. *History Compass* 9, no. 1 (2011): 45–60. https://doi.org/10.1111/j.1478-0542.2010.00746.x.

A Social History of Disability in the Middle Ages: Cultural Considerations of Physical Impairment. London: Routledge, 2013.

More, Max. 'The Philosophy of Transhumanism'. In *Transhumanist Reader: Classical and Contemporary Essays on the Science, Technology, and Philosophy of the Human Future*, edited by Max More and Natasha Vita-More, 1–18. Somerset: Wiley, 2013.

More, Max and Natasha Vita-More, eds. *Transhumanist Reader: Classical and Contemporary Essays on the Science, Technology, and Philosophy of the Human Future.* Somerset: Wiley, 2013.

Mounsey, Chris. 'Variability: Beyond Sameness and Difference'. In *The Idea of Disability in the Eighteenth Century*, edited by Chris Mounsey, 1–28. Cranbury: Bucknell University Press, 2014.

Moyer, Ann E. 'Sympathy in the Renaissance'. In *Sympathy: a History*, edited by Eric Schliesser, 71–102. Oxford: Oxford University Press, 2015.

Neely, Carol Thomas. *Distracted Subjects: Madness and Gender in Shakespeare and Early Modern Culture.* New York: Cornell University Press, 2004.

Nevitt, Marcus. 'The Insults of Defeat: Royalist Responses to Sir William Davenant's *Gondibert* (1651)'. *The Seventeenth Century* 24, no. 2 (2009), 287–304.

Nussbaum, Felicity. *The Limits of the Human: Fictions of Anomaly, Race and Gender in the Long Eighteenth Century.* Cambridge: Cambridge University Press, 2003.

Ochs, Sydney. *A History of Nerve Functions: From Animal Spirits to Molecular Mechanisms.* Cambridge: Cambridge University Press, 2004.

O'Connell, Mark. *To Be a Machine: Adventures among Cyborgs, Utopians, Hackers, and the Futurists Solving the Modest Problem of Death.* London: Granta Books, 2017.

Oldridge, Darren. *Strange Histories: the Trial of the Pig, the Walking Dead, and Other Matters of Fact from the Medieval and Renaissance Worlds.* Florence: Taylor and Francis, 2004.

'Paré A (1575)', *James Lind Library*, 26 May 2010. Accessed 7 November 2019. www.jameslindlibrary.org/pare-a-1575/.

Parkes, Pamela. 'Leg-Loss Patients Left in Limbo'. *BBC News*, 17 January 2016. www.bbc.co.uk/news/uk-england-somerset-34879100.

Parton, Chloe M., Jane M. Ussher, and Janette Perz, 'Women's Construction of Embodiment and the Abject Sexual Body after Cancer'. *Qualitative Health*

Research 26, no. 4 (2016), 490–503. https://doi.org/10.1177/
1049732315570130.

Paster, Gail Kern. *The Body Embarrassed: Drama and the Disciplines of Shame in Early Modern England*. New York: Cornell University Press, 1993.

'Nervous Tension: Networks of Blood and Spirit in the Early Modern Body'. In *The Body in Parts: Fantasies of Corporeality in Early Modern Europe*, edited by David A. Hillman and Carla Mazzio, 107–25. New York: Routledge, 1997.

Patterson, Sarah. 'Descartes on the Errors of the Senses'. *Royal Institute of Philosophy Supplement* 78 (2016), 73–108.

Pennell, Sara. 'Consumption and Consumerism in Early Modern England'. *Historical Journal* 42, no. 2 (1999), 549–64

Peschel, Enid Rhodes, and Richard E. Peschel. 'Medical Insights into the Castrati in Opera'. *American Scientist* 75, no. 6 (1987), 578–83.

Porter, Martin. *Windows of the Soul: Physiognomy in European Culture, 1470 – 1780*. Oxford: Clarendon Press, 2005.

Porter, Roy. *Flesh in the Age of Reason*. London: Allen Lane, 2003.

Price, Douglas B., and Neil J. Twombly. *The Phantom Limb Phenomenon: a Medical, Folkloric, and Historical Study. Texts and Translations of 10th to 20th Century Accounts of the Miraculous Restoration of Lost Body Parts*. Washington: Georgetown University Press, 1978.

Priest, Stephen. *Merleau-Ponty*. London: Routledge, 1998.

'Prosthetic FAQs for the New Amputee'. *Amputee Coalition* (blog). Accessed 11 May 2018. www.amputee-coalition.org/resources/prosthetic-faqs-for-the-new-amputee/.

Ramachandran, V. S., and D. Rogers-Ramachandran, 'Synaesthesia in Phantom Limbs Induced with Mirrors'. *Proceedings: Biological Sciences* 263, no. 1369 (1996), 377–86.

Raven, James. *Publishing Business in Eighteenth-Century England*. Woodbridge: Boydell and Brewer, 2014.

Rey, Roselyne. *The History of Pain*. Translated by Louise Elliot Wallace, J. A. Cadden, and S. W. Cadden. Cambridge: Harvard University Press, 1995.

Robinson, Benedict S. 'Thinking Feeling'. In *Affect Theory and Early Modern Texts: Politics, Ecologies, and Form*, edited by Amanda Bailey and Mario DiGangi, 109–27. New York: Palgrave Macmillan, 2017.

Robinson, Douglas. *Estrangement and the Somatics of Literature: Tolstoy, Shklovsky, Brecht*. Baltimore: Johns Hopkins University Press, 2008.

Rosselli, John. 'The Castrati as a Professional Group and a Social Phenomenon, 1550–1850'. *Acta Musicologica* 60, no. 2 (n.d.), 143–79.

Rousseau, George Sebastian, and Roy Porter. *Sexual Underworlds of the Enlightenment*. Manchester: Manchester University Press, 1987.

Rowe, Katherine. 'God's Handy Worke'. In *The Body in Parts: Fantasies of Corporeality in Early Modern Europe*, edited by David A. Hillman and Carla Mazzio, 285–311. New York: Routledge, 1997.

Row-Heyveld, Lindsey. *Dissembling Disability in Early Modern English Drama*. Basingstoke: Palgrave, 2018.

'Dissembling Disability: Performances of the Non-Standard Body in Early Modern England'. Ph.D. University of Iowa, 2011. http://ir.uiowa.edu/etd/4906/.

Rowlands, Mark. *The New Science of the Mind: From Extended Mind to Embodied Phenomenology*. Cambridge: MIT Press, 2010.

Ryan, Frances. 'We Wouldn't Accept Actors Blacking up, so Why Applaud "Cripping up"?'. *The Guardian*, 13 January 2015. www.theguardian.com/commentisfree/2015/jan/13/eddie-redmayne-golden-globe-stephen-hawking-disabled-actors-characters.

Savoia, Paolo. *Gaspare Tagliacozzi and Early Modern Surgery: Faces, Men and Pain*. London: Routledge, 2019.

Sawday, Jonathan. *The Body Emblazoned: Dissection and the Human Body in Renaissance Culture*. Abingdon: Routledge, 2013.

'"I Feel Your Pain": Some Reflections on the (Literary) Perception of Pain'. In *The Hurt(Ful) Body: Performing and Beholding Pain, 1600–1800*, edited by Tomas Macsotay, Cornelis Van der Haven, and Karl Vanhaesebrouck, 97–114. Manchester: Manchester University Press, 2017.

Schoenfeldt, Michael C. *Bodies and Selves in Early Modern England: Physiology and Inwardness in Spenser, Shakespeare, Herbert, and Milton*. Cambridge: Cambridge University Press, 1999.

'Shakespearean Pain'. In *Shakespearean Sensations: Experiencing Literature in Early Modern England*, edited by Katharine A. Craik and Tanya Pollard, 191–207. Cambridge: Cambridge University Press, 2013.

Schwarz, Kathryn. 'Death and Theory: Or, the Problem of Counterfactual Sex'. In *Sex before Sex: Figuring the Act in Early Modern England*, edited by James M. Bromley and Will Stockton, 52–88. Minneapolis: University of Minnesota Press, 2013.

Tough Love: Amazon Encounters in the English Renaissance. Fordham: Duke University Press, 2000.

Shapiro, Lisa. 'Elisabeth, Princess of Bohemia'. In *The Stanford Encyclopedia of Philosophy*, edited by Edward N. Zalta. Stanford: Metaphysics Research Lab, Stanford University, 2014. https://plato.stanford.edu/archives/win2014/entries/elisabeth-bohemia/.

'Princess Elizabeth and Descartes: the Union of Soul and Body and the Practice of Philosophy'. *British Journal for the History of Philosophy* 7, no. 3 (1999), 503–20. https://doi.org/10.1080/09608789908571042.

Shepard, Alexandra. *Meanings of Manhood in Early Modern England*. Oxford: Oxford University Press, 2006.

Shepherd, Simon. *Amazons and Warrior Women: Varieties of Feminism in Seventeenth-Century Drama*. Brighton: Prentice Hall/Harvester Wheatsheaf, 1981.

Silvers, Anita. 'Feminism and Disability'. In *The Blackwell Guide to Feminist Philosophy*, edited by Linda Martín Alcoff and Eva Feder Kittay, 131–42. Oxford: Blackwell, 2007.

Skinner, Patricia. 'The Gendered Nose and Its Lack: "Medieval" Nose-Cutting and its Modern Manifestations'. *Journal of Women's History* 26, no. 1 (2014), 45–67. https://doi.org/10.1353/jowh.2014.0008.

Skuse, Alanna. *Constructions of Cancer in Early Modern England: Ravenous Natures*. Basingstoke: Palgrave Macmillan, 2015.

'"Keep your Face out of my Way or I'll Bite off your Nose": Homoplastics, Sympathy, and the Noble Body in the *Tatler*, 1710'. *Journal for Early Modern Cultural Studies* 17, no. 4 (2018), 113–32.

'Missing Parts in *The Shoemaker's Holiday*'. *Renaissance Drama* 45, no. 2 (2017), 161–79. https://doi.org/10.1086/694329.

'"One Stroak of His Razour": Tales of Self-Gelding in Early Modern England'. *Social History of Medicine* 33, no. 2 (2020), 377–93. https://doi.org/10.1093/shm/hky100.

'Wombs, Worms and Wolves: Constructing Cancer in Early Modern England'. *Social History of Medicine* 27, no. 4 (2014), 632–48.

Slatman, Jenny. 'Is It Possible to "Incorporate" a Scar? Revisiting a Basic Concept in Phenomenology'. *Human Studies* 39, no. 3 (2016), 347–63. https://doi.org/10.1007/s10746-015-9372-2.

Slatman, Jenny, and Guy Widdershoven. 'Hand Transplants and Bodily Integrity'. *Body and Society* 16, no. 3 (2010), 69–92. https://doi.org/10.1177/1357034X10373406.

Smith, Bruce R. 'Premodern Sexualities'. *PMLA* 115, no. 3 (2000), 318–29. https://doi.org/10.2307/463453.

Snyder, Sharon L., and David T. Mitchell, *Cultural Locations of Disability*. Chicago: University of Chicago Press, 2010.

Sobchack, Vivian. 'A Leg to Stand On: Prosthetics, Metaphor, and Materiality'. In *The Prosthetic Impulse: From a Posthuman Present to a Biocultural Future*, edited by Marquard Smith and Joanne Morra, 17–42. Cambridge: MIT Press, 2006.

'Living a "Phantom Limb": On the Phenomenology of Bodily Integrity'. *Body and Society* 16, no. 3 (2010), 51–67. https://doi.org/10.1177/1357034X10373407.

Solga, Kim. *Violence against Women in Early Modern Performance: Invisible Acts*. Basingstoke: Palgrave Macmillan, 2009.

Stevens, Scott Manning. 'Sacred Heart and Secular Brain'. In *The Body in Parts: Fantasies of Corporeality in Early Modern Europe*, edited by David A. Hillman and Carla Mazzio, 263–84. New York: Routledge, 1997.

Stoyle, Mark. '"Memories of the Maimed": the Testimony of Charles I's Former Soldiers, 1660–1730'. *History* 88, no. 290 (2003), 204–26. https://doi.org/10.1111/1468-229X.00259.

Strickland, Lloyd. 'The Doctrine of "the Resurrection of the Same Body" in Early Modern Thought'. *Religious Studies* 46, no. 2 (2010), 163–83.

Sutherland, James. *The Restoration Newspaper and its Development*. Cambridge: Cambridge University Press, 2004.

Sutton, John. 'Spongy Brains and Material Memories'. In *Environment and Embodiment in Early Modern England*, edited by Mary Floyd-Wilson and Garrett A. Sullivan, Jr., 14–34. Basingstoke: Palgrave Macmillan, 2007.

Tarlow, Sarah. *Ritual, Belief and the Dead in Early Modern Britain and Ireland*. Cambridge: Cambridge University Press, 2010.

Tilmouth, Christopher. 'Passion and Intersubjectivity in Early Modern Literature'. In *Passions and Subjectivity in Early Modern Culture*, edited by Freya Sierhuis and Brian Cummings, 13–32. Farnham: Ashgate, 2013.

Tribble, Evelyn. *Cognition in the Globe: Attention and Memory in Shakespeare's Theatre*. New York: Palgrave Macmillan, 2011.

Tucker, Holly. *Blood Work: a Tale of Medicine and Murder in the Scientific Revolution*. New York: W. W. Norton, 2012.

Turner, David M. *Disability in Eighteenth-Century England: Imagining Physical Impairment*. Abingdon: Routledge, 2012.

Turner, David M., and Kevin Stagg. *Social Histories of Disability and Deformity: Bodies, Images and Experiences*. Abingdon: Routledge, 2006.

Turner, David M., and Alun Withey. 'Technologies of the Body: Polite Consumption and the Correction of Deformity in Eighteenth-Century England: Technologies of the Body'. *History* 99, no. 338 (2014), 775–96. https://doi.org/10.1111/1468-229X.12087.

van Dijkhuizen, Jan Frans, and Karl Enenkel. *The Sense of Suffering: Constructions of Physical Pain in Early Modern Culture*. Leiden: Brill, 2009.

Wade, Nicholas J. 'The Legacy of Phantom Limbs', *Perception* 32, no. 5 (2003): 517–24. https://doi.org/10.1068/p3205ed.

'The Vision of William Porterfield'. In *Brain, Mind and Medicine: Essays in Eighteenth-Century Neuroscience*, edited by Harry Whitaker, C. U. M. Smith, and Stanley Finger, 163–77. New York: Springer, 2007.

Wade, Nicholas J., and Stanley Finger. 'Phantom Penis: Historical Dimensions'. *Journal of the History of the Neurosciences* 19, no. 4 (2010), 299–312. https://doi.org/10.1080/09647040903363006.

'William Porterfield (ca. 1696–1771) and His Phantom Limb: an Overlooked First Self-Report by a Man of Medicine', *Neurosurgery* 52, no. 5 (2003), 1196–9. https://doi.org/10.1227/01.NEU.0000057837.74142.68.

Wagner, Darren N. 'Body, Mind and Spirits: the Physiology of Sexuality in the Culture of Sensibility', *Journal for Eighteenth-Century Studies* 39, no. 3 (2016), 335–8. https://doi.org/10.1111/1754-0208.12336.

Walker, Garthine. *Crime, Gender and Social Order in Early Modern England*. Cambridge: Cambridge University Press, 2003.

Waskul, Dennis D., and Pamela van der Riet, 'The Abject Embodiment of Cancer Patients: Dignity, Selfhood, and the Grotesque Body'. *Symbolic Interaction* 25, no. 4 (2002), 487–513. https://doi.org/10.1525/si.2002.25.4.487.

Weaver, Darren, Corey Protin and Paul Szoldra. 'The Military Just Built the Most Advanced Prosthetic Arm We've Ever Seen'. *Business Insider*. Accessed 28 May 2018. http://uk.businessinsider.com/advanced-darpa-prosthetic-arm-2016-5.

Wegenstein, Bernadette. *The Cosmetic Gaze: Body Modification and the Construction of Beauty*. Cambridge: MIT Press, 2012.

Wheeler, Roxann. *The Complexion of Race: Categories of Difference in Eighteenth-Century British Culture*. Philadelphia: University of Pennsylvania Press, 2000.

'William Porterfield | Portraits of European Neuroscientists'. *Neuroportraits*. Accessed 7 August 2017. http://neuroportraits.eu/portrait/william-porterfield.

Williams, Gerhild Scholz, and William Layher, *Consuming News: Newspapers and Print Culture in Early Modern Europe (1500–1800)*. Amsterdam: Editions Rodopi, 2008.

Williams, Katherine Schaap. 'Performing Disability and Theorizing Deformity'. *English Studies* 94, no. 7 (2013), 757–72. https://doi.org/10.1080/0013838X.2013.840125.

Wilson, Margaret Dauler. *Descartes*. London: Routledge and Kegan Paul, 1978.

Woods, David. 'Nero and Sporus'. *Latomus* 68, no. 1 (2009), 73–82.

Yong, Amos. *Theology and Down Syndrome: Reimagining Disability in Late Modernity*. Waco: Baylor University Press, 2007.

Zigarovich, Jolene. 'Preserved Remains: Embalming Practices in Eighteenth-Century England'. *Eighteenth-Century Life* 33, no. 3 (2009), 65–104.

Index

prostheses, limb (cont.)
  incorporation of, 94
  legs, 90–4
  modern innovations in, 167–8
  as proof of military service, 88–9
  social effects of, 97–8
  and supercrip trope, 104–5
  Titus Andronicus, 81–2, 102–7
  trusses, 95
prostheses, theory of, 62–3, 66, 82–3
Pulter, Hester, 'To Sir W.D. upon the
      Unspeakable Loss of the Most
      Conspicuous and Chief Ornament of
      His Frontispiece', 76–9

Rabelais, François, *The Life of Gargantua and
      Pantagruel*, 3
race
  and Amazons, 41, 48–9
  and castrati, 18–30
  and female sterilisation, 54
  in the miracle of the black leg, 128–9
  in *Titus Andronicus*, 101
Raleigh, Sir Walter, *Discovery of the Large, Rich,
      and Beautiful Empire of Guiana*, 40–1
Read, Alexander, 71
  Chirurgorum Comes, 61
  Somatographia Anthropine, 142–3
religion. *See* miracles; resurrection
resurrection, 110–25
  and the 'cannibal problem', 114–15
  disabilities in resurrected bodies, 119–22
  nature of resurrected bodies, 111–12, 116–21
  scriptural basis, 110–11
rhinoplasty
  grafts from third parties, 71–9
  history of, 70
  method, 70
rogue literature, 89
Royal Society, the, 73
Ryder, Hugh, *New Practical Observations in
      Surgery*, 83

Salmon, William, *Ars Chirurgica*, 90–2
scars, 49, 79
Scultetus, Johannes, *The Chyrurgeon's Store-
      House*, 43–5
Senesino, 20
senses, 61
  nociception. *See* pain: theories of; phantom
        limb pain
  smell, 77
  vision, 145–6

sex
  and bodily difference, 49–50
  sexuality, 23–6
  See also Amazons; castrati
Shakespeare, William
  2 Henry IV, 89
  Henry V, 99
  A Midsummer Night's Dream, 47
  Titus Andronicus, 81–2, 98–107
Sinibaldi, Giovanni Benedetto, *Rare Verities*, 54
Smollet, Tobias, *Roderick Random*, 86
social cognition, 171
  See also 4E cognition
soul. *See* dualism; resurrection
sterilisation. *See* castrati; castration (medical);
      female sterilisation
supercrip trope, 104–5
surgeons. *See* Beckett, William; Cooke, James; de
      la Charriere, Joseph; de la Vauguion,
      M.; Dionis, Pierre; Moyle, John; Paré,
      Ambroise; Read, Alexander; Salmon,
      William; Scultetus, Johannes;
      Tagliacozzi, Gaspare; van Horne,
      Johann; Woodall, John
surgeries. *See* amputation; castration; female
      sterilisation; mastectomy; rhinoplasty
sympathy, 73–5

Tagliacozzi, Gaspare
  De curtorum Chirurgia per Institionem,
        70–2
  'Letter to Hieronymus Mercurialis', 70
  See also rhinoplasty
teeth
  false teeth, 61–2, 65–6
  transplants, 62–4
Tenducci, Giusto Ferdinando, 29–30
transhumanism, 167–9
transplants
  dental transplant. *See* teeth
  hand transplant (modern), 130–2
  limb transplant (miraculous), 127–8
transvestism, 32–3
travesti, 32–3

vagrancy, 89, 105
van Helmont, Jean-Baptiste, 74
  *A Ternary of Paradoxes. The Magnetick Cure of
        Wounds*, 72
van Horne, Johann, *Micro-Techne*, 59–60
venereal disease, 68–70
Venette, Nicholas, *Mysteries of Conjugal Love*,
      54

For EU product safety concerns, contact us at Calle de José Abascal, 56–1°, 28003 Madrid, Spain or eugpsr@cambridge.org.

www.ingramcontent.com/pod-product-compliance
Ingram Content Group UK Ltd.
Pitfield, Milton Keynes, MK11 3LW, UK
UKHW020351140625
459647UK00020B/2410